VIRTUAL SELLING

Other Books by Jeb Blount

The Virtual Training Bible: The Art of Conducting Powerful Virtual Training that Engages Learners and Makes Knowledge Stick (Wiley, 2020)

Inked: The Ultimate Guide to Powerful Closing and Sales Negotiation Tactics that Unlock YES and Seal the Deal (Wiley, 2020)

Fanatical Military Recruiting: The Ultimate Guide to Leveraging High-Impact Prospecting to Engage Qualified Applicants, Win the War for Talent, and Make Mission Fast (Wiley, 2019)

Objections: The Ultimate Guide for Mastering the Art and Science of Getting Past No (Wiley, 2018)

Sales EQ: How Ultra-High Performers Leverage Sales-Specific Emotional Intelligence to Close the Complex Deal (Wiley, 2017)

Fanatical Prospecting: The Ultimate Guide to Opening Sales Conversations and Filling the Pipeline by Leveraging Social Selling, Telephone, E-mail, Text, and Cold Calling (Wiley, 2015)

People Love You: The Real Secret to Delivering Legendary Customer Experiences (Wiley, 2013)

People Follow You: The Real Secret to What Matters Most in Leadership (Wiley, 2011)

People Buy You: The Real Secret to What Matters Most in Business (Wiley, 2010)

A QUICK-START GUIDE TO LEVERAGING VIDEO

VIRTUAL

TECHNOLOGY, AND VIRTUAL COMMUNICATION CHANNELS

SELLING

TO ENGAGE REMOTE BUYERS AND CLOSE DEALS FAST

JEB BLOUNT

WILEY

Published by John Wiley & Sons, Inc., Hoboken, New Jersey.
Published simultaneously in Canada.

For general information on our other products and services or for technical support, please contact our Customer Care Department within the United States at (800) 762-2974, outside the United States at (317) 572-3993 or fax (317) 572-4002.

Wiley publishes in a variety of print and electronic formats and by print-on-demand. Some material included with standard print versions of this book may not be included in e-books or in print-on-demand. If this book refers to media such as a CD or DVD that is not included in the version you purchased, you may download this material at http://booksupport.wiley.com. For more information about Wiley products, visit www.wiley.com.

Library of Congress Cataloging-in-Publication Data is Available:
ISBN 9781119742715 (Hardcover)
ISBN 9781119742777 (ePDF)
ISBN 9781119742791 (ePub)

Cover Design: Paul Mccarthy
Cover Art: © Istock | Shuoshu

Printed in the United States of America

SKY10020043_072320

To Carrie. The love of my life.

Contents

Foreword

Virtually Yours . . .

For the past 100 years, letters and emails have been signed with – sincerely yours, very truly yours, or some form of pleasant goodbye. No more. "Virtually yours" has taken over. By storm. Actually, by hurricane. And it's here to stay.

Virtual selling will become the new normal, and the only question is: Are you ready?

Virtual meetings are not the new black—they're the new normal, and most salespeople, sales leaders, executives, and entrepreneurs were and are woefully unprepared. They're (you're) looking at customers and coworkers from a laptop or phone, poorly dressed, poorly lit, in front of a closet or worse, in front of an unmade bed, trying to conduct a meeting or make a sales call that they (you) are unprepared for, BOTH mentally and technologically.

YIKES!

Luckily, you have this book. *Virtual Selling* will catapult you to the top of virtual Mt. Everest. IF, and only IF, you read it, study it, get prepared, make a game plan, and put it into action. (It's the same for climbing real Mt Everest, just warmer.)

Just a little background . . . I have been a fan and friend of Jeb Blount for more than a decade, and if you know him like I do, you know his passion, his positivity, and his performance are without peer. Not just a leader, an innovator. He is the perfect person to write this book because he lives in (and make bank in) the virtual world.

I have named Jeb "the hardest working man in sales business." And his trademarked challenge, "one more call," has forever branded his work ethic and his philosophy.

On one of Jeb's visit to our home, he spotted his book *Sales EQ* on my nightstand. He was proud—but it was there because I am TOTALLY interested in what Jeb Blount writes, says, and does, both face-to-face and ESPECIALLY virtually—and you should be, too.

Jeb Blount was, is, and always will be a student. A life-long student. A keen observer. A risk taker. And a winner.

He is always ahead of the curve, and this book is the CLASSIC example. Jeb is setting the standard in virtual webinars, virtual seminars, virtual training, virtual meetings, virtual studio, and as a result is the leader in virtual selling.

This book has the ANSWERS you need right now.

A playbook, a manual, and a bible about the new virtual world of sales. You see, the virtual sales world has been here for 20 years. It used to be optional. It was "one way to communicate. One way to sell."

During the "pandemic period," virtual was the ONLY way to communicate and sell. Tomorrow, *virtual* will be the BEST way, and the most cost-effective way, to communicate and sell. And *Virtual Selling* tells you the virtual "why" and "how to" that's not only impressive, it's an imperative.

From foundation to the top floor, this book takes you step by step through the virtual world of selling whether you take the fire escape or the elevator.

I promise you that *Virtual Selling* is GOLD. New gold. Unmined gold that every sales organization and salesperson is looking for to gain a leadership position and a competitive advantage in the mind, the pocketbook, and the loyalty of your customer—the only places it matters.

This book is a (virtual) roadmap for the future of sales and selling. It addresses everything in detail with elements of understanding, strategies, tactics, and game plans that any salesperson—beginning or advanced, tech savvy or technophobe—needs to emerge as a winner in this new sales world.

NOW IS THE TIME. Jeb Blount delivers the virtual answers you can put into action and turn into actual money. And all you have to do is read the pages and take the actions.

Virtually yours,

Jeffrey Gitomer,
author of *The Little Red Book of Selling*

PART

I

Foundation

1

And, Just Like That, Everything Changed

A global pandemic. Panic. Social distancing. Working from home. An economic crisis.

In a heartbeat, we went from happy hours to virtual happy hours. From conferences to virtual conferences. From the classroom to the virtual classroom. From selling to virtual selling.

To be sure, we've sought out and used virtual communication channels since the dawn of man. It began with smoke signals and then written letters. We've even used carrier pigeons.

Innovation in virtual communication accelerated in the nineteenth century with the telegraph—which was essentially very slow text messaging. The telegraph was soon disintermediated by the telephone.

In the 1980s, we fell in love with the fax machine, which was, likewise, disintermediated by email in the 1990s. In the ensuing decades, the online chat rooms of the 1990s morphed into texting, direct messaging, interacting on social media, and then interactive chat.

As early as 1880, an inventor named George Carey proposed a video phone. His idea was published in *Scientific American*. Forty-seven years later, in 1927, Herbert Hoover stepped into a video booth at Bell Labs and made a video call.

By the 1960s, AT&T had developed video technology to the point that it went to market with the *Picturephone*, but it was a flop. For the next 30 or so years, video calling failed to launch.[1] Then, in 2003, Skype kicked off the modern age of video calling.

In 2007, the iPhone changed everything. This was quickly followed by FaceTime in 2010, Zoom in 2013, and then Facebook Messenger video calls in 2015. Finally, the convergence of broadband internet and inexpensive hardware made the video call accessible to all.

Today video calling, though underutilized by sales professionals, is the most powerful and effective virtual communication channel of them all.

Technology Meets the Moment

The global coronavirus pandemic of 2020 accelerated the adoption of virtual selling much like the global financial crisis of 2007–2009 accelerated the emergence of inside sales teams and the division of sales labor into business development, selling, account management, and customer success (land, expand, and retain).

Except that this was faster, compressing what might have taken 10 years to fully actualize into a matter of months. In an instant, to remain relevant and competitive, salespeople, account managers, entrepreneurs, and business professionals had to shift the way they were engaging prospects and customers. Likewise, prospects and customers had to shift the way they interacted with vendors.

The evolution of virtual selling technology finally met its moment. Digital transformation, which for the past 20 years had been an inevitable yet slowly building tide, rolled over us like a tsunami. Suddenly, virtual selling became king.

Unlike so many other pivotal points in history, in which smart people were forced, out of necessity, to invent technology in order to meet the moment, this time the technology was ahead of us. We simply needed to catch up.

This is where we find ourselves. Virtual selling is the new normal. There is no turning back.

The Purpose of This Book

My objective is to teach you techniques that turn virtual communication platforms into powerful and effective sales tools, no matter what you sell, the complexity or length of your sales cycle, or whether you are an inside rep, field rep, or hybrid of the two. *Virtual Selling* is the most comprehensive and practical resource on video-based and digital sales skills ever developed.

This book will help you:

- Become more effective with virtual communication tools so that you can connect, engage, and build deep and lasting relationships with other people.
- Leverage technology, digital tools, and virtual communication channels to increase the number of connections you make and accelerate the speed at which you make those connections.
- Blend virtual selling channels and tactics into your sales process to increase productivity.
- Master virtual techniques to allow you to separate from competitors and gain a distinct competitive edge.
- Make virtual selling more human.

As you dive into these powerful insights, and with each new chapter, you'll gain greater and greater confidence in your ability to leverage virtual communication channels and conduct successful virtual sales calls. And, with this newfound confidence, your success and income will soar.

2

Is Face-to-Face Selling Dead?

I want to be clear from the start that I'm not an evangelist. I'm not an ideologue.

I despise and have no respect for the so-called "experts" and "gurus" who get on their high horse and shove their evangelism for a preferred technology platform or sales method down your throat. These are the same people who pontificate that their way is the ONLY way. They shout loudly that everything else in sales and business is dead.

These sad charlatans couldn't sell their way out of a paper bag. Somewhere, there is a graveyard full of the carcasses of former blowhard sales gurus who made a lot of noise, produced unimpressive results, and then died a quick death because their message was so shallow and self-serving (see *social selling evangelists*). Thankfully, real, frontline sales professions easily see through this bullshit.

This book is titled *Virtual Selling*. But this does not mean I am against face-to-face selling or, for that matter, against any particular type of selling. There are many products and services perfectly suited to field sales and physical face-to-face selling. Likewise, there are many products and services perfectly suited to inside sales and pure virtual selling. In the same vein, there are plenty of products and services that can be sold without the need of a salesperson.

Over the past decade, many companies have replaced field sales teams with inside sales, only to add field sales back when they realized that not having a face-to-face sales presence was costing them market share. Likewise, companies with pure inside sales teams have added a field sales presence to allow them to be more competitive and responsive to buyers.

Thousands of companies these days operate and sell through blended teams of inside and outside sales professionals, along with phone, email, chat, text and ecommerce. These forward-thinking organizations understand that there are different types of buying journeys, differing complexities, different risk profiles and different sales cycles.

The key is applying the right sales channel and approach to meet buyers where they are and how they prefer to buy. This will give you the highest probability of inking a deal at the lowest cost. Win probability—and your ability to bend win probability in your favor—is all that matters.

Probability versus Ideology

In sales, context matters. There are few black-and-whites, few right ways or wrong ways. In sales, no matter how hard the so-called experts might want it to be so, there is no one-size-fits-all. There is no "one way."

What works in a transactional sale will not work in an enterprise-level sale. Selling to the government is different from selling to a business or consumer. Selling a physical product is different from selling a service or software. Selling complex, high-risk products and services is vastly different from selling a one-call-close product.

Can you close a high-risk, enterprise-level deal over the phone without ever meeting face-to-face? Of course you can. Can you sell SaaS software solutions face-to-face? Absolutely. Can you do business over email or chat? You bet. You can conduct sales and close business face-to-face and through any virtual communication channel. In sales, everything works some of the time.

This is why, instead of ideology, I'm a student of probability. Probability is how I play the game of sales. Every move I make, every question I ask, every word I say, each sales communication channel I deploy, and when, where, and how I deploy it in the sales process is based on the probability that the specific move will generate the outcome I desire.

Virtual Is NOT the Same as Face-to-Face

Still, if your primary go-to market sales communication channel has been face-to-face, it's natural to fear that you won't be able to communicate effectively, build relationships, be as competitive, or make the same impact through virtual channels. You fear that virtual selling will lower your probability of closing sales.

This fear is not unfounded. The most effective way to build relationships and trust, resolve conflict, brainstorm ideas, gain consensus, present ideas, negotiate, and close deals is a physical face-to-face meeting. You know this and I know this, because we are human.

Successful face-to-face sales pros are masters at reading other people, responding to nuance, and using charisma as a competitive advantage. They have the ability to intuitively sense the emotions of other people and respond appropriately.

This is why so many field sales professionals were paralyzed with fear when the coronavirus pandemic made face-to-face interaction impossible. It was as if their sense of sight had suddenly been taken away. And, in reality, it had been.

The eyes manage roughly 80 percent of the information and communication you take in. Visual interpretation of the world and people around you consumes at least 50 percent of your brain's computing power. In fact, a far larger part of the brain is dedicated to vision than to hearing, taste, touch, and smell combined.[1]

When you are on face-to-face sales calls, you can see and interpret the *entire* picture. You see not only the person you are meeting but also their surroundings and how they interact with their environment. You also have the luxury of reading their eyes, the micro-expressions on their face, and the entirety of their body language. If there are other people in the room, you're able to read their reactions and nonverbal signals as well.

Emotional contagion is another form of *sight* that is significantly diminished in quality and clarity when you are communicating through virtual channels versus face-to-face.

Emotional contagion[2] is a subconscious response that allows us to pick up on the emotions of other humans without much conscious effort.[3] Like invisible vibrations, emotions are easily transferred from one person to the other when we are together.

We are constantly scanning those around us for clues about their emotional state. We read between the lines, interpret those clues, and alter our approach to people based on our perceptions.

Though you can see the other person on a video call or hear their voice over the phone, it is not the same as being in person. It's cloudy, and never as clear as when you are selling face-to-face.

When you are face-to-face with prospects and customers, it is easier to:

- Ask for the next step—and know when to ask for the next step.
- Tour facilities, get hands-on, and understand their real issues and problems.

- Communicate clearly and minimize miscommunication.
- Know when what you are saying or presenting is off-base or missing the mark.
- Accurately read stakeholders and develop discovery questions organically, in the moment.
- Compare the words that stakeholders say to their nonverbal communication for congruency.
- Keep people engaged, because it is far less likely that they'll drift into social media, look at their email, or become distracted when you are sitting in front of them.
- Build relationships.
- Gain commitments. It is much harder for stakeholders to say no to your face.

Face-to-face human interaction is powerful, persuasive, and compelling. When you are there, face-to-face, it sends the message that the meeting is important, and it makes the person with whom you are meeting feel important. It demonstrates your credibility and allows you to fully leverage your personal brand.

Because face-to-face meetings require both parties to make a significant investment of time, it increases the probability that there will be meaningful outcomes and that your deal will move to the next step.

All of this and more are why face-to-face selling and human interaction are going nowhere. Going out on physical sales calls and meeting prospects at trade shows, networking events, or conferences face-to-face are not going away (at least not while we are alive on Earth).

3

Necessity Is the Mother of Virtual Selling

When I started my company, Sales Gravy, in 2007, right at the cusp of the global financial crisis, I found myself in unfamiliar waters. For my entire career, I'd sold face-to-face. I was damn good at it. I never considered that there was any other way.

But, my prospects were spread out all across the country. I had limited startup funds and could not afford to take the risk of buying a plane ticket, only to lose the deal. If I wanted to grow my business (and I did), my only choice was virtual selling—face-to-face was not an option for me.

It required a massive mindset shift. I had to change my belief system about selling. Most of all, it required me to get past my fear and just do it. Out of pure necessity, and many mistakes later, I eventually mastered virtual selling.

Today, Sales Gravy has grown into one of the most successful training and consulting firms in the world. We have customers on every continent except Antarctica. Virtual selling is how we go to market because it is the most practical and cost-effective means of engaging prospects across the globe. We regularly close six- and seven-figure deals within a completely virtual sales process.

Everything Works—Blending Works Best

This, of course, begs the question: Do we ever make face-to-face sales calls? The answer is yes. When we have big, company-changing deals on the line, and it is practical, we visit face-to-face—usually late in the sales process when it matters most. Likewise, in cities like San Francisco, where we have salespeople in the market, we make face-to-face calls.

When we are onsite with our clients, delivering training or providing professional services, we leverage those in-person engagements to interact with our stakeholders to anchor relationships and expand our business inside those accounts—often displacing competitors who are not engaging face-to-face.

When our trainers and consultants are already in a city for a client engagement, we set up face-to-face meetings with prospects in the same city. Since we are already there and the cost to schedule an additional face-to-face meeting is low, it makes sense to meet in person because those face-to-face meetings almost always give us a leg up over our competitors.

The two early enterprise-level deals that made my company what it is today were closed on face-to-face calls. At the final presentation stage, I took the risk, purchased the plane ticket, and delivered my closing presentation in person. These deals were game changers and were so important that the cost of the face-to-face engagement to seal the deal in person was well worth it.

This is called *blending*, and it is the key to leveraging virtual selling to become more productive and win more often, at a lower cost to you and your company.

I'm a student of probability rather than an evangelist. As we've established, everything works. You just need to calculate the probability that using a particular approach, at a particular time, with a particular opportunity will improve the probability that you get the appointment, advance the opportunity, close the deal, expand the revenue within your account, or renew the contract—AND—that the approach you choose, relative to its probability, is worth the cost.

Will Customers and Prospects Accept Virtual Selling?

Here are five truths:

1. Most of your prospects and customers would prefer to meet with you face-to-face prior to making an important or risky decision. They want to know they can trust you. Since so much of human communication is visual, seeing you face-to-face helps them feel that they are making a better decision.
2. If prospects and customers are given a choice to meet face-to-face, most will.
3. If the only option to meet with you is on a virtual call— phone or video—most prospects and customers will accept that option.
4. The majority of your prospects and customers will be comfortable with at least some of the steps of the sales process being virtual.
5. Most of the mental hang-ups about virtual selling are with you, not your stakeholders.

When I'm working with inside sales professionals on virtual selling skills, the biggest fear they have is engaging stakeholders by phone (weird, but true) and on video calls. They say, "You don't understand, Jeb; our customers prefer to communicate through email." Or, "It's really hard to get our customers on video calls."

Field sales teams universally fear the phone and video sales calls. They whine, "You don't understand, Jeb; our customers prefer to meet face-to-face." Or, especially when it comes to prospecting, "Nobody answers the phone and I'm so much better face-to-face."

Jeb, you don't understand. I hear those same words every week, in every training session, wherever I am in the world.

When I'm overseas, it's, "Jeb, you don't understand because you are an American." When I'm in North America, it's, "Jeb, you don't understand, because our company, product, service, customers, buyers, niche, vertical, geographic region [pick a card, any card] is different."

I've heard it all. From Moscow to Milan, Lisbon to London, Shanghai to Sau Paulo, Dubuque to Dubai, and Atlanta to Amsterdam, there are a thousand excuses and justifications for why salespeople can't do something.

- "Our buyers are different."
- "Our culture is different."
- "Our product is different."
- "It doesn't work like that in our industry [company, culture, country]."
- "The buyers we deal with won't get on a video call."
- "My customers only meet face-to-face."
- "The buyers in our industry just commoditize us."

It's mostly bullshit. Just lies, excuses, and delusions that sales professionals throw at me to justify their fear of a particular tool or technique. It's easier to blame it on their prospects than to look in the mirror.

So, let's just cut to the chase. The people you call on will happily schedule and jump on virtual calls with you. You just have to ask.

How do I know? Because there are real stories everywhere, including my own (above), about how prospects and customers quickly adapted to virtual sales calls because there was either no other choice or because it was faster and more convenient.

Think about it: During the coronavirus pandemic, no one had a choice and we quickly adapted to virtual sales calls. Or, how many times has a customer with a problem demanded that you get on a plane or in your car and visit them right at that moment? When you explained that it was impossible for you to get there, didn't they manage to work it out with you on the phone?

One of my sales training clients sells used commercial trucks over the phone, sight unseen. These deals run from $20,000 to $200,000. Their customers can see only a picture of the truck. No test drive, no kicking the tires, no making a deal belly-to-belly. This group sells tens of thousands of trucks a year this way. It is one of the largest resellers of used commercial trucks in the world.

Is this a weird way for people to buy used commercial trucks? You bet. Do customers push back and say they have to see the truck before they buy? Absolutely. But this is the only option, and therefore thousands of buyers accept it. Once they experience how easy and painless virtual can be, they become loyal customers and buy more trucks.

This is one of the keys to successful virtual selling. When you make it a great experience for your stakeholders, they'll begin to trust the process and be open to more virtual calls. One thing you can take to the bank, though, is that *prospects and customers won't accept virtual sales calls if you never ask for them.*

Author's note: I use the terms *prospect, stakeholder, customer,* and *buyer* interchangeably and regularly change up terms to avoid repeating myself and boring my readers.

4 | Virtual Selling Definition and Channels

Before we move further into the book, and to avoid confusion surrounding the term, let's stop and define *virtual selling*.

Traditionally, *virtual* has been thought of as something purely digital that takes place online versus in the physical world. Though true for software programs, online experiences, and gaming, this limited definition of *virtual* when applied to selling is what causes consternation within the sales community.

When salespeople or leaders hear the word *virtual* paired with the word *selling,* it's natural for many to think "robots." They envision sales activity devoid of any human-to-human contact. This, of course, makes those who make their living through face-to-face interaction recoil. Face-to-face is their comfort zone and their skill set. It's difficult to conceive that it's possible to sell any other way.

Virtual selling is simply leveraging virtual communication channels in place of physical, face-to-face interaction.

These channels include:

- Video calls
- Video messaging
- Telephone calls
- Interactive chat
- Text messaging
- Email
- Voicemail and audio messaging
- Social media
- Direct messaging
- Snail mail

If you look closely at the list above, you'll notice that you are already using some, if not all, of these channels. You are already engaging in some level of virtual selling activity.

You'll also notice that all of the tools and technology that you need to engage in virtual selling—communicating with prospects and customers without physically being there—already exist. In addition, there are hundreds of software platforms that facilitate and simplify the use of these communication channels, both individually and working in concert.

Therefore, since the tools, technology and platforms already exist and every salesperson is engaging in some level of virtual selling, this is not a showdown between virtual selling and face-to-face selling. It is not about "revolutionizing" the way you sell.

Rather, it's a laser focus on applying virtual selling tools more effectively to engage and connect with other humans while boosting your sales productivity. It's about helping you improve your virtual communication, interpersonal, and selling skills along the three main journeys of the sales continuum (see Figure 4.1):

1. *Business development:* Engaging prospects and moving them into the pipeline (targeting, qualifying, engagement)
2. *Selling:* Advancing opportunities through the pipeline (initial meetings, discovery, demos, presentations, negotiating, closing)

Figure 4.1

    3. *Account management:* Servicing, expanding and growing existing accounts (onboarding new customers, delivering products and services, up-selling, cross-selling, developing relationships, adding new products and services, retention)

Human-to-Human

Videoconferencing, the telephone, text messaging, video messaging, live chat, social media platforms, email, and direct messaging: What do all of these virtual channels have in common?

Each was developed by humans as a facsimile for physical, face-to-face interaction. From the beginning of human self-awareness, we have been driven to develop virtual communication tools, techniques, methodologies, and technologies to facilitate human-to-human connection when we are far apart.

The digital transformation of the twenty-first century has aimed to break down barriers to human-to-human connection while removing inefficiencies that slow down the pace of communication. Today, we have the capacity to interact and engage with people across the globe at breakneck speed.

The tools have changed, but what has not changed, since the dawn of mankind, is the innate human craving for emotional connection. We are compelled to interact with other humans.

In the virtual world, though, everything moves fast, and I don't want to discount just how challenging virtual selling can be. It requires constantly learning, adopting, and adapting to new technology while practicing and honing the interpersonal skills and emotional intelligence required to build relationships and influence others.

It requires a mindset shift, applying interpersonal skills in new ways, learning how to influence and persuade without the help of some of your senses, moving at a faster pace and, getting out of your comfort zone.

Sales Communication Approaches

Virtual sellers are adept at communicating through a complex web of interconnected communication channels—synchronous and asynchronous—often at the same time. *Interconnected* is the key word. There isn't one best way. Communication channels are not siloed.

There are two primary forms of virtual communication that you need to master and, learn to blend (interconnect) together to be effective:

1. *Synchronous (talking with people).* Communication channels are dynamic and require both parties to be available and engaged in a conversation at the same time.
2. *Asynchronous (talking at people).* Communication channels do not require both parties to be available and engaged at the same time.

Synchronous Channels (Talking with People)	Asynchronous Channels (Talking at People)
Face-to-face (not virtual)	Email
Video calls	Video messaging
Phone calls	Direct messaging
Live chat	Voice mail
Texting	Social media posting and commenting
	Snail mail

We live in a time when attention spans have contracted. The modern world moves at light speed. Information overload is a state of being for most people.

Attention is currency. Leveraging as many channels as possible improves your probability of gaining attention. With attention, you can win mindshare. With mindshare comes wallet share.

5

The Asynchronous Salesperson

The inside sales professional I was coaching had been underperforming for a while. The year before, on a team of 30 inside sales reps, he'd been a top performer and made it to the President's Club. Recently, however, his productivity had dropped off and it had not recovered.

We were sitting face-to-face at one corner of a large conference table. I asked questions in an attempt to diagnose his performance problem over the last few months—a problem that, despite the evidence, he denied he had—the sad delusion of an underperformer.

I asked him to walk me through his day and describe his outbound prospecting process. I sat back in my chair in disbelief as he told me that his primary prospecting methodology was sending out hundreds of bulk emails to the buyers in his database each day.

Seeing the, "Oh shit, I can't believe you just said that" look on my face, he defended this practice. "It works," he said, while

25

barely hiding the defensive tone in his voice. "People respond to my emails looking for more information."

I let him talk in circles, justifying why he wasn't talking with people, for a few more minutes before interrupting him. "Eric, here's the thing. If you are telling me that sending emails is the most effective means of engaging buyers and closing business, then we don't need you. It would be a lot cheaper to get a robot to do your job."

The look on his face was that of a hurt puppy that had just been whacked with a rolled-up newspaper for peeing on the floor. But I could see the wheels turning as he tried to cobble together a response. He shot back, "I'm really offended that you would say that."

"Well," I responded, "I'm really offended that you are collecting a $75,000-a-year salary to do what a $19-a-month robot can do better than you."

Once I was able to get his attention and shake him out of his delusion, we were able to get him back on track. Today he is a sales leader. But he almost got fired because he forgot that his job was to talk with people.

A Robot Can Do Your Job—If You Are Not Doing Your Job

In today's digital world, it is easy to avoid talking to people. It's easy to justify that the people who buy from you would like to avoid talking with you, too.

Talking with people is difficult. You must pay attention, listen, and flex your communication style. You must put the other person at the center of your attention. It can make you vulnerable and expose you to the potential for rejection.

This is exactly why thousands of misguided salespeople have deluded themselves into believing that staring at a computer screen all day, researching, posting on social media, and using automated tools to effortlessly send thousands of generic emails and direct messages is selling.

This behavior is why so many sales floors are dead silent. It is why so many sales teams and organizations are woefully behind their forecasts and business plans. It's *transacting* versus *engaging*. Which is why so many buyers are left longing for real human-to-human interaction.

It's also a big reason why there are so many new tech companies popping up that claim they can replace your sales team with an AI driven software application. They are partially right. If all you do is send emails all day long, you can be replaced. Robots are not that great at complex, real-time conversations, but they are pretty good at sending one-way bulk emails.

If we learn nothing else from the great coronavirus pandemic, it's that real human connection matters. And you are just not going to get that from an email.

The more complex the sale, the longer the sales cycle, the higher the dollar amount, the greater the risk to the stakeholders and the more emotions are involved in the decision to purchase, then the more companies need salespeople who are intelligent, creative, insightful, influential, and persuasive to shift win probabilities in the organization's favor. The more they need you to talk with people.

Talk with People

There is no doubt that asynchronous communication channels have an important place in virtual selling. These channels allow you to move fast and get a lot done, communicate when you are unable to get together in real time with the other person, and use written communication to ensure clarity and build familiarity.

With prospecting, asynchronous channels allow you to build sequences of touches to improve the probability that you will get a response.

But there is a downside. Asynchronous channels don't feel as personal. It's almost impossible to build real relationships with stakeholders through these channels. Furthermore, asynchronous communication may result in miscommunication and misinterpretation that can damage relationships and your reputation.

I subscribe to a basic sales truth: *The more people you talk with, the more you will sell.* If I'm an evangelist for anything, it's talking with people through as many channels as possible, building emotional connections and helping them solve problems. In the land of the complex sale, real-time, human-to-human communication is the key to success for you and your customers.

Talking with people is what we as sales professionals get paid to do. It's just that simple. The good news is, with virtual selling it's easier than ever to have real-time conversations with people, wherever they are.

Synchronous communication is where you earn your chops as a sales professional. It helps you gain a much deeper understanding of the motivations, desires, needs, wants, fears, aspirations, and problems of each stakeholder. It allows you to make emotional connections and build relationships.

6 | Blending

When I got my start in sales, back in my early twenties, I worked in an assigned territory in a local market. I could drive to all of my sales calls.

I called on local service businesses and manufacturers. To be effective at making recommendations that addressed their unique needs, I needed to physically walk through their operations. It was the most effective way to both build relationships and get hands-on with the problems my stakeholders faced.

My industry was also insanely competitive. Because the competition was so fierce, and the products, services, and prices offered by each company were essentially the same, it was the relationship that mattered most. People bought *me* first and then my company.

Those face-to-face interactions mattered dearly, because it was there that I built trust, reduced risk, differentiated and locked my competitors out.

Still, I spent a lot of time driving. My territory was four hours from top to bottom. Windshield time was, and still is, the biggest time sucker for field sales reps.

Then, as today, most field salespeople preferred to prospect for new business with their feet—in-person prospecting and door-to-door canvassing. I remember one of my first managers telling me to "go get lost in my territory" and that he "didn't want to see me in the office during the day."

I quickly realized that this approach—driving around in my territory looking for new business opportunities—was stupid. Driving was not an accomplishment.

Time is money, and prospecting by foot is an expensive use of time. So, I learned to hide from the boss and use the phone for prospecting (virtual) so that I could maximize my face-to-face time for selling (physical).

Shifting to virtual prospecting made me highly productive. I could make far more prospecting calls by phone than on foot. This made my pipeline robust, giving me more at-bats.

Though in-person prospecting could be more effective because of the face-to-face interaction, the sheer number of touches I could make by phone versus on foot improved my statistical probability of adding more opportunities to my pipeline. It allowed me to outgun everyone on my team.

While most of my peers closed one deal a month, I was closing one a week. My commissions soared, and I set every sales record in my company's history. That was my first experience with *blending*.

Map Your Sales Process to Communication Channels

Blending is the active and intentional strategy of leveraging multiple communication channels (synchronous and asynchronous) in the sales process to give yourself the highest probability of engaging a prospect, scheduling an appointment, advancing to the next step, closing the sale, expanding your account, or retaining your customer.

Every sales leader and sales professional should be focused on blending right now. You should be actively mapping communication channels to the sales process, buying journey, and sales cycle. Even pure inside sales teams should reevaluate the communication channels you are leveraging and how you are using them, relative to the steps in the sales process.

You see, sales is a blend of art and science. The art is influencing people to comply with your requests. The science is influencing the right people, at the right time, with the right message, through the right channel to give yourself the highest statistical probability of inking the deal at the lowest cost.

For example: A company could deploy a field sales force to sell subscription-based SaaS software to small companies in local markets across America. These salespeople would likely be very successful and have much higher raw win ratios than an inside sales team.

Yet, the SaaS sales organization can lower costs significantly, move faster, touch far more prospects, and do it with fewer people via telephone and video sales calls. The cost savings and sheer volume of touches make the trade-off of a lower win ratio worth it.

To the consternation of CFOs everywhere who manage travel and entertainment budgets, there are many salespeople who'll jump on a plane, train, or automobile at a moment's notice to go see a prospect or customer, regardless of the cost.

The CFO for one of my customers, upon hearing about this book, exclaimed that he was going to buy a copy for every salesperson working for the company—figuring he'd get his money back "a hundred fold" if he could get the salespeople to stop traveling so much and use virtual communication tools instead.

As you objectively evaluate and map communication channels to both the stages of the sales process and micro-steps within those stages, answer these questions and more:

- Which sales communication channel is most effective at the lowest cost at each step in the sales process?
- When does communication need to be face-to-face?
- When should you use video versus phone?

- What are the right sequences of touches when prospecting based on targeting and segmentation?
- How should you deploy social media, video messaging, and texting in the sales process?
- What is the appropriate use of email and direct messaging in the sales process?

As you go through this analysis and build a sales communication playbook, you'll find that there are times when virtual communication should be the first choice and times when it should be the last. Times when asynchronous makes the most sense and times when it will hurt your efforts. You'll leverage different blends by account size, product, service, and sales team.

If there is one lesson you should take away from this book, it is this: Virtual selling is omnichannel communication. It's blending your communication channels along the steps of the sales and account management processes or sequencing channels when prospecting, to give yourself the highest probability of achieving your desired outcome, at the lowest cost.

We'll be diving into techniques for leveraging each virtual communication channel in upcoming chapters. First, though, we're going to discuss important human-to-human virtual communication skills.

PART II

Emotional Discipline

7 | The Four Levels of Sales Intelligence

Virtual sales excellence and acumen requires that you:

- Become adept at connecting disparate ideas, data, and patterns; and leverage these mashups of information to offer insights and solve problems via virtual communication channels.
- Have insatiable curiosity for and courage to explore and learn new technology.
- Possess an *evolve-or-die* mentality.
- Be willing to invest in acquiring new knowledge and skills.
- Become a keen observer of nuanced human behavior—your own and that of others.
- Hone the ability to accurately sense, respond to, and influence the emotions of stakeholders, while advancing toward a defined sales outcome in both synchronous and asynchronous communication.
- Have the discipline to be aware of and in control of your emotions.

A combination of innate intelligence (IQ), acquired knowledge (AQ), technology acumen (TQ), and *sales-specific* emotional intelligence (EQ) allows you to seamlessly blend and balance multiple sales communication channels. You become more agile and flexible. You move faster with less effort. You make a bigger impact. You become a person with whom people want to do business.

These four types of intelligence are tightly intertwined, each connecting, affecting, and amplifying the others. With virtual selling, people who combine high IQ, AQ, and TQ with high EQ dominate any field or discipline they pursue. These "high Q" people are at the very top of the food chain.

- IQ—how smart you are—is fixed. It is baked into your DNA.
- AQ—how much you know—makes IQ relevant.
- TQ—how fast you assimilate and leverage technology for low-value tasks—gives you more time for human relationships.
- EQ—your acuity for dealing with emotions—amplifies the impact of IQ, AQ, and TQ because it allows you to relate to, respond to, influence, and persuade other human beings.

Innate Intelligence (IQ)

Your intelligence quotient is an indicator of how smart you are. Innate intelligence is a talent no different than athleticism. It is baked into your DNA. You are either born with a certain IQ or you are not. IQ is immovable. In other words, you are as smart as you will ever be.

It's almost impossible to blend and effectively navigate the complexity of the interconnected virtual communication channels if you do not possess a certain level of intelligence. The speed and complexity of virtual selling and communication in the modern marketplace is the domain of intellectual agility. In a low-IQ versus high-IQ battle, I'll put my money on the high-IQ person any day.

Sales professionals with a high level of intelligence tend to be curious, rapidly assimilate and learn new information, are strategic and can see the bigger picture, hold themselves to high standards, and have superior reasoning skills.

They can easily see relationships among seemingly unrelated objects, ideas, or facts and develop unique and original solutions to problems from these relationships. This is a critical competency in sales for discovery, challenging the status quo, and developing unique solutions and recommendations.

But there is a dark side. Because high-IQ people tend to explore, assimilate, and connect disparate ideas faster and more rationally than other people, they have the tendency to damage relationships through:

- Impulsiveness.
- Impatience.
- Talking down to people.
- Talking over people.
- Failure to listen and hear people out.
- Failure to empathize with others.
- Overwhelming people with elaborate solutions to basic problems.

These behaviors are a massive Achilles' heel in a virtual selling environment in which the visual cues that help guide and temper our behavior in face-to-face settings are either not present or, on video calls, hard to discern because you are unable to see the entire picture.

Many extremely intelligent people fail at virtual selling because it requires a much higher level of patience and emotional intuition than face-to-face selling. Highly intelligent salespeople who cannot make the leap, often become asynchronous sellers who eventually fail.

There is absolutely no doubt that being smart gives you a distinct competitive edge, but it is only one part of who you are. Innate intelligence only becomes relevant, useful, and powerful when combined with acquired, technological, and emotional intelligence. It is useless on its own and must be honed and developed through learning, exercise, and experience.

In sales, where emotions rather than rational decision-making carry the day, IQ is but part of the equation. To effectively navigate relationships and influence the emotions of others, you must learn to temper and complement innate intellectual ability with emotional intelligence.

Acquired Intelligence (AQ)

While delivering a seminar for a client, I noticed that a couple of the participants were disengaged. The rest of the group were participating and energetic. But these two were on the edge of hostile and disrupted the class with their "this will never work here" comments and remarks.

At lunch, I asked the sales leader if there was something going on. He confided that everyone had been excited about the training except for them. "They think they know it all," he explained. "They're both really smart, but trust me, these guys need this training badly because they are struggling to hit their numbers."

Salespeople who think they know it all—I see it every day. Far too many of these people, at some point, just quit learning. This is the "nothing is new here" crowd.

This mindset is a death sentence in modern virtual selling. The moment you quit learning is the moment you become extinct. It is critical that you develop both the courage and the curiosity to seek out new ideas. You must learn how to apply the proven fundamentals and basics of selling to new communication channels.

Unlike innate intelligence, acquired intelligence is not static. Regardless of your IQ, you can grow your AQ with schooling, training, reading, and other learning experiences, along with practice and experience. In other words, you may not be able to become more intelligent, but, through study and practice, you can get a whole lot smarter.

Technological Intelligence (TQ)

Virtual selling requires that you learn and adopt new technology. Because technology is always evolving, you must be willing to evolve with it. It is also important that you quickly assimilate new technology and master the complexity of multichannel virtual selling to facilitate human–to–human synchronous communication.

In the future, there will be three types of salespeople: low–TQ sellers, asynchronous sellers, and high–TQ sellers.

Low–TQ Sellers

These sellers are hopelessly stuck in their ways. They are either unwilling or unable to learn new technology. They complain that that they are "not computer savvy" or that they "are not good with learning new technology." They shun virtual communication channels because the technology seems daunting. These sellers will be left behind and out of a job.

Asynchronous Sellers

These salespeople put barriers between themselves and buyers, replacing human–to–human engagement with technology. Because they replace talking to people with technology, this group of people will eventually be replaced by technology.

High–TQ Sellers

These sellers interact with technology and weave it seamlessly into their sales day. They easily integrate emotional intelligence and interpersonal skills with technology to expand their ability to communicate and connect with prospects and customers. These sellers leverage technology to remove mundane tasks so that they have more time to build relationships with people.

High-TQ sellers leverage technology using three As:

- *Adopt:* They tend to be early adopters of new, cutting-edge technology, and leverage it to achieve a game-changing, competitive edge.
- *Adapt:* They adapt new technology to their unique sales process; and, leverage technology to automate low-value tasks so as to gain more time for focusing on high-value human interactions and strategies.
- *Adept:* They rapidly assimilate technology into their sales day, blend it into their sales process, and become adept at using it.

Emotional Intelligence (EQ)

The ability to perceive, correctly interpret, respond to, and effectively manage your own emotions and influence the emotions of others is called emotional intelligence.

In our tech-dominated society, interpersonal skills (responding to and managing the emotions of others) and intrapersonal skills (managing your own disruptive emotions) are more essential to success in sales than at any point in history. This is good news for high-TQ, virtual sellers because buyers are starving for authentic human interaction.

Emotional intelligence is the key that unlocks virtual selling excellence. Emotional discipline, combined with empathy and the ability to develop and maintain emotional connections with other people through virtual communication channels, is the rocket fuel of sales performance.

Sales EQ—sales-specific emotional intelligence—equalizes the investment in interpersonal relationships, accelerating the speed of communication, expanding the number of connections you can make, lowering the cost of those connections, *and* achieving your primary objective of advancing opportunities through your pipeline and getting ink.

Sales professionals who leverage sales-specific emotional intelligence are able to seamlessly manage technology, emotions, relationships, and outcomes.

8 | Emotions Matter

These days there are more and more "experts" popping up who are quick to tell you that relationship building is old school. They say emotional connections don't matter.

This is the dark side of virtual selling. Distance deludes us into believing that putting effort into human connections is a waste of time.

This false and dangerous narrative leads to asynchronous sales behaviors. It is appealing to salespeople who feel vulnerable developing human-to-human connections and to sellers who focus on getting as much as they can from buyers, as fast as they can, with the least amount of human interaction.

But the people who tell you this are dead wrong. They are wrong because science tells us they are wrong.[1] Although we might be certain that we make choices based on rational logic, our own best interests, or organized facts, science says that we often don't.

From complex to completely transactional impulse purchases, emotions drive buying decisions. Science is stacking up one study after another demonstrating the influence emotions exert on the choices we make.

Emotion is why well-educated executives make multimillion-dollar decisions with massive implications for their companies because they *feel* that one sales team cares more about them than another. Despite all the tools, information, and data at their finger-tips, in our tech-connected virtual world, buyers continue to make irrational decisions.

Am I saying that product features, quality, specs, delivery options and speed, service, technology, locations, price, and other tangible attributes of your offering don't matter? Of course not. These things absolutely matter. All are tickets to the game. A deficiency in one of these areas can eliminate you before you ever get started.

Selling is human. Buying is human. Both pursuits are woven into the imperfect fabric of human emotions. No matter what you sell, how you sell, your sales cycle, or the complexity of the sales process, emotions play a crucial role in the outcomes of your sales conversations, interactions, and deals.

This is why emotions matter. Influence matters. Relationships matter. Interpersonal connections matter. It is why virtual selling through the lens of human emotions matters.

Each time you (and the members of your selling team) interact with stakeholders though a virtual channel, you are creating an emotional experience that they feel and remember.

Your stakeholders' emotional experience while working with you is a more consistent predictor of outcome than any other vari-able. This is because, as humans, we feel and then we think.

There is an oft-expressed maxim: *They'll forget what you said, they'll forget what you did, but they will never forget how you made them feel.*

People Buy You

People buy you first (emotion), and then your product or service (logic). They buy how they feel about you and what you are selling before buying the outcomes your product delivers. This brings us back to the importance of synchronous human-to-human communication.

In sales, perceiving, interpreting, and reacting to your own emotions and the emotions of stakeholders are critical capabilities. To be effective, you must learn to manage your own disruptive emotions in order to respond appropriately to and influence the emotions of stakeholders, resident within the logical, linear, systematic sales, and buying processes.

The most successful sales professionals are virtuosos with people. They shift win probability in their favor through perceiving, controlling, managing, and influencing nonconforming, irrational, human emotions. They possess a toolbox full of influence frameworks, along with the agility to apply them in any situation to improve the probability of getting the outcome they desire.

Emotion is the glue that connects all the disparate elements of the sales equation and virtual selling technology. It's the ability to leverage technology and emotion to create the highest statistical chance of winning that separates ultra-high-performing salespeople from everyone else.

As a sales professional, understanding how emotions dominate and drive buying decisions is critical to mastering virtual selling, because in virtual selling you must be better than when you are in person to influence people the same way.

When all things are equal—and in today's marketplace there are rarely huge gaps or differences between competitors (at least from the prospect's viewpoint)—your ability to influence the emotions of stakeholders while regulating your own disruptive emotions, as you move deals through the sales pipeline, gives you a distinct competitive edge.

9 | Relaxed, Assertive Confidence

In every sales conversation the person who demonstrates the greatest emotional control has the highest probability of getting the outcome they desire. In these conversations, your most powerful emotional state is relaxed, assertive confidence.

Nothing pulls stakeholders toward you, makes you more believable, and causes stakeholders to have confidence and trust in you more than relaxed, assertive confidence. When you pair relaxed, assertive confidence with a sound strategy for blending communication channels and excellence throughout the sales process, you bend *win probability* decidedly in your favor.

Stakeholders are always subconsciously scanning you for clues about your emotional state and trustworthiness. When communicating through virtual channels, however, people put you under an especially powerful microscope.

They observe your facial expressions, body language, the tone and inflection of your voice, and the words you use. They interpret those clues and alter their perception of you based on how your behavior makes them feel. Even though you are not face-to-face, you still transfer your emotions to other people. This is known as emotional contagion.

I've spent most of my life around horses. Horses have an innate ability to sense hesitation and fear. They test new riders and take advantage of those riders the moment they sense that the person is afraid or lacks confidence. Horses have a 10-to-1 weight and size advantage over the average person. If the horse doesn't believe that you are in charge, it can and will dump you. Stakeholders are no different. Your emotions influence their emotions.

When you approach virtual sales calls (and horses) with relaxed, assertive confidence, stakeholders respond in kind. They lean into you, engage, and respect your positions. They are more willing to trust you, open up and be transparent, engage, collaborate, and make micro-commitments that advance you to the next step.

10 | Deep Vulnerability

I've spent three chapters talking about emotions rather than how to make a video call, phone call, send a text, email, direct message, or conduct a web chat. I expect that most people who are reading this book are seeking "how-to" answers rather than a lecture on emotional discipline.

So, why would I frontload the book with this discussion? The reason is simple. Let's go back to a statement I made in chapter seven (and one that I've been hinting at since Chapter 1). I'll paraphrase:

If you fail to rapidly adopt and assimilate omnichannel virtual selling into your business development, sales, and account management processes, you will either become extinct or be replaced by a robot. That's a brutal and absolute fact.

Yet, almost daily I watch as otherwise-competent sales professionals are pushed to emotional extremes when forced into situations in which they must use virtual selling platforms, particularly video calling, phone calling, and interactive web chats.

I've watched veteran salespeople completely shut down when asked to interact with prospects and customers on both reactive and proactive web chats. I've observed sales professionals who can command any room they walk into, cower in fear when faced with video calls. At least 50 percent of the work we do at Sales Gravy is focused on getting salespeople (inside and outside) to use the telephone.

So yes, I can teach you HOW to use virtual communication platforms, but I cannot make you get past your fear or emotional hang-ups that hold you back from using them. Only you have the power to master the disruptive emotions that erode your confidence with virtual selling.

Vulnerability

The truth is that synchronous virtual sales channels make most people feel uncomfortable and vulnerable, which is why we prefer asynchronous communication:

- When you are calling invisible strangers on telephone prospecting calls, everything in your body and mind screams at you to *stop*.
- When chatting, you fear that you'll say the wrong thing and then freeze.
- Few of us haven't felt the instant wave of insecurity the moment we look into the lens of a video camera or webcam.

Interacting with people through synchronous virtual communication channels requires you to put it all out there and be vulnerable. It's emotional risk with no guarantee that your approach will be accepted or appreciated by the other person.

In the back of your mind, there is always that little voice warning you that you'll butcher your words, look foolish on camera, come across the wrong way on the phone, that people will laugh at you, that you'll blow it. This can cause you to become nervous and to feel and act insecure.

You begin focusing your attention on what could go wrong rather than what will go right. On video calls, this nervousness makes it far more likely that in your haste, you will click the wrong link or hit the wrong button and self-generate a technical malfunction. It makes it more likely that if something does go wrong, you freeze.

On virtual selling platforms, you hesitate, become hypercritical, and beat yourself up over small mistakes that no one else notices. Then, in this state of insecurity, revert back to a communication channel that makes you feel more comfortable—typically face-to-face for field reps and email or social media for inside sales reps.

Vulnerability, according to Dr. Brene Brown, author of the *Power of Vulnerability*, is created in the presence of uncertainty, risk, and emotional exposure. This vulnerability conjures up the deepest and darkest of human fears: *Being rejected, ostracized, criticized, or embarrassing yourself in front of others.*

Rejection is a painful demotivator. It is the genesis of deep-rooted fear. The anticipation of being rejected generates worry, doubt, stress, and hesitation. The fear and avoidance of the emotional pain caused by rejection is why salespeople become asynchronous sellers. It allows them to avoid rejection altogether.

These fears are the number one reason why sales professionals fail to adopt and master virtual communication channels.

You can, like so many people do, wish that you didn't have to use them. Wish that prospects would always be nice and never reject you, wish that you could go back to the good old days, wish that it was easier. Yet, to be successful in the brave new world that is dominated by virtual selling, you are going to need to ditch your wishbone and grow a backbone.

Developing Emotional Self-Control

As you've learned, the most consistent predictor of outcome is your stakeholders' emotional experience working with you. When you lack confidence in yourself, stakeholders tend to lack confidence in you.

Yet with a relaxed, assertive demeanor, you gain the power to influence the emotions of the other people. For this reason, you must develop and practice techniques for building and demonstrating relaxed confidence, even when you feel the opposite. Even if you must fake it because you are shaking in your boots on virtual sales calls, you must appear relaxed and poised.

Disruptive emotions produce destructive behaviors that fog focus, cloud situational awareness, cause irrational decision-making, lead to misjudgments, and erode confidence.

To master virtual selling, you must first learn to master and rise above the disruptive emotions of fear, worry, doubt, and insecurity. You'll need to rise above your egotistical need to always look good and never be seen making mistakes.

There Are Only Three Things You Control

You have a choice. Either become extinct, be replaced by a robot, or learn to control your emotional responses, gain confidence, and start leveraging virtual sales channels. If you want to succeed in sales today, you must master an omnichannel communication approach. There is no way around this.

Getting past the emotions that disrupt confidence when using synchronous virtual communication channels is among the most formidable challenges for sales professionals. It's natural to feel intimidated and insecure. It's natural to doubt yourself. It's natural to want to retreat to communication channels that you feel you can control. But the truth is, you can only control three things:

1. Your actions
2. Your reactions
3. Your mindset

That's it—nothing more. You can choose to learn new technology. You can choose to try. You can choose to dust yourself off when you make a mistake and try again. You can choose your attitude and self-talk. You can choose awareness over delusion. And in emotionally tense situations, you have absolute control over your response.

Self-Awareness

Mastering your emotions begins with your awareness that the emotion is happening, which allows your rational mind to take the helm, make sense of the emotion, rise above it, and choose your behavior and response. Awareness is the intentional and deliberate choice to monitor, evaluate, and modulate your emotions so that your emotional responses to the people and environment around you are congruent with your intentions and objectives.

Self-awareness opens the door to self-control. There is a big difference between experiencing emotions and being caught up in them. Awareness allows you to gain rational control over your emotions and choose your actions appropriately.

Once you become aware that the emotion is happening, self-control allows you to manage your outward behavior despite the volcanic emotions that may be erupting below the surface. Like a duck on the water, you appear calm and cool on the outside even though you're paddling frantically just below the surface.

Obstacle Immunity

Self-awareness and self-control are like muscles. The more you exercise them, the stronger they get. And the best way to exercise them is to face adversity, challenges, and emotional obstacles head on. In other words, practice.

During World War II, Lawrence Holt, who owned a merchant shipping line in Britain, observed something that launched a movement. His ships were being targeted and torpedoed by German U-boats. Strangely, the survivors of these attacks were more likely to be old sailors than younger, more physically fit men.

This phenomenon led Holt to turn to Kurt Hahn, an educator who before the war had been imprisoned by the Nazis for criticizing Hitler. Holt engaged Hahn to help him understand why the younger, stronger, more physically fit members of his crews died at an alarmingly higher rate after attacks.

What Holt and Hahn eventually concluded was the difference between the two groups came down to emotional resilience, self-reliance, and inner strength. Even though the younger men possessed superior physical strength and agility, it was the emotional resilience to endure grueling emotional obstacles that helped the older, more experienced sailors survive.

Holt is famous for saying, "I would rather entrust the lowering of a lifeboat in mid-Atlantic to a sail-trained octogenarian than to a young sea technician who is completely trained in the modern way but has never been sprayed by saltwater."

The findings led Holt and Hahn to found Outward Bound, an organization that, ever since, has been helping people develop mental strength, confidence, tenacity, perseverance, resilience, and obstacle immunity by immersing them in harsh conditions.

Joe De Sena's Spartan Races and military training are designed for the very same purpose—to build obstacle immunity. People are pitted against challenging and painful tests of will. Through adversity and suffering, participants learn how to change their mental state and gain control of disruptive emotions.

You build your "emotional discipline muscle" when you put yourself in a position to experience a perceived obstacle, like engaging prospects on video calls, and the accompanying emotions again and again.

Once you intentionally begin to face your fears in emotionally uncomfortable virtual selling situations, you'll learn to disrupt and neutralize the anxiety that comes right before the obstacle. You'll begin rising above your emotions.

The more often you do it, the more your emotional self-control will improve and the easier it will become. Soon omnichannel virtual selling will become routine. You'll gain a sense of mastery and confidence. This leads to higher self-esteem and improved effectiveness with virtual selling.

PART III

Video Sales Calls

11 | Video Calls— The Closest Thing to Being There

Being there face-to-face makes it much easier to build relationships, solve problems, collaborate, navigate the sales process, meet all of the stakeholders, and close the deal. This is why sales professionals spend so much time on planes, trains, and automobiles traveling to visit with prospects and customers.

If you can't be there face-to-face, or if an in-person sales call is not practical or cost effective, the next best thing is a video call. According to a Forbes Insight study, 62 percent of executives said that video improved communication versus the phone.[1] It is the closest facsimile to in-person interaction and the reason smart people were dreaming about video calling all the way back in the nineteenth century.

As you've learned, at least half of our brain capacity is dedicated to our eyes. The primary way we interpret the world around us is through visual stimulus. This is exactly why video calls are a powerful and effective virtual sales communication channel when human to human connection matters most.

Video is more personal than any other form of virtual communication. It feels more human. On video calls, you may observe facial expressions and body language and pick up on emotional nuance. Just as with face-to-face calls, you are able to use this information to quickly adjust your approach based on these reactions.

Video makes you appear more human than on a phone call. Because people can see you, emotional connections, relationships, and trust are established faster. This is why video calls are the most powerful and effective virtual sales channel.

Video Is Underutilized by Sales Professionals

Video sales calls are easy, convenient, and cost-effective. Today, you can make a video call on any device, at anytime, anywhere, from a growing list of platforms, apps, and messaging tools.

Likewise, you can record video messages for prospects and customers that help you open up opportunities, stay top-of-mind between sales calls, advance opportunities through the pipeline, and nurture relationships (we'll discuss video messaging in Chapter 18).

Yet, video calls and video messaging are way underutilized by sales professionals, for several reasons:

- Salespeople default to face-to-face before considering that a video call may be just as effective and more efficient.
- Salespeople default to the phone rather than considering that a video call may be far more effective.
- Stakeholders have not been explicitly asked to participate on video sales calls.

- Training is lacking in how to conduct highly effective video sales calls.
- Technology and equipment make people uncomfortable.
- Appearing on video makes people nervous or anxious.

Sales Gravy has a sister company called *Knowledge Studios.* This organization collaborates with commercial and governmental organizations to design and create customized e-learning content. When working with clients, we often interview their leaders on video to include in the course work. I've watched the most confident, high-powered executives who easily command any room lose the ability to speak the moment we put a camera in front of them.

We always poll participants before our Virtual Selling Bootcamps about their biggest challenges. Number one, by a wide margin, is "being uncomfortable on camera." This self-conscious fear of appearing on video is real, and it holds more salespeople back from taking advantage of video than any other issue. In a recent survey, 59 percent of people said they felt less attractive on video than they do in real life, and 48 percent worried more about how they looked than preparing for the meeting.[2]

I get it, because I've been in those same shoes and experienced that same fear. You would never believe this today, because I'm on video all of the time. There are more than 500 videos on my YouTube channel at https://youtube.com/salesgravy.

However, there was a time when I was terrified of being on video. I was self-conscious, self-critical, and a perfectionist to the point that I would plan, to plan, to plan to shoot videos but never would. Even though I could stand in front of 20,000 people and deliver a keynote, I sounded like a blithering idiot when speaking to the camera. I hated video.

I realized, though, that my fear of the camera was holding me and my entire company back. So, I resolved to make a change.

I started by just doing it. I'd set my phone up and record a video, then force myself to post it online. I started showing my face on webinars and presentations rather than hiding behind slides. I set a goal to make a new video every day, often in crowded places like airports to force myself to let go of the fear that other people were judging me.

There were some incredibly embarrassing moments, like the time I did a webinar with over 2,000 people on the call. I was so nervous that I didn't notice that people could only see half of my face. I looked like a Muppet. I was so mortified I thought I'd die. I remember saying that I'd never do it again. But I made myself get back on the horse.

I've made a ton of bad videos. Bad audio. Bad lighting. Bad framing. Over time, though, the more I did it, like everything else in life, the better I became.

I developed immunity to my fear of the camera. My confidence grew. I learned how to talk to the camera like it was a person standing in front of me. I became comfortable with video equipment and technology. Along the way, the quality of my videos and video calls improved dramatically.

Mastering video has given me and my company a huge competitive advance. It allows us to be more agile. We are able to connect with clients and fans all over the world. We have become so good with video production that Sales Gravy has set the standard for how virtual training should be delivered.

If you fear or are uncomfortable with video, I promise that you can learn to master it. I know this to be true because I've watched so many other people do it. There is no easy button, though. You must make the choice to face this obstacle again and again. You must allow yourself to feel embarrassed and make mistakes until the camera becomes your friend.

Free Resources: I've developed a Video Selling Playbook as a supplemental resource for this book. I'll reference it often over the upcoming chapters. With the purchase of this book you get 12 months of access. To claim these free resources, go to https://www.salesgravy.com/vskit and use code **VSKIT2112RX** when you check out. (No credit card or payment of any kind is required.)

12 | Blending Video Calls into the Sales and Account Management Process

In modern sales, speed matters. Channels like email, text, direct messaging, and the phone help you move faster. However, far too often, speed is prioritized over human connection. When these channels are overused, it can leave both you and your stakeholders feeling emotionally disconnected.

Trust is not built over text messages or emails. It is built most effectively through face-to-face connections. Because stakeholders are able to see your facial expressions and body language, your words carry more credibility. Video calls open the door to deeper relationships, emotional connections, and trust.

Blending video sales calls into your sales and account management processes helps you become more agile and productive. It accelerates pipeline velocity.

Initial Meetings

One of the most effective points in the sales process to leverage video calls is the initial meeting. The initial meeting is the first step in the sales process. It is the appointment you (or your sales development rep) set during outbound prospecting or on an inbound call.

The objective of the initial sales meetings (which are often the first step in the discovery process) is threefold:

1. Make a great first impression and develop an early emotional connection with the stakeholder(s).
2. Fully qualify the opportunity to determine if it makes sense for you to move to the next step with the prospect.
3. Generate enough interest with the stakeholder(s) to motivate them to advance to the next step in the sales process.

An effective initial meeting should be about 30 minutes in length and no more than 60 minutes. Your primary goal is to close for the next meeting—discovery, demo, or presentation based on the complexity and length of your sales cycle.

In cases where the opportunity is not a good fit, the stakeholder does not have the ability to buy, or the timing is wrong, you'll want to walk away. Sometimes the stakeholders will not have enough interest to move forward and won't set the next meeting with you. A good rule of thumb and my personal experience is that I disqualify between 30 percent and 50 percent of prospects on initial meetings and never move forward with the next step.

For example: If you conduct 10 initial meetings over the course of a week, about half will advance to the next step. Depending on your closing ratio, one or two of those will close. Of course, some delusional salespeople throw proposals at every prospect, regardless of how they check the qualification boxes. This is a terrible drain on productivity and a waste of resources. You cannot be successful and delusional at the same time.

For a field rep, 10 good-quality initial meetings a week is about all you can handle and still have time for prospecting, discovery calls, demos, presentations, installations, account management, and admin work. There just isn't enough time for more.

That is . . . unless, you cut out all of the windshield time and shift your initial meetings from in-person to video. There are several benefits to conducting initial meeting video calls:

- You will increase the number of initial meetings you can conduct a week, which, in turn, increases the number of new opportunities advancing through your pipeline—which, in turn, increases the number of deals you close.
- Because video sales calls tend to be shorter than in-person calls *and* you eliminate drive time, you immediately become more efficient.
- Prospecting objections are reduced. More prospects will agree to meet with you because a short video call (to determine if it makes sense to work together) is easier for them to consume and lowers their risk of wasting time with you.
- Travel costs are reduced.

For many field salespeople, the idea of conducting initial meetings via video seems unimaginable. Likewise, there are many inside sales account executives who cringe at moving their initial meetings from a pure telephone call to a video call.

What I want to impress on the field sales professional is that even though we know that an in-person meeting is more effective, the efficiency you gain by shifting initial meetings to video calls more than makes up for not being there face-to-face. You'll be able to meet with and qualify more prospects, resulting in a bigger pipeline and more sales.

For the inside sales account executive, you will find that even though the video call will take just a little longer, which can potentially reduce the number of initial meetings you can conduct, the connections, credibility, and trust you build over video will result in a higher show rate on next steps and a higher conversion rate overall.

Discovery

Discovery is the most important step in the sales process and where 80 percent or more of your time should be spent. It is the key to building your business case and trust.

Depending on the complexity of the deal, discovery may last a few minutes or span many months and require meetings with a broad array of stakeholders.

Discovery is hard work. It can be slow and time-consuming. It requires intention, strategy, and planning. You must ask open-ended questions, demonstrate sincere interest, and listen.

One of the primary reasons so many salespeople struggle to ink more deals is that their discovery is weak and inadequate. It's so much easier to run quickly through a handful of self-serving, closed-ended questions, with a single stakeholder, email over a proposal, and hope for the best than it is to take the time to truly understand what is important to your stakeholders.

During discovery, you must be patient, strategic, and methodical. The objective is to leverage strategic, artful, and provocative questions to:

- Create self-awareness that causes stakeholders to realize that there is a need to change.
- Challenge the status quo and shake stakeholders from their comfort zones.
- Eliminate perceived alternatives to doing business with you.

Discovery done well also allows you to get high, wide, and deep, and build relationships with multiple stakeholders. The more discovery you do, the more people you meet, the more questions you ask, the more stakeholders who trust you and become your advocates, the stronger and more competitive your position and the higher the probability that you will close the sale.

In the discovery phase of the sales process, especially with complex deals, there are situations in which you absolutely must be there face-to-face. You need to see the entire picture, get hands-on with the problem, assess where your competitor is making mistakes, and see things that a video camera cannot capture so that you may develop unique solutions. With complex, high-value, high-risk deals when you can be there in person for discovery, you probably should be.

However, in-person discovery is not always practical or cost-effective. If you are in inside sales, face-to-face, in-person discovery may never be possible. If you have a multistep discovery process with a wide array of stakeholders who are located in many locations, the cost in both time and expenses may be too high and too risky. This is where video becomes a powerful tool.

Video discovery gives you the ability to meet more stakeholders and ask more questions. In some situations, you can even ask stakeholders to use their mobile devices to show you around their facility to give you a closer look. With video discovery calls, you can be far more agile and shorten the sales process.

One of the best features of video discovery calls is that on platforms like Zoom, you can both record the conversation and get a transcript. I find this invaluable when I'm building proposals. I'm able to go back and view the video recording and transcripts for anything I might have missed or misunderstood. This has saved my hide more than once.

For inside sales professionals who are used to working exclusively on the phone, video discovery calls help you build deeper connections and get a much bigger view of your prospect's issues. It may take you a little bit more time to do discovery this way. However, the connections you make and relationships you build will have a significant and positive impact on your closing ratio.

My team recently conducted video discovery calls with 27 stakeholders in cities spanning the United States, Canada, and Europe on a monster deal that we eventually won. Only one (the last) discovery call was in person, and that was with the company's top executives at their headquarters. We scheduled that in-person meeting once we determined that the probability of closing the deal was high and traveling to meet with them was worth the risk.

Video allowed us to connect with key influencers in the organization and turn them into advocates. We moved faster than our competitor in the deal, covered more ground, and the breadth of our discovery allowed us to build an unassailable business case that impressed the stakeholders and sealed the deal.

Presentations

Inside and field reps have been delivering presentations to remote stakeholders via videoconferencing since the technology became available. Before videoconferencing, I would overnight presentation decks to remote stakeholders and give my final presentation over the phone.

There are certainly some high-stakes situations when being there in-person matters. It's about making a statement and anchoring the relationship. There is an art to delivering powerful in-person presentations, and I've won my fair share of accounts by showing up when it counts.

However, it is so much more cost- and time-effective to deliver presentations through virtual meetings. Presentations tend to be short meetings. You are there to deliver information and close the deal. You typically spend far more time in transit, traveling to the meeting, than you do in the meeting.

By the time you get to the presentation, you've already made a significant investment in building relationships with your stakeholders. At this point, they are either going to buy from you or not. Therefore, being there has minimal impact on whether you close the deal. You'll get far more mileage investing that time in face-to-face meetings in the discovery phase of the sales process.

Stakeholders are busy, too. They prefer the convenience of a virtual presentation. In today's environment, they are comfortable consuming presentations on a video sales call. You'll find that giving your prospect a virtual option will make it easy to get past the "just email it to me" micro-commitment objection.

It also puts you in control. Most sales professionals have had the frustrating experience of handing out meticulously prepared presentation books to a group of stakeholders, only to watch them flip right to the price page and start grilling you with questions before you even start your presentation. This doesn't happen on video sales presentations because you have complete control of the deck and the pace.

Demos

Account executives at SaaS companies have been using videoconferencing for platform demos for years. These types of demos make total sense with an intangible product like software.

The good news, as enterprising salespeople learned during the coronavirus pandemic, is with today's technology and inexpensive video equipment (including your smart phone), you can deliver video demos of almost any product.

From capital equipment, tradeshow booths, real estate, and even walk-throughs at senior living facilities, video makes it easy for you to give virtual hands-on demos to remote buyers. The key is that you need to develop a system and process for your demo, make it interactive, and invest in a little bit of equipment to deliver a great experience. You'll find a list of recommended equipment here: https://www.salesgravy.com/vskit.

Closing and Negotiating

If you are managing the sales process correctly, you should be asking for the sale at the final presentation. Sometimes, though, stakeholders want to meet again just to feel good that they are making the right decision, or they want to negotiate. These are usually short meetings, with specific questions or issues. Leveraging video for these meetings allows you to work out the details and close the deal faster.

Account Management

When it comes to important customers, there really isn't anything like being there. With your top accounts, those face-to-face meetings are gold. They help you get high, wide, and deep in your accounts, strengthen relationships, find opportunities to add more value, expand the relationship, and lock out your competitors.

But you know as well as I do that if you own a large number of managed accounts, it is nearly impossible to visit them all on a regular basis. Nor are the infrequent quarterly or annual account review meetings with your top accounts enough.

Video calls help you connect more often to keep your fingers on the pulse of your accounts at a lower cost. This allows you to cover your accounts, protect your turf, and keep your competitors locked out.

For inside account managers who typically interact with customers by phone, video puts a face with a name, makes the interaction more human, improves problem solving, and anchors important relationships.

13 | Brain Games

The good news is, most of us have become comfortable interacting with family and friends via video. We'll FaceTime Grandma on a whim. With our smart phones, we are constantly capturing our lives on video and posting them online.

However, as you likely know, making a video call to your mom on FaceTime is far different than conducting a professional video sales call with prospects and customers. On video sales calls, the stakes are higher. You are always on stage. People are observing everything about you, including:

- Your appearance
- Facial expressions and body language
- Video and audio quality
- Your backdrop
- How you are framed in the video window

They use this information to make both conscious and sub-conscious decisions[1] about whether they like you, trust you, and want to work with you. Because as humans we feel first, then we think, it is incumbent on you to deliver the best possible emotional experience for your stakeholders on video calls.

Video Calls and the Problem with Cognitive Load

On video sales calls, you must never discount the power of the subconscious mind and how it holds sway over your stakeholder's perceptions, emotions, behavior, interpersonal interactions, likes, dislikes, and decisions.

Their brains are hard at work, looking at the patterns on screen and attempting to make sense of them to decide if they like you, determine if you are trustworthy, compare you to your competitors, and decide whether they should advance to the next step in the sales process.

Imagine if TV shows and movies looked like most virtual calls. You'd be instantly turned off by the cheap production quality. You certainly wouldn't want to pay for them.

The quality of most video calls is awful. Bad lighting, audio, video, backdrops, and framing all contribute to a poor emotional experience. And, it turns out, these calls hurt your brains.[2]

On video calls the brain must expend energy as it attempts to interpret the picture it sees on the screen and compare it with the way it expects a person to look like in person. When that picture does not look natural, when the clues and cues that are normally present in an in-person conversation are not there, the brain must work harder to fill in the gaps.

Poor-quality video calls increase cognitive load, causing your brain to work harder to fill in those gaps—to the point that it can become overloaded. This is why even 30 minutes on a video call can leave you feeling exhausted.[3]

Much like a computer, your brains can process only so much information at one time. As the cognitive load[4] grows, the brain must work overtime to process what it sees. It slows down and becomes less efficient. It is unable to focus. Attention control diminishes, and both short- and long-term memory are negatively impacted.

From an evolutionary standpoint, this is a bad thing. When your brain gets overloaded, you cannot focus on potential threats in your environment. This puts you in danger of being removed from the gene pool.

Therefore, in these situations, rather than wasting even more precious cognitive resources on rational thinking, the brain uses mental shortcuts called *heuristics* to make snap judgments.[5] These heuristics allow you to think fast in complex situations.

For example, if you position yourself in the frame so that the stakeholder cannot see your hand gestures, their brain diverts some of its computing power from paying attention to what you are saying, in an attempt to work out what you might be doing with your hands. As cognitive load increases, their brain uses a mental shortcut (heuristic) to make a snap judgment about you and protect its limited cognitive resources. *"If I can't see your hands, you must be doing something other than paying attention to me, and I don't like people who don't pay attention to me."*

This heuristic is a form of the *negativity bias* that causes your stakeholder to assume a "what's wrong with this picture" stance rather than to seek out what is right. In situations like this, humans almost always focus on the negative and assume worst.

You Are Always on Stage: Neutralizing Cognitive Biases

Cognitive biases[6] are the dark side of cognitive heuristics, and they are always in play. These hasty, pattern-based judgments cloud objectivity. In his book *Thinking, Fast and Slow*, Daniel Kahneman, the father of heuristic and cognitive bias research, writes:

> *Organisms that placed more urgency on avoiding threats than they did maximizing opportunities were more likely to pass on their genes. So, over time, the prospect of losses has become a more powerful motivator on your behavior than the promise of gains.*[7]

Humans tend to be attracted to safe choices and safe environments. Salespeople, as a rule, are not perceived as safe. You pose a threat.

Stakeholders are scrutinizing you. They are looking for congruence in your words, nonverbal communication, and actions. Your every behavior, every word, every action is being observed. This *safety bias* causes your stakeholder's brain to be more aware of bad things (what could go wrong) than good things (what could go right).

This is why the number one reason buyers choose not to move forward with buying decisions is not price, product specs, delivery windows, or any of the things salespeople too often blame. It's the fear of negative future consequences.

The trap salespeople fall into, though, is the false belief that good intentions are enough. They show up on video calls with the belief that the logical substance of the call is all that matters, forgetting about the perceptions they are creating within their video frame.

Think about it. Would you walk into a corporate boardroom to deliver an important presentation to a group of C-level executives wearing a T-shirt, shorts, and flip-flops? Of course not, because no matter how good your presentation, no matter how well placed your intentions, the image of you dressed that way would create such a deep negative perception that you would lose the deal.

Stakeholders are not judging your trustworthiness based on *your* rational intentions. They make those judgments based on their emotional perceptions. They worry that:

- If they make a change, things could go wrong.
- You won't live up to your promises.
- The change will disrupt their business.
- You'll manipulate them.

In a form of *confirmation bias*, their brain begins to seek out things about you that support their fears. Their subconscious mind magnifies anything in the video frame that seems out of place. Though they are consciously unaware of how or why their perceptions have been negatively impacted, they feel uncertain, unsure, and afraid but don't always know why. "I can't put my finger on it, but something just doesn't seem right."

This is why you must never forget that you are always on stage! Yes, you must follow the sales process, build your business case, and present a solution that delivers the outcomes your stakeholders desire. Yet, at the same time, you must neutralize the potential negative subconscious biases that can hurt you on video sales calls (and, for that matter, with all virtual communication).

14 | Seven Technical Elements of Highly Effective Video Sales Calls

The directors and producers of TV shows and movies invest hundreds of hours into perfecting their sets, lighting, and audio. On the major shoots I've been on with professional crews, twice as much time was spent on getting the set right as I spent actually working in front of the camera.

They do this because they know that viewers know what looks right and know what looks wrong, even if they are unaware of it at the conscious level. Directors and producers are acutely aware that the more natural and "right" things look to the viewer's brain, the lower the cognitive load and the easier the content is to consume.

This is your primary goal with video sales calls. You'll need to invest time to create a video sales call experience that makes you look natural on camera and as closely as possible to how you might look if you were there in person.

It takes effort to get it right. You need to care about the details and your audience. You must optimize every aspect of your *video sales call set*.

Videoconferencing technology is good and getting better. Professional-level video equipment continues to become less expensive and easier to use. Today, you can build an impressive video sales call set for a few hundred dollars that will make you look professional and feel confident.

In the next chapter, we will take on the human elements that give you a competitive edge on video sales calls. First, though, we will dive into the technical elements. Because technology and equipment are always evolving, I am not going to provide specific equipment recommendations here. Instead, we keep an updated list of recommended equipment for your virtual selling kit at https://www.salesgravy.com/vskit.

When you make the investment, you'll wow stakeholders on video sales calls and separate yourself from your competitors because most salespeople will be far too lazy to go the extra mile and do it right.

Audio

Even though we are discussing video calls, the most important element is audio. High-quality audio matters. If people can see you, but cannot hear you, your call will be a failure. If your audio quality is poor, it creates a bad impression of you. This is why audio comes first. There are four keys to good audio:

Good Internet Connection and Speed

Your internet connection has a great deal of impact on the quality of the audio portion of your call. If it is poor, there will be times when your voice cycles in and out or becomes distorted—no matter how good of a microphone you have. If you have poor or inconsistent speed, dial into the video call with your phone. That way, no matter what happens to the image on screen, they'll be able to hear you.

Background Noise

Do not run video sales calls in rooms where irritating and random background noise is an issue. Trains, alarms, traffic, doorbells, pets, and random loud noises affect your audience's experience and *your* ability to maintain attention control.

Room Echo

There is a reason why film studios build expensive sound stages. *Few things are more irritating than audio that is echoing off the walls.* When your voice is echoing, people have a hard time hearing and paying attention to you.

Most offices and rooms in your home have walls made of sheet rock. Sound bounces off of these walls like a rubber ball off of concrete. If your room is sparsely furnished or has high ceilings, it will be worse. You will sound like you are in a cave.

The key to cleaning up this sound is installing acoustic panels on stands or affixed to ceilings and walls. I also suggest *sound blankets* built onto mobile stands and corner base traps to clean up echoes. Learn more about these tools here: https://www.salesgravy .com/vskit.

Professional Microphone

If you listen to most people on video calls, their voice is distorted. It's not deep, natural, or flattering. This is because they are either using a cheap headset or, worse, the microphone on their laptop.

I am not a fan of wearing headphones of any kind. It creates a poor visual. Even though the person on the other side of the video call knows why you are wearing them, their subconscious brain does not compute. We are used to staying at arm's distance from people wearing headphones. Headphones or wireless earbuds send a clear message, "Do not bother me."

That said, some of the new wireless earbuds like the Apple's AirPods Pro have far better audio quality than the microphone in your laptop. They are still not ideal, but, in a pinch, they are better than wearing earphones.

Some of the high-quality external webcams have built-in microphones. Because you don't need to wear earphones, you look much more natural. Though the sound quality isn't great, it's better than your laptop mic and most earphones.

A good, professional microphone will make your voice sound full and natural. It will also help dampen background noise and reduce the impact of echo. One option is a good-quality podcasting microphone. In many cases, these mics can be placed out of the scene, creating a more natural look.

Personally, I prefer wearing a high-end lavalier mic. This delivers superior audio quality and eliminates the telltale signs that I am miced up, making it feel more natural, as if I am there face-to-face. Learn more about audio options here: https://www.salesgravy.com/vskit.

Lighting

Next to audio, lighting is the most important technical element of a video sales call. Just like your eyes, cameras require the right amount of light to render a good image.

Great lighting makes you look natural and accessible and reduces stakeholder brain strain. It also illuminates your facial expressions, making you appear more human and trustworthy. Fortunately, it is relatively easy to get lighting right on your video sales call set.

The first step to good lighting is to eliminate bright light sources behind you (like windows and bright white walls). Webcams and many cameras automatically adjust to and record the brightest source of light in the frame. When that light is behind you, you're no longer the focus and your face becomes a dark blob. We call this look "witness protection."

If you are in a room with a window, face toward the window. Natural light helps accentuate skin tone and features. On the other hand, if it is too bright or there are harsh glares, it can be distracting and wash you out. Manage and regulate natural light sources with shades or sheers.

For the best lighting, place a professional light source directly behind the camera and at face level. Typically, one or two good-quality light sources will do the trick. You'll want the light source to be roughly the same level as the camera and directly behind it. Don't place your lights above you because it can create distracting shadows that pull attention away from you.

I recommend either LED ring lights or LED panel lights made specifically for shooting video. Place lights on light stands so that you may adjust the height and angle. Make sure that the lights you choose have a dimmer and temperature control so that you can adjust the brightness. If your light source is too bright, it will wash out your face and make it difficult to concentrate on your facial features.

You'll find several recommendation and options for lighting your video call set here: https://www.salesgravy.com/vskit.

Framing

Proper framing on video sales calls makes you look professional and confident. How you are positioned within the video frame has a massive impact on cognitive load and how you are perceived. It determines whether you look natural, as if you are right there in front of your stakeholder, or look like a distorted version of you that causes their brain to hurt.

Six Frames That Cause Negative Perceptions of You

There are six framing positions that hurt your appearance on video calls. We gave them names to help you easily identify and remember these poor frames (see figure 14.1):

1. *Skydiver:* This is the most common framing mistake. In this position, you are looking down into the camera. This is typically caused by your laptop computer being lower than your face. In extreme cases, you can even see the skydiver's ceiling.

Figure 14.1   Improper Video Framing

2. *Bobblehead:* In this position you are too close to the camera, causing your head from the neck up to fill the entire frame. In extreme cases, parts of your head are cut off.

3. *Stargazer:* In this position, the camera is above you and you are looking up. This causes your image on video to become weirdly distorted.

4. *Witness protection:* In this position, the light is behind you – typically, a bright window. This causes your face to be obscured and dark on the screen. In extreme cases, with very bright lights you appear completely blacked out.

5. *Max Headroom:* In this position, there is too much space between the top of your head and the top of the video frame. With severe headroom issues, your head appears teeny tiny at the bottom of the frame (we call this look "Mini-Me").

6. *Grim Reacher:* You'll notice this look when a person is using their laptop's internal webcam. As you reach to touch the keyboard your hands become massively large compared to your head. It is not a flattering or natural look.

The most common cause of poor framing positions is that you are using the webcam on your laptop so that where your laptop is positioned, your camera is positioned.

Proper Framing

The best way to visualize proper framing for a video sales call is to think about how a newscaster is positioned on screen. If you take a moment to turn on your favorite news show, you'll notice that when the newscaster is in the frame, the horizontal and vertical axis lines are symmetrical—straight up and down and across rather than tilted, as with the skydiver and stargazer positions. See Figure 14.2.

You should be positioned in the center of the frame with your sight line camera level, making eye contact just as if you were meeting with someone in person. Ensure that there is reasonable space between the top of your head and the top of the frame, but not too much so that you avoid the Max Headroom framing mistake.

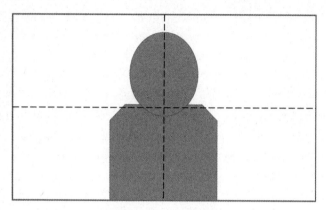

Figure 14.2   Proper Video Framing

The best way to achieve eye-level framing is to use an external webcam or professional camera. Place the webcam on a tripod that can be adjusted to eye level. If you must use your laptop, place it on books or a stand so that the camera is at eye level.

You should be far enough away from the camera that your torso above the waist is visible. This ensures that your face is not too close to the camera and distorted, as in the Bobblehead position, and your hands are visible when you speak.

Hands are a big part of our body language. In order to trust you, stakeholders need to see that your words and body language are congruent.

Camera

Do not use your computer's built-in camera! These cameras tend to produce a subpar image, making it difficult to achieve proper framing. Using your laptop's internal webcam also turns you into the Grim Reacher.

Choosing the right camera setup can make a huge difference in the quality of your video frame and how you appear on screen. Choose a camera that is external from your laptop and place it on a sturdy, adjustable tripod. There are excellent, high-quality webcam options available that will make you look professional without breaking the bank.

You may also want to consider a professional setup. I achieve professional look and sound with a Sony mirrorless, full-frame camera paired with a high-quality wide-angle lens. My wireless lavalier microphone runs through the camera, which is connected to my laptop with an easy-to-set-up capture card.

You'll find several recommendation and options for cameras here: https://www.salesgravy.com/vskit.

Backdrop

Your backdrop is essentially everything that is visible in your video frame other than you. Your backdrop represents your company and personal brand. Treat it that way. What people see when they are on calls with you sends a powerful message.

Backdrops to Avoid

- Clutter and trash
- Unflattering personal items that do not reflect well on your personal brand
- Blank walls—especially white or beige
- Distracting paintings and art
- Bright windows
- Big cavernous rooms (like your family room)—this has tendency to pull the viewers eyes away from you and into the room

Backdrops to Consider

Background Image Replacement.   This is a feature offered by some videoconferencing technology platforms like Zoom. It allows you to replace your background with an image.

Do not use the stock images provided with the platform. Instead, use a tool like Canva to create your own. This will allow you to experiment with multiple versions to find the one that looks best with your lighting and room. When I use background replacement on calls, I like to place my customer's logo in the background image.

This technology is getting better but has its limitations. The benefit is that it is inexpensive and allows you to have infinite backdrops. The downside is that fast movements and hand gestures can cause blurs and break the background replacement, making you look distorted and unnatural.

Your lighting configuration will also affect how it looks, so you'll want to experiment. You may also want to consider placing a greenscreen behind you. Though not necessary, I've found that this delivers the highest-quality background replacement results with the least amount of distortion.

Bookcase. A well-crafted, built-in bookcase (white is the best color), neatly filled with books and a limited number of tasteful knick-knacks that support your personal brand makes for an excellent backdrop. This backdrop offers enough variety to be interesting but not distracting. Just be sure that what is on the shelves is not offensive or in any way controversial.

Credenza. A credenza paired with tasteful artwork or your company logo centered on the wall behind you is another good choice. Even better is a credenza paired with a flat screen TV on which you may display your logo or other visuals, including PowerPoint slides. Choose a TV with a matte screen to avoid glare from your lighting.

Working Office. If you conduct video sales calls from your office, it is absolutely acceptable for your backdrop to be people working behind you, as long as you are able to manage the background noise. A working office sends a strong message about you and your brand.

Tradeshow Style Display. A branded tradeshow-style display or stand-and-repeat (like what you might see at a press conference) is my favorite backdrop. It eliminates any potential distractions, supports your brand, and always looks professional. Most of these displays are portable, making it easy to relocate your set.

We've included resources for building a professional backdrop here: https://www.salesgravy.com/vskit.

Internet Connection

No internet connection, no video sales call. Poor internet connection, poor video sales call.

If you live in an area with fiber or super fast internet speeds, count yourself lucky. No matter what your situation though, spend the money to upgrade to the fastest *upload* speed your broadband provider offers.

Most providers tout their download speeds. That's great for streaming movies but doesn't help a bit with delivering a video sales call stream. For this, you need to max out your upload speeds.

Like many people, you may live in an area or work in an office where speed and bandwidth go up and down, depending on the day, weather, node, or how many people are on at the same time. For this reason, I highly recommend investing in a backup connection source like a mobile hotspot. Having a backup source has saved me on many occasions when my main broadband source went down.

We've included tools to check your internet speed here: https://www.salesgravy.com/vskit.

Platform and Tech Stack

There are many good options on the market for videoconferencing platforms. I recommend investing in at least two different platforms so that you have a backup and can give your prospects and customers multiple options.

The most important action you can take with your platform and technology stack is to invest time into exploring the features and taking the tutorials. Become an expert so that you can quickly troubleshoot issues and help other people who may have trouble connecting.

You should also practice and perfect making video sales calls on apps like FaceTime, Messenger, and WhatsApp. You'll find a list of supporting apps for enhancing video calls, from noise reduction, virtual backgrounds, and testing your equipment here: https://www.salesgravy.com/vskit.

Invest in Your Set

What if my company won't provide the equipment I need?

I hear this complaint from salespeople all of the time. My response: Suck it up and make the investment yourself. It's your commission check on the line.

I remember when PowerPoint first came on the scene in the early 1990s. Only a few people were using it. I begged my company for a laptop and the software so I could deliver more compelling presentations. They refused.

So, I took a calculated risk and dropped five grand (a huge sum of money at that time) on a laptop and the software. It gave me an instant competitive advantage.

This might not seem like a big deal now because everyone uses PowerPoint. But back then, no one had ever seen anything like it. I walked into presentations and blew stakeholders away. That year, I made more than $300,000 when most of my peers were making less than $40K.

I learned an important lesson from that experience, and ever since, I've made investments in technology that keep me ahead of the curve. Stop whining. Make the investment. Be better than everyone else. Separate from your competitors before they catch up.

15 | Five Human Elements of Highly Effective Video Sales Calls

In simple terms, your brain is like a Russian nesting doll.

- The big doll on the outside is the neocortex. This is your gray matter—your rational brain.
- The middle doll is the limbic system—your emotional brain.
- The smallest doll is your cerebellum or autonomic brain—it manages all the little (but still important) things, like breathing, so you can concentrate on thinking.

All three brains are connected by the amygdala, a small structure within the brain, which is housed in the limbic system.

The amygdala is the hub that processes all sensory input, connecting the rational, emotional, and autonomic parts of your brain. It is the center for emotions, emotional behavior, and motivation.

To help your brain avoid wasting precious cognitive resources on things that don't matter, the amygdala ignores boring patterns and focuses on and responds to environmental disruptions – anything different, out of place, unexpected, bright, shiny, sexy, new, or threatening.

This simple cognitive shortcut of ignoring boring patterns and being alert to anything that disrupts those patterns is a key survival mechanism. Pattern disrupters can be threats or opportunities, so it makes sense to pay attention to them.

The amygdala exerts a massive and compulsory influence over emotional behavior. At a foundational level, your stakeholder's amygdala decides whether or not you are safe, likeable, and worthy of attention. This happens long before the person is consciously aware of these decisions. The amygdala acts as a gate to their neo-cortex, letting things in that it deems important and blocking those it deems unimportant to avoid wasting cognitive resources.

As you've already learned, most video calls are awful. They hurt the brain. To deal with this pain, over time, your brain begins to ignore bad video frames and tune them out. Simply said, those frames become boring patterns.

When your virtual behaviors fall into this expected pattern, when your video frame looks and feels like every other awful video frame, you will not differentiate. You are not interesting. You are not memorable. Your stakeholder's amygdala closes the gate.

Painting this boring gray pattern with bright colors changes everything. When you disrupt expectations on video calls, you pull stakeholders toward you and grab their attention. Pattern painting works because the amygdala loves different.

The beautiful thing about video sales calls is that, to stand out, you don't need to stand on your head. You just need to be good. In the last chapter you learned how to upgrade the technical elements of your virtual sales call set—audio, lighting, camera, framing, backdrop—to instantly separate yourself from 90 percent of the salespeople you compete against.

In this chapter, we're going to focus on the elements that make you accessible, warm, credible, human, and memorable on camera.

Body Language

People are listening to the words you *say* and comparing them to the body language they *see* to judge whether you are trustworthy. If there is not congruence, they begin to question your motives. For example, on video calls, when they cannot see your body language because you are in the *bobble-head* position in your video frame, it causes them to trust you less.

There are five elements of body language that you must manage and control to be an effective, approachable, trustworthy communicator on video sales calls.

1. Facial expressions
2. Body movement and posture
3. Gestures
4. Voice tone and inflection
5. Eye contact

When you observe other people's body language and interpret it for meaning, it's called *decoding* or deep listening. When you are sending cues to other people—like buyers—it is called *encoding*.

A distinguished list of researchers, including Dr. Albert Mehrabian[1] and Dr. Paul Eckman,[2] have done extensive research on the impact of nonverbal cues on human communication. They have concluded that somewhere between 70 percent and 93 percent of human communication is nonverbal.

What this tells us is that our nonverbal signals have a massive impact on our ability to connect with and influence other people. This is why encoding is a meta-skill for virtual selling where nonverbal communication is being put under a microscope and scrutinized by stakeholders for meaning.

Simply put, message matters. What you say, and more importantly how you say it, is critical with all forms of communication. On video sales calls, though, it is everything. Which is why you must be more disciplined with managing your message—from your set, to your wardrobe, to your body language.

Facial Expressions

Research conducted over the past fifty years tell us that that we can truly read a face like a book. Your face is expressive. It reveals how you are feeling—happiness, concern, fear, anger, and surprise.

When we are interacting with other humans in person, we are constantly scanning their faces in an attempt to judge their emotions. This same process is in play on video calls.

On video calls, though, it is much harder to read facial expressions than in person:

- When you are speaking into the camera, you cannot see the other person's face. This is called the *eye-contact paradox*. I'll explain this later in the chapter.
- Most video frames suffer from poor lighting and positioning, which makes it difficult to read microexpressions[3] that help us discern emotional nuance.

It is because of these challenges that you'll want to upgrade your camera and lighting and improve your framing. This instantly makes your face and expressions easier for your stakeholder to see and thus makes you seem friendlier and more trustworthy.

To be successful at encoding, you must ensure that you don't miscommunicate your intentions or that stakeholders make misjudgments about your facial expressions. You've already learned that one of the great problems with video calls is that we are unable to see the entire picture—as we can when interacting in person.

Inside this limited picture, the stakeholder's brain works to fill in the gaps that are missing. Therefore, your facial expressions take on greater importance. You must carefully control your facial expressions and be more intentional and expressive than you would be in person.

For example, consider your resting facial expressions. This is your normal expression when you are listening to someone or concentrating.

Often when I'm reading, thinking, or writing a book, my wife will ask me if I'm mad. It surprises me, because the assumptions she is making about me based on my facial expression could not be further from the truth.

What she is responding to is my RBF (resting bitch face) or RAF (resting asshole face), as she likes to call it. Most people have some form of this resting facial expression which confuses other people. It can be a big miscommunication problem on video calls.

Demonstrates Lack of Confidence, Insecurity, and Fear	Demonstrates a Relaxed, Confident Demeanor
Jaw clenched, tense look on face.	Relaxed smile. The smile is a universal nonverbal sign that relays, "I'm friendly and can be trusted."

Victor Borge once said, "The shortest distance between two people is a smile." From the moment we are born, we learn that smiling is the fastest way to get others to pay attention to us. A baby's smile lights up the room. Smiles attract. Even dogs understand this. A wagging tail, an upturned mouth, and bright, wide eyes are the fastest route to a pat or treat.

Smiling is a primary communication tool used to connect and bind us to others. Numerous scientific and psychological studies have shown that the smile is a universal language that is recognized across cultures and ethnicities around the globe.[4] Excitement, humor, pleasure, confidence, happiness, welcome, love, understanding, caring, kindness, and friendship are all communicated through the smile.

On video calls, the smile is the most powerful and effective facial expression. Period. It makes you instantly likeable. It's welcoming and makes the best first impression. A sincere smile humanizes business relationships and conveys authenticity. It sets stakeholders at ease and creates a relaxed environment.

Your sincere smile says, "I mean no harm. I'm open." In this more relaxed state, you will find that people are more likely to engage, more willing to answer your questions, more forgiving of mistakes, and more open to connecting and developing a relationship.

Smiling is encoding at the highest level. From the moment the video sales call begins and until it ends, I am focused on and intentional about smiling. And because people respond in kind, stakeholders tend to smile back at me. Because smiling has a positive impact on mood, once they begin smiling, they feel good. When your actions make your prospects and customers feel good, they will naturally become more emotionally connected to you.

Posture and Body Movement

Consider the perceptions and judgments that stakeholders can make about you based on your posture, stance, and body movements.

Demonstrates Lack of Confidence, Insecurity, and Fear	Demonstrates a Relaxed, Confident Demeanor
Hunched over, head down, arms crossed.	Straight posture, chin up, shoulders straight and back. This posture will also make you feel more confident.
Shifting back and forth on your feet or rocking your body.	Standing still in a natural power pose.
Stiff posture, tense body.	Relaxed, natural posture.

How you position yourself in the frame and move on camera sends clear nonverbal messages. If you take an objective look at people who are sitting down while on video calls, you'll notice a number of poor behaviors that create a negative impression:

- Leaning in too close to the camera = Face distortion, hiding something
- Slumped or hunched over = Low energy and insecure
- Leaning back in the chair = Disinterested, not enthusiastic
- Fidgeting in the chair, back and forth or side to side = Insecure, untrustworthy, distracting

None of the positions make you look confident and enthusiastic. Yet when you are sitting at your desk, these positions are all too easy to assume. Because you sit at your desk all day, they've become habitual—making these posture and positioning mistakes almost impossible to break.

This is exactly why I *stand up* when I'm on video calls. The two emotions I want to transfer to my prospect are confidence and enthusiasm. I want them to feel my energy and passion. When I'm standing up, those messages come through the screen loud and clear.

When I stand up, I'm framed better in the shot. It allows me to move toward or away from the camera. Just like when I'm in person, I can lean in when something is important and move back when I want to reduce intensity and set people at ease. Standing up also makes it much easier to keep the sightline between my eyes and the camera level.

Standing up keeps my shoulders and chin up which makes me not only look confident, it makes me *feel* confident. Research by Amy Cuddy of Harvard University demonstrates that "power posing," physically standing in a posture of confidence, causes you to *feel* more confident.[5]

Standing up not only elicits a change in emotions[6] but it also triggers a neurophysiological response, which releases the hormones cortisol and testosterone, which play a significant role in creating the feeling of confidence.[7]

When you feel confident you transfer that emotion to stake-holders (emotional contagion). When they feel confident in you, win probability bends in your favor.

Gestures

We talk with our hands.[8] People watch our hand gestures and use those signals to connect the dots between facial expressions, voice inflection, tone, and words. Generally, we use our hands while we are speaking without thinking and people interpret the meaning of our gestures subconsciously.

When you don't use hand gestures or your hand gestures are awkward, your behavior is interpreted as stiff, cold, aloof, or uninterested.[9] Making your hands visible on video calls is also important because when people can't see your hands, they don't trust you.

Demonstrates Lack of Confidence, Insecurity, and Fear	Demonstrates a Relaxed, Confident Demeanor
Hands in your pockets.	Hands by your side or out in front of you as you speak. This may feel uncomfortable but makes you look powerful and confident.
No hand gestures.	Appropriate, natural hand gestures that meet the moment and are congruent with your words and pace.
Wild gesticulations or hand motions.	Using hand gestures in a calm and controlled manner.
Touching your face, hair, or putting your fingers in your mouth—a clear sign that you are nervous or insecure.	Your hands in a power position—by your side or out in front of you in a controlled, nonthreatening manner.

This is exactly why I stand up on video sales calls. It keeps my hand gestures natural and in the correct position. It also helps me avoid becoming a *Grim Reacher* (see Chapter 14).

Keep hand gestures natural and relaxed. Try not to move too fast because your gesture can break the background replacement and cause you to look distorted. Wild gestures can also cause stakeholders to lose trust in you. If you are conducting sales calls with stakeholders in other countries, do your homework to ensure that you don't accidentally use hand gestures that your audience may find offensive.

Human touch is a nonverbal communication channel that we lose on video calls—it's impossible to shake hands, bump fists, and engage in other friendly human rituals that connect us. The good news is you can easily and effectively replace these rituals with waving.

Waving is friendly, inviting, and a universal gesture that says, "I'm not a threat." It is considered good manners to wave at neighbors. Nice people wave.

A wave, accompanied with a smile, is like a virtual handshake. Just like with handshakes, you should wave hello at the beginning of the call and wave goodbye before you leave. Because people respond in kind, when you wave and smile, they almost always smile and wave back. This creates a positive emotional experience that connects you.

Voice

What you say matters. HOW you say it matters more. While your stakeholder's neocortex (rational brain) is busy interpreting the words you use, the emotional center of their brain is listening closely to your tone, timbre, pace, and inflection for hidden meaning.

Demonstrates Lack of Confidence, Insecurity, and Fear	Demonstrates a Relaxed, Confident Demeanor
Speaking with a high-pitched voice.	Speaking with normal inflection and a deeper pitch.
Speaking fast. When you speak too fast, you sound untrustworthy.	Speaking at a relaxed pace with appropriate pauses.
Tense or defensive tone of voice.	Friendly tone—a smile in your voice and on your face.
Speaking too loudly or too softly.	Appropriate voice modulation with appropriate emotional emphasis on the right words and phrases.
Frail or nervous tone of voice with too many filler words, "ums," "uhs," and awkward pauses.	Direct, intentional, properly paced tone and speech that gets right to the point.

How you say words can convey irritation, sarcasm, insecurity OR conviction, confidence, passion, and enthusiasm. It is important that you are careful to ensure that there is congruence between the words you say and the way you say them.

Flex your voice tone, inflection, and pace to match that of the stakeholder you are interacting with. Be careful not to speak too fast or too slow. Ensure that inflection emphasizes the right words.

Video sales calls tend to move at a faster pace than in-person calls. This can be challenging when you feel nervous, uncomfortable, and insecure in front of the camera.

The most effective way to increase your confidence and reduce the chance for miscommunication is pre-call planning. To ensure that your message is clear and congruent and that your brain is prepared to stay on track:

- Research, profile, and map stakeholders.
- Know your objective and targeted next step.
- Prepare your questions in advance for discovery calls.
- Practice presentations and demos.
- Plan for and run through multiple scenarios before closing and negotiation calls.
- Run "Murder Boarding Sessions" on complex deals.[10]

We know that when you dress your best, you feel your best. When you put your shoulders up and chin up, you look and feel confident.

For the very same reason, when voice inflection and pace are relaxed, assertive, and confident, you will feel confident and sound professional and believable. Likewise, when you put a smile in your voice and lead with a pleasant tone, you reduce the chance of misinterpretation and misjudgment and, like a magnet, you pull others toward you.

Eye Contact

The eyes really are the windows to the soul.[11] The eyes and the microexpressions around the eyes are how we gauge a person's mood, truthfulness, and approachability. When I want to know what my wife is feeling, I don't ask, I look at her eyes. They tell me everything.

The reason why in-person meetings are the most effective form of sales communication is because we have the chance to see each other eye-to-eye. The eyes connect us at an emotional level like nothing else.

Consequently, if you want to build emotional connections with stakeholders on video calls, if you want video calls to be as close a facsimile to in-person meetings as possible, then you must be intentional about making eye contact.

It is much easier to make and maintain eye contact in-person than it is on video. On video, because people cannot see the entire picture, they are much more likely (negativity bias) to assume the worst when they feel that you are not making eye contact.[12] They may think that you are:

- Insecure and lack confidence.
- Lying.
- Hiding something.
- Uninterested and detached.
- Not paying attention.
- Not listening.
- Uncaring.

Demonstrates Lack of Confidence, Insecurity, and Fear	Demonstrates a Relaxed, Confident Demeanor
Lack of eye contact—looking away. Nothing says "I can't be trusted" and "I'm not confident" like poor eye contact.	Be direct. Use appropriate eye contact.

Sadly, eye contact is the most challenging aspect of video sales calls. So much so that Apple (with other platforms soon to follow) is working to perfect software that creates the illusion of eye contact on video calls.[13]

One of the big reasons why maintaining eye contact on video calls is so difficult is that we tend to look at ourselves. There are a number of studies and surveys that indicate that most people spend between 30 percent and 70 percent of the time on video calls looking at their own face.

According to a survey conducted by Steelcase, 72 percent of people get distracted by their own appearance on video calls.[14] Why are we so distracted? Because we believe we look horrible on video.

When you are on camera, it is very difficult not to look at yourself because you know that people are looking you. It can be nerve wracking and cause you to be incredibly self-conscious. We stare at the gargoyle we see on screen and pick apart everything about ourselves until we are utterly disgusted.[15] This can have a significant and negative impact on your confidence and self-esteem in front of the camera.

Of course, at an in-person meeting, if you spent half the time looking at yourself in a mirror, you'd likely have a similar reaction. But you would never do this. It would be considered rude and vain. For this same reason you need to break the habit on video calls:

1. Make an intentional choice and commitment to stop looking at yourself.
2. Minimize your video frame and maximize the frames of the other people on the call. When possible, hide your frame from yourself.
3. Look at the camera instead of the screen.

Looking at the camera instead of the screen takes effort, though. The Steelcase survey also found when people were not looking at themselves on screen, they were looking at the other people on their screen. Thus, breaking eye contact. Herein lies the great video call *eye-contact paradox*:

> *When you look directly into the camera, the stakeholder feels that you are making eye contact. Yet, when you are looking into the camera, you cannot see them. When you can't see them, it does not feel to you that you are making eye contact. This causes you to feel uncomfortable and disconnected. In this state, you look down at their image on your screen to make eye contact, which causes the other person to feel that you are not making eye contact.*

Since you are the salesperson, it is your responsibility to connect with them, not their responsibility to connect with you. To build that connection, you must make eye contact. So despite what your brain is telling you, when you are unable to see their eyes, you must have faith that when you are making eye contact with the camera, you are making contact with the stakeholders—and they will like you more, become more engaged, and feel more comfortable.[16]

The good news is, when you are standing with your torso visible, it creates more distance between your eyes and the camera. With this increased distance, you gain a wider view of the screen. If you lift your computer up so that it is just below your camera, you'll be able to see stakeholders in your peripheral vision and glean insight from their body language without breaking the sightline. This takes some practice, but with repetition you can absolutely train your brain to do this.[17]

On my video call set, I have installed a large, 75-inch TV monitor positioned about two feet behind my camera so that the camera is near the center of the screen. This allows me to "look through" the camera and see the other person. The screen is positioned so that I never need to look down in order to see them. This keeps my eyes on the proper sightline.

From time to time, though, you may need to look away from the camera to look at your notes, find a resource, or even deal with people who stick their head in your office. What you must not forget is that your stakeholder cannot see the entire picture.

The moment you look away, their brain attempts to fill in the gap. Because of the negativity bias, it assumes the worst. The easiest and most effective way to neutralize this bias is to simply announce or pre-frame what you are doing. "I need to look away for a moment to find something in my notes," is all it takes.

On my set with the big screen TV, when I have multiple people on the call, I pre-frame breaks in eye contact at the beginning of the call. It works like a charm. So much so that people often complement me on being so considerate.

As I'm going over the agenda, I'll gesture outward and say, "I have a massive screen in front of me on which I can see each of you. Since there are several of us on the call, I've set it to gallery view so I can see everyone. If you notice me looking away from the camera and at another part of my screen, while we are having a discussion, it's because I'm looking at you." Once they know why I'm breaking contact, and it makes sense to them, their negativity bias is neutralized.

You can learn more about my video call monitor setup here: https://www.salesgravy.com/vskit

Attention Control

The late Jim Rohn said, "Wherever you are, be there." This is essential advice when it comes to video sales calls.

If you've ever been in a conversation with another person and they look away, get distracted by something or someone else, or interrupt your conversation to return a text message or email, you know how disrespected this makes you feel. When you don't feel like the other person is listening to you, it hurts your feelings, makes you feel unimportant, and can cause you to become angry.

In today's demanding work environment, it is easy to become distracted. We are constantly looking at our devices. Phone calls interrupt conversations. Email, text messages, and social media distract us. When you are working at home, there are any number of interruptions that can pull your attention away from the people on the screen. Add to this the problem of video call fatigue[18] and you have a perfect storm of distractions and diminished willpower.

It's a challenge to:

- Tune out the distracting noise from the world around you.
- Be patient and wait for your turn to talk.
- Avoid looking down at your phone screen.
- Turn off your thoughts and pay attention to another person.
- Remain interested when you find the other person boring.
- Bite your tongue when you feel the urge to interrupt so you can tell your story or prove how much you know.

Because people are on screen rather than right in front of us, it is much more challenging to stay focused. We are so accustomed to multitasking when working on our computers, playing on our devices, and watching TV that we don't even think about it when we drift away into something else and lose focus on the video call.

Attention control discipline is similar to impulse control. It's sacrificing what you want now, like checking Facebook for the latest cat video, for what you want most, connecting with your stakeholder, and making a sale. When you are on a video sales call, failing to focus on the person you are interacting with is a fast track to becoming unlikeable and harming your relationship.

You must be present in the conversation. Turn everything else off, remain completely focused, and do not let anything distract you. Turn the sound off on devices so that beeps, dings, and buzzes don't cause you to look away. Keep your eyes off papers and screens so as to avoid the burning desire to multitask.

Controlling your eyes keeps you there. *As go your eyes, so goes your attention.*

The moment you make the mistake of looking away, not only will you lose concentration, but you'll also offend the other person. This is especially true on video calls because the stakeholder has no insight into your surrounding environment and will usually assume the worst—that you are not interested in them.

When you zone out on video calls, you miss crucial information. Often, you end up asking people to repeat themselves or ask questions that have already been answered. This gives proof that you were not listening, which destroys your relationships and your credibility.

Listen

Effective listening is the ability to actively understand information expressed by your stakeholder while causing them to feel that you are paying attention, interested, and care. It is listening with the intent to understand rather than a desire to respond.

For all the technology and tools, no single skill is more important for excellence in virtual selling than effective listening. Listening is the heart of virtual selling. It's the key to effective discovery, tailoring solutions that differentiate you from your competitors, and developing deep emotional connections with prospects and customers. Yet, listening is the weakest link in virtual selling.

I'm not going to sugarcoat this. Salespeople suck at listening. They forget a basic rule of human communication: *The person asking the questions is always in control.* Far too many people believe that they are in control when their mouth is moving.

However, because of the natural limitations of virtual communication channels, listening requires more focus and patience on a virtual sales call. Talking rather than listening is a much easier mistake to make. In person, there are far more visual cues that signal when you need to shut up.

This is easy to observe. Just watch a few video call replay videos. If people aren't awkwardly talking over each other in their eagerness to express their own self-important point of view, they are waiting impatiently for the other person to stop talking so they can start.

The Failure to Listen Damages Relationships

Think about a time when you were trying to explain something to another person. Recall the moment, right in the middle of your story, that the other person held up a hand and said, "Stop! Could you just get to the point?" Consider how that made you feel—hurt, unappreciated, angry, enraged? Were you left with the feeling that the other person didn't understand you?

How about the time you were trying to have a conversation with a friend, and they kept looking down at their phone at incoming text messages? Remember how it made you want to rip the phone from their hand and smash it on the floor!

Or, have you ever been excited to tell your significant other about your day? You talked, but the other person was not paying attention because he or she was watching TV, playing a video game, or typing away on a computer.

"You're not even listening to me!" you complained in disgust. "I don't know why I even bother." As your significant other replied with a "Huh?" while barely averting attention from the screen, did you feel more emotionally connected or in love in that moment?

You know the truth, and so do I. When people don't listen to you, it makes you feel small, unappreciated, and unimportant.

Win Others Over

Abraham Lincoln once said that to win a person over, "first convince him that you are his sincere friend." In other words, you must build an emotional connection.

The most insatiable human desire, our deepest craving, is to feel valued, appreciated, and important. The key to connecting and winning others over is, therefore, extremely simple: Make them feel important.

The real secret to making others feel important is something you have at your disposal right now. It's listening. Listening is powerful. When you listen, you make people feel important, valued, and appreciated.

The secret to influence and persuasion is not what you say; it's what you hear. The discipline to control your disruptive emotions and listen requires you to have faith that when you are listening, you are in control, and by listening you win others over.

Whether in synchronous or asynchronous conversation, your ability to tune it, turn on, and truly listen to other people is the key to effective virtual selling. You must not only hear what they say, you must also become adept at reading between the lines and accurately interpreting what they are not saying.

Active Listening

Effective listening on video sales calls begins with active listening. This is a set of behaviors that provide tangible proof that you are listening. Active listening rewards your stakeholder for talking and keeps them talking. The more they talk, the more they'll reveal about their unique situation; and, the more they reveal, the more compelling your business case and proposal will be.

Active listening behaviors include the following:

- Acknowledge that you are listening by looking directly at the camera and making eye contact.
- Affirmative body language and facial expressions demonstrate that you are listening. Smile. Lean forward toward the camera, and nod your head. Make sure that your hands are idle and by your side; otherwise, it will appear that you are distracted.
- Summarize and restate what they have said. This not only tells them you are listening but aids understanding.
- Ask relevant follow-up questions that build on the conversation. This validates that you are paying attention.
- Supporting phrases like "Yes, I see," "That makes sense," and "That's exciting" encourage them to open up and reveal more. However, because of the intrinsic issues with virtual communication, you need to be careful that your verbal acknowledgment is not misconstrued as you talking over them.

Deep Listening

People communicate with far more than words. To truly hear another person, you must listen with all your senses—eyes, ears, and intuition. This is called *deep listening*.

Opening your senses to become aware of the entire message affords you the opportunity to analyze the emotional nuances of the conversation. As you listen, observe your stakeholder's body language and facial expressions.

Be observant and tune in to the emotional nuances. Pay attention to the tone, timbre, and pace of the stakeholder's voice. Focus on the meaning behind the words they are using. Be alert for emotional cues—both verbal and nonverbal.

Since people tend to communicate in stories, listen deeply to pick up unsaid feelings and emotions. As you perceive emotional importance, ask follow-up questions to test your hunch. For example: "That sounds pretty important. How are you dealing with it?"

This opens the door for other relevant follow-up questions that encourage your stakeholder to share the issues that are most important to them.

Pause to Avoid Video Awkwardness

One sure way to kill a conversation is to blurt out your next question or statement and talk over a stakeholder before they have finished speaking. Nothing makes your stakeholder feel like you aren't listening more than when you talk over them. It becomes transparent that you are not listening with the intent to understand, but rather, to formulate the next thing you plan to say.

When you feel that the other person has finished speaking, pause and count to three. This affords you time to fully digest what you have heard, before responding. Pausing leaves room for others to finish speaking and prevents you from cutting them off if they have not. You'll often find that this moment of silence triggers stakeholders to continue talking and reveal important information they were holding back.

Learn to listen without jumping to conclusions or making snap judgments. Remember that the speaker is using language to represent their thoughts and feelings. Don't assume that you know what those thoughts and feeling are and finish their sentences.

When your stakeholder slows down or is trying to gather their thoughts or find a way to express their feelings or an idea, it is easy to become impatient, jump in, and finish the sentence for them. More often than not, when you do this you end up way off base because you had no idea what they were actually thinking. This uninvited interruption instantly makes you unlikeable, shuts the other person down, and impedes understanding.

When you are unclear about what your stakeholder is saying, or you don't understand something they are trying to express, you'll want to clarify. In this moment, it is easy to make the mistake of interrupting them mid-sentence.

Don't do this. Instead, just make a note, wait until they pause, and then ask your clarifying question. Well-timed clarifying questions demonstrate to the other person that you are listening and are interested in understanding them. Never forget that the person asking the questions is in control of the conversation.

Prepare to Listen

Effective listening on video calls requires emotional control, self-discipline, practice, intention, and planning. This is why it is critical that before sales conversations, you prepare yourself to listen.

- *Be empathetic.* Consider how you feel when people are not listening to you. Then step into your stakeholders' shoes and consider how they feel when you dominate the conversation or demonstrate through your actions that you're not *really* listening.
- *Focus on what you really want.* Listening is the fastest path to achieving better virtual selling outcomes. Focus on what you *really* want as motivation to regulate your disruptive emotions of boredom, attention control, and the need for significance.
- *Practice intentional attention control.* Make a deliberate choice to remove all other distractions, including your own self-centered thoughts and impulse to interrupt, and give the stakeholder your complete attention. Tell yourself to shut up and listen— make it a conscious, intentional choice.

- *Prepare to listen.* Before each virtual sales call, prepare yourself mentally to listen. Be aware of your urge to blurt out your idea when you feel the impulse to make a point and stop yourself.

When you learn to listen effectively, you'll gain complete control of the conversation, move past emotional walls, and uncover the stakeholder's real pain, needs, issues, desires, motivations, and problems. The more you listen, the more emotionally connected stakeholders feel to you.

Be Video Ready

A recent study from Princeton University concludes that people judge your competence based on what you wear and how you look. "These judgments are made in a matter of milliseconds, and are very hard to avoid."[19]

Grooming and makeup matter. It turns out that people who are well-groomed are also deemed more competent and earn more.[20]

- If you think for a moment that just because you are on a video call rather than face-to-face you can relax your discipline to look your best, think again.
- If you think that since you are working at home it's OK to use that as an excuse for looking like a slob, you are dead wrong.
- If you think because you work on a hip inside sales floor on the west coast that you can show up to a video call with a business owner in Iowa wearing a hoodie and baseball cap, then you need to get a clue because this is a big mistake.

"But this is just the authentic me," you say. "People are just going to have to accept me as I am."

Again, wrong! Authenticity, without regard for your audience, is arrogance. If you want to "keep it real," go sling coffee at Starbucks. You are in sales. Your job is to close deals. Not make a statement about the "authentic you." Let me say this again for the folks who are still not tracking: *Your job is to close deals.* If people don't like you, they won't trust you. If they don't trust you, you are not going to close deals.

On video sales calls, you are on stage. The way you look—your physical appearance—is a key element in making a great impression and projecting credibility and competence. Both of which lead to trust.

Therefore, you need to dress and groom like your job is to close deals. And, in today's world in which video calls are easy and ubiquitous, you must dress like you mean it every day. Always on. *Always video ready.*

Wardrobe

Rule number one for wardrobe is that you must dress at the same level you would if you were going into a face-to-face meeting with your stakeholders. In most cases, this means conservative business casual.

However, as with all face-to-face calls, it makes sense to adjust the way you dress to flex to your customer. For example, if you sell farm equipment, you wouldn't wear a suit and tie to visit your customer on site at an agricultural operation. Nor would you wear work boots and jeans into the boardroom at a meeting with a banking client.

My rule of thumb has always been to dress the way my client dresses but just one step above. The goal is to project professionalism without making stakeholders feel uncomfortable. Back in my days as a field sales rep, I kept several outfits in my car. I'd often pull a Clark Kent and change clothes before meeting with different customers to ensure my wardrobe met the moment.

I do the same thing now on video calls. I have several outfits available on a rack near my video call set and will often make wardrobe adjustments between calls.

Rule number two is, you must dress for the camera. It is important to consider how what you wear will look in the video frame on screen.

Things to avoid:
- Avoid black, which can negatively impact lighting and accentuate unflattering shadows and dark circles under your eyes.
- Avoid very bright colors like white, neon, pastels, or vibrant reds.
- Avoid white shirts unless covered with a vest, sweater, or other garment that minimizes it.
- Avoid colors that clash with your backdrop or are the same color as your backdrop.
- Avoid shiny fabrics.
- Avoid patterns. Patterns can create a weird strobe effect on camera called a moiré effect.[21]
- Avoid garments with too much drape and fold. These types of outfits cause shadows and are not flattering on camera.
- Avoid garments that are stained and wrinkled.

Good choices:
- Choose colors that look best on the camera like blues, greens, deep reds, and pinks. I'm a big fan of blue.
- Choose a light blue shirt.
- Choose an outfit with a collar. Collars are professional and send the message that you mean business.
- Choose clothes that are properly fitted and flatter your build and body shape. Be sure they fit well and do not bunch or ride up.
- Choose clothes that are comfortable and breathable. It can get hot under the lights.
- Choose clothes that are clean.

Should You Wear Pants?

Beth Maynard, Sales Gravy's Vice President of Curriculum Development and a senior master trainer, says that most salespeople treat video calls like the infamous mullet hairstyle. Business on the top. Pajamas on the bottom.

Which begs the question: *Should you wear pants on video sales calls?* There are two reasons why the answer is *yes!*

First, your brain knows when you are not wearing pants (or a structured outfit), and this affects the way you think, your mood, attitude, and behavior. Scientists calls the effect clothes have on your psychological processes, including emotions, self-esteem, and interpersonal interactions, *enclothed cognition.*[22]

When you dress your best, you feel your best. You have more emotional control, are more relaxed, and feel more confident. When you feel good, you are more likeable and approachable on video. Wearing a complete, professional outfit puts you in the frame of mind for the business of sales.

Second, you don't want to "get caught with your pants down." Embarrassingly, this happened to an ABC news reporter who was doing a segment from home.

"Camera framing and digital graphics made it appear as though he was fully dressed in the beginning of the segment. But toward the end, his bare legs began to show onscreen," wrote Hannah Yasharoff in a column for *USA Today.*[23] Suddenly, millions of people were left to wonder whether or not he was wearing shorts or only his underwear. For reporter Will Reeve, it was "hilariously mortifying."

We'll chalk Reeve's situation up to unintentional wardrobe malfunction but trust me, you don't want this to happen to you. A wardrobe malfunction on live TV during the 2004 Super Bowl halftime show almost cost Janet Jackson her career.[24] So, lose the sweatpants, shorts, and pajamas. Put your pants on. Complete your outfit.

Accessories

Choose conservative and understated accessories. These items should support your outfit, without becoming the center of attention.

You should avoid wearing any large accessories that reflect light, that make noise, dangle, or move. If you wear glasses, be sure they have a nonreflective coating.

I recently sat through a video presentation with a rep who was wearing a bracelet that made a loud sound each time she put her arm on her desk. It was such an irritating noise. By the end of the meeting, instead of being motivated to buy, I wanted to get off of the call as fast as I could to get away from that sound.

Grooming

On video, good grooming is essential. The camera is unforgiving, and poor grooming sticks out like a sore thumb. Your hair, face, teeth, makeup are being scrutinized by stakeholders, and you are being judged.

Makeup can make you look healthier on camera. For this reason, I wear a little bit of concealer on camera to even out dark circles under my eyes and cover up imperfections and blemishes. I also brush on a very light coat of translucent powder to reduce shine.

For women, your normal makeup routine should make you look good on camera. A little blush on your cheeks can add dimension and help avoid wash-out in bright light. Using moisturizer on your skin can give you a healthy and nourished look.

For gentlemen with facial hair, keep it trimmed neatly. Unkempt facial hair looks extremely unflattering on camera. Make sure your hair is styled and neat. A little hair gel or paste can go a long way toward making you look phenomenal.

For women and men with long hair, style it back away from your face. This will prevent it from casting unflattering shadows and keep you from fidgeting with your hair.

Video platforms like Zoom have a touch-up feature that can make you look younger and smoother. This is essentially a blur effect, and it works! However, because it is a blur effect, if you plan to show anything behind you like a whiteboard or graphics on a TV, Smartboard, or screen, it may negatively impact the clarity of those visuals. Make sure you test it first.

Video Sales Call Calendar Invitation

It happens every day. You schedule a video sales call and one or more of the stakeholders on your call does not show their face. I've conducted plenty of video calls in which I'm the only one on video. This can be disconcerting, but it shouldn't be. It is your opportunity to shine.

When I'm in these situations, I act as if they are on camera with me—always making eye contact. Even if they dialed in, I treat the call as if they are there. I know that I'm making a great impression, and what I have found is that on the next call, they turn on their camera.

The best way to avoid this situation, though, is to send a proper meeting invite that clearly indicates that you intend it to be a video call. This means you must avoid taking the lazy route and just sending the generic invitation produced by your video conferencing platform. Instead, customize the invitation.

If your meeting is intended to be a phone call only, do not include the link to the online meeting. This will help you avoid the awkwardness of your stakeholders being in the online meeting waiting for you to show your face or share your screen while you are on the phone.

If you intend the call to be a video call, you should only include the online meeting link. Remove all other superfluous information.

Wrong Way to Send a Video Meeting Invite

Jeb Blount is inviting you to a scheduled Zoom meeting.
Topic: Virtual Selling Book Example
Time: May 14, 2020 08:30 AM Eastern Time (US and Canada)
Join Zoom Meeting
https://zoom.us/j/94348310511
Meeting ID: 943 4831 0511
One tap mobile
+13017158592,,94348310511# US (Germantown)
+13126266799,,94348310511# US (Chicago)
Dial by your location
+1 301 715 8592 US (Germantown)
+1 312 626 6799 US (Chicago)
+1 646 558 8656 US (New York)
+1 253 215 8782 US (Tacoma)
+1 346 248 7799 US (Houston)
+1 669 900 6833 US (San Jose)
Meeting ID: 943 4831 0511
Find your local number: https://zoom.us/u/aKGmKJ5xc
Join by SIP
94348310511@zoomcrc.com
Join by H.323
162.255.37.11 (US West)
162.255.36.11 (US East)
115.114.131.7 (India Mumbai)
115.114.115.7 (India Hyderabad)
213.19.144.110 (EMEA)
103.122.166.55 (Australia)
209.9.211.110 (Hong Kong China)
64.211.144.160 (Brazil)
69.174.57.160 (Canada)
207.226.132.110 (Japan)
Meeting ID: 943 4831 0511

Right Way to Send a Video Meeting Invite

Video Call: Jeb Blount (Sales Gravy) & Rachael Watkins (AMCO)
Topic: Virtual Selling Skills Training for AMCO Sales Team
Time: May 14, 2020, 10:30 AM Eastern Time
Platform: Zoom
Video Meeting Link to Join: https://zoom.us/j/94348310511
Meeting ID: 943 4831 0511

Profile Picture

One final tip. Set up your profile on your videoconferencing platform. Use a professional headshot. This way, people see your face in the frame prior to you joining the call on video and if your video feed goes down.

16 | Virtual Presentations and Demos

I have no doubt that you've sat through an online presentation that was excruciating. A voice droning on and on over heavily bullet-pointed slides.

Somewhere in the middle, you quit paying attention and started playing on your phone. That's 60 minutes of your life you will never get back.

Boring, impersonal, and hard to remember. Sadly, this is exactly how many virtual sales presentations and screen-sharing software demos are delivered; and, this is what stakeholders expect.

It doesn't need to be this way. You can easily deliver engaging and memorable virtual demos and presentations that WOW stakeholders. You just need to plan, practice, and follow a few important rules.

Keep It Visual

When your on-screen visuals are hard to see and read, it creates cognitive overload. The more your stakeholder's brain has to work to read your presentation, the more likely they will tune out.

If you want your presentation to be memorable, tell your story with images and limited text. Scientific studies have proven that humans are much more likely to remember a picture than words.[1] This is why a picture is worth a thousand words. Literally.[2]

Images also make it easier for your audience to consume your virtual presentation. The human brain processes images 60,000 times faster than text.[3]

Memorable matters because of something called the human availability bias. When making decisions, stakeholders tend to place more importance and trust in things they can easily remember.[4]

- The most impactful slides will consist of full slide images with a single sentence description, either on the slide or in the header.
- When you need to include bullet points (and you will), include no more than five bullet points per slide, stay under seven words per bullet point, and include a large image on the slide.
- Keep flow charts and other graphics simple and easy to understand.
- Use primary colors that are easy to see on-screen.
- Use easy-to-read fonts in the sans-serif family such as Helvetica, Arial, and Calibri with large font sizes of 24 points or larger.

When you have more detailed information or supporting data, send it via email either before or after your presentation. My rule of thumb is to send information before presentations when I'm working with existing accounts and after when I'm working with new opportunities.

I've included presentation slide examples at https://www.salesgravy.com/vskit

Show Your Face

Shockingly few salespeople show their face on camera and interact with stakeholders during presentations and demos. This is a bad move.

Showing your face on-screen makes your presentation or screen-share demo more personal and memorable. It also builds trust, because when people are able to see you, they are more likely to believe you.

- Begin presentations and demos with your face on screen.
- During the presentation, while you share your screen use the picture-in-picture option so that your face is visible as you walk through the slides or the screen-share.
- When you pause to interact, get feedback, or ask and answer questions, put your face back on the full screen.

Be Relevant

During discovery, you learned about the issues that are most important to your stakeholders. Limit your presentation to those lanes. People buy for their reasons, not yours, so focus your presentation or demo on their reasons.

Especially with virtual presentations, you should avoid front-loading it with slides and information about your company. This is the fastest path to boring stakeholders and turning them off.

The real secret to keeping stakeholders engaged is talking about them. As long as what you are presenting or demonstrating is relevant to them, they will pay attention and your presentation will be memorable.

Be Brief

When presenting in-person, either standing in front of a group of stakeholders or in a one-to-one meeting, it is much easier to grab their attention; and, make adjustments on the fly to keep their attention. In person, they are far less likely to drift into a social media app or incoming email.

On a virtual call, however, you can lose your audience in a heartbeat. Online, people tend to have very short attention spans, and the temptation to multitask burns hotter the longer your presentation goes on.

For this reason, you should keep your presentation to 10–20 minutes. Total presentation time is measured from the first slide (or first screen with a screen-share demo) all the way through to the last, with zero interaction or interruptions.

Ten minutes is optimal because after that, people begin to tune out.[5] Of course, when you are interacting with your stakeholders and answering questions, the total time of your meeting will be longer.

Use Structure and Practice

The most effective way to keep your presentation short and relevant is to work from a consistent framework. Structure keeps you on track and makes your presentation easier to consume.

- Confirm the time frame for the presentation with all of the participants.
- Set the agenda.
- Review what you plan to cover (tell them what you are going to tell them).
- Check with the stakeholders to confirm that they are OK with the agenda.
- Use a "parking lot" white board to capture off-topic issues and questions that arise during your presentation so that you remain on track.
- Deliver the meat of your presentation (tell them).
- Summarize your key points (tell them what you told them).
- Gain agreement on next steps.

Once you have created your presentation, practice until you can deliver it in the allotted time frame, without rushing through slides.

Be Interactive

It is far more challenging to get stakeholders to interact during a virtual presentation than in person. Sometimes they are so quiet that you'd swear you were on the call by yourself. Their silence and lack of feedback can be disconcerting.

Because you are not getting verbal or visual feedback (body language) from the audience, it makes you nervous and insecure. In this emotional state, you begin to talk fast and forget to stop and interact. For this reason, interaction begins with pace and pause.

You must not move too fast or too slow. Your speed should give your audience the time they need to fully digest your key points.

Pausing and checking is crucial with virtual presentations because you are not getting the visual cues that you would, were you presenting in person. Checking keeps you connected to your audience, encourages them to interact, allows you to get feedback, and brings potential concerns to the surface.

Pause after each slide or after important points within a slide to check stakeholder temperatures.

"Does that make sense?"

"May I answer any questions about that?"

"It sounds like that recommendation didn't hit the mark."

"It seems like you might have some concerns about this particular feature."

"How is my pace? Am I moving too fast or too slow?

When you are presenting to multiple stakeholders, there will usually be a couple of people asking many questions and a few that are hanging back. Sometimes it is hard to get anyone to talk.

The most effective technique for getting stakeholders to engage when there are more than one on the call is to say their name when you check with them. Check with everyone on the call at least once. Use the information you gleaned during discovery to frame your questions, mixing them in with your presentation, so it doesn't sound like a roll call:

> *"Bob, you said during our conversation last week that this feature was important to you. Does this demonstration make you feel more comfortable?"*
>
> *"Emily, does this answer your question about the way we handle service issues?"*
>
> *"Praveen, I know you were concerned about quality specs. Have I fully addressed your concerns?"*
>
> *"Maria, does this make sense?"*

The true art of delivering a memorable virtual presentation is stakeholder interaction. The good news is that once stakeholders get over their own trepidation and begin interacting, they tend to keep interacting. When they are interacting, you know that they are engaged. When they are engaged, your presentation will be memorable.

Beware of Red Herrings

On a Wednesday morning at 10:00 a.m., our team gathered in our conference room in front of a big wall-mounted flat-screen TV for the virtual demo and presentation. The account executive (AE) was already on when we joined the call and had with him a specialist to take us through the software demo.

After the basic introductions and pleasantries, the AE asked if we had any questions. I chimed in with the one question we had not yet asked: "How much does this cost?" But that's not how I asked the question. It was more of a direct challenge:

"Before we get started, I think it is important for you to know that we are on a very tight budget. We aren't a big company, so we can't afford to pay what you are charging those big company logos that you have on the screen right now [referring to the brag slide where he'd listed a "who's who" of his company's clients]. I really don't want to waste your time if this is outside of our budget. So why don't you walk us through the costs we can expect."

Then *bam*—like a bass hitting a lure—he took the bait and ran. He stuttered through a vague and noncommittal answer that sounded defensive. That's when our COO hit him.

"We're going to need you to be more specific than that. Sounds like you aren't giving us the whole story. Walk us through the entire cost structure."

More stuttering and sputtering. His rational brain was warning him not to give us cost information out of context, but emotion was overriding logic, causing his mouth to run out of control.

That's when our VP of curriculum development chimed in. "We've been burned by hidden costs in the past, so let's get everything on the table."

At this point, the AE was talking in circles, sounding more defensive each time he opened his mouth. His defensiveness and argumentativeness served only to create more resistance.

My team pushed him harder. It turned into a feeding frenzy. They challenged him with questions about the stability of his company, getting references, why he wasn't showing us logos of companies that were our size, and on and on.

Finally, he relented. He laid out the cost of his program, line by line, before the demo, and completely out of context. The cost of the program was in line with what we had expected, but he made the grave mistake of explaining that there would be a "professional services fee" that was 30 percent of the total cost of the program because "we'd need help getting it set up."

"Are you telling us that your software is so complicated that we need to pay you over $10,000 to train and babysit us? That's ridiculous."

"Do you think we are so incompetent that we can't learn how to use your platform? We are already using your competitor's program. We're talking to you because we want to upgrade. We know how to use this kind of system and don't need your help."

Knocked back on his heels, he attempted to defend his position on the professional services fee. In doing so, he dug the hole deeper. He argued his point, and my team became intractable.

"We're not paying a professional services fee! If that is a requirement, there is no reason for us to move forward."

He attempted to shift to the demo, but it was too late. We'd spent most of the 30 minutes allotted for the meeting arguing about this price structure. We were exasperated with his defensiveness, had lost trust, and were bumping up against other scheduled meetings. We politely declined and moved on with our day.

Later that afternoon, he called me and explained that the professional services fee was negotiable and if we felt like we could set up the program on our own, he'd be happy to waive it. He wanted to reschedule the demo. I brushed him off.

"We're going to be super busy with client projects and don't have any more time available on our schedule. Give me a call next month, and perhaps we can schedule another demo."

The account executive had blown it, allowing a *red herring* to derail his demo.

Avoid Chasing Red Herrings

A red herring is something your stakeholder does, says, or asks that distracts you and diverts attention from the objective of your presentation.

Red herrings are treacherous in face-to-face situations. But chasing them on a virtual presentation is a suicide mission. Once you get drawn into one, it's almost impossible to recover. Figure 16.1 provides some strategies for avoiding them.

Figure 16.1 Getting Past Red Herrings

The term *red herring* is thought to originate from the practice of dragging a dead fish across a trail to pull hounds off the scent. And this is exactly what happens to salespeople who abandon the objective of their call to chase a red herring. Red herrings often seem innocuous—just simple statements or questions:

"Look, before we go any further, I need to know that you aren't too expensive."
"You need to know that we are not going to sign a long-term contract."
"Just so you know, we're not buying anything from you today."
"We tried this with your company before, and it didn't work out."
"Why are your online reviews so bad?"
"There are several things about your software that we don't like. We're going to need you to add some features."
"We are already in discussions with your competitor."
"Which companies in our industry do you serve?"
"That was a pretty bad report on your CEO in the news today."

Do not take the bait! Red herrings are emotional hijackers that turn virtual presentations into train wrecks.

Because stakeholders respond in kind, instead of becoming defensive or argumentative, respond in a relaxed, calm tone. Acknowledge the issue and take control of the conversation. Most red herrings go away as you move deeper into your presentation.

Let the stakeholders know that you heard them. You might say, "That makes sense," or "I get that," or "This sounds important."

My favorite way to acknowledge a red herring is to write it down. Because you are on a virtual call, it is important to say that you are writing it down "That sounds important, I'm going to put that in the parking lot." I keep a white board behind me where I write down "parking-lot items." The parking lot allows me to acknowledge the red herring without getting pulled in.

I generally ignore the red herring unless it comes up again, because I've learned, over a lifetime in the sales profession, that they almost never do. I simply acknowledge the concern, then continue on my path.

If there is a real concern or legitimate question, it will need to be addressed at some point. But because dealing with it in the moment will derail the conversation or inject the issue out of context, it is best to save it for a more appropriate time.

If you do choose to deal with the issue or question on the spot, be careful not to answer questions without first clarifying the meaning behind the questions.

Virtual Demos

Conducting demos of software and presenting intangible services has always been relatively easy to do on virtual calls. The traditional means for demonstrating a physical, tangible product or physical space like a building, however, has been in-person.

This makes sense. People become more connected to and feel more comfortable with buying things that they have experienced first-hand.

Sometimes, though, as so many salespeople learned the hard way during the global coronavirus pandemic, it is not possible to conduct in-person demos. In these situations, video is the closest thing to being there.

Holdcroft Nissan, for example, never missed a beat during the pandemic. They began inviting customers into their showroom for live "test drives."[6] Many other forward-thinking sales professionals and organizations did the same. Thrive Senior Living conducted live video tours of their facilities, while Ellison Technologies sales professionals leveraged videoconferencing to demo machining centers for their manufacturing customers.

Tips for an Effective Video Demo

Videoconferencing platforms make it super easy to conduct remote demonstrations and give stakeholders an interactive experience.

To be most effective, video demos require two people, one person to operate the camera and one person to conduct the demo. This allows you to focus on the demo and interact with stakeholders while the camera operator follows you and points the camera in the direction you or your stakeholders want.

My preference for a virtual demo camera setup is an Osmo three-axis gimble, paired with an iPhone, that is connected to the Zoom videoconferencing platform. Because the Osmo tracks your movements, it can also act as a stand-in when you don't have a camera operator. Using Zoom allows for interacting with multiple stakeholders and creates a replay recording that can be sent to stakeholders afterwards.

Even though virtual demos are interactive, and stakeholders will guide some of the engagement, you still need a scripted framework for conducting demos—step by step by step. Then you need to practice until you can deliver it in your sleep.

When you master virtual demos, you'll be able to reach far more prospects, increase pipeline velocity, and shorten your sales cycle.

I've included more information on video demo equipment at https://www.salesgravy.com/vskit

17 | Be Video Ready

Winging it on video sales calls (and for that matter, all sales calls) is stupid. Wickedly stupid.

Murphy's law states, "Anything that can go wrong, will go wrong." Enter the video sales call. Here, the things that can go wrong, will. Always at the worst possible time, when you are least prepared to deal with it.

What is most important to understand about video calls is that even if what goes wrong is not your fault, you will still take the blame. For example, if your stakeholders' internet connection is slow, their computer reboots in the middle of your call, they don't understand the technology, can't get their mic to work, or it's Wednesday. No matter the situation, the stakeholders will blame you.

Then there is your own stress and anxiety about being on camera, working with videoconferencing technology, video and audio equipment glitches, and the never-ending challenge of getting consistent internet upload speeds. When there is a problem during a call, it can be embarrassing and induce panic.

Ten years ago, when I was first beginning to use videoconferencing technology, I scheduled a public webinar. After advertising it for a month, 1,000 people signed up to attend.

The webinar began without a hitch. Six hundred people joined the live presentation. About 15 minutes in, I noticed in the chat box that dozens of people were complaining that they could not hear me. I panicked. I felt a wave of embarrassment roll over me as I realized how bad I looked in front of all of those people. My fingers hit the keyboard of my computer, searching for a solution.

As the clock ticked, I couldn't breathe. I tried to think, to troubleshoot, but I couldn't focus. Then, I did the worst thing I've ever done on a video call. In my panic-stricken state, I accidentally ended the meeting for everyone. I wanted to crawl under my desk. I still cringe when I think about it.

The biology that drives your neurophysiological and emotional responses when things go wrong on a video call are powerful. Your pulse quickens, breathing gets shallow, and anxiety increases. It is challenging to maintain composure. Attention control is difficult. It's hard to think. Studies have proven that even your IQ drops in these situations—a big problem when you need 100 percent of your intellectual acuity.

The human brain, the most complex biological structure on Earth, is capable of incredible things. Yet, despite its almost infinite complexity, your brain is always focused on one fundamental responsibility—to protect you from threats so that you remain alive.

Harvard professor and psychologist Dr. Walter Cannon first coined the term *fight-or-flight response* to describe how the brain responds to threats.[1] This response, in one circumstance, can save you from certain death, but in another, unleashes a wave of disruptive emotions that can derail you on a video call when things go wrong.

Fight-or-flight is your autonomic, instinctive response to either standing your ground and fighting or running away when threatened. In some cases, you freeze (cognitive overload). Freezing is a very bad thing. In life-threatening situations, it can permanently remove you from the gene pool.

Your brain and body respond to two types of threats:

1. *Physical:* Threats to your physical safety or the safety of someone close to you.
2. *Social:* Threats to your social standing, banishment from the group, looking bad in front of other people, nonacceptance, diminishment, ostracism, and rejection.

The fight-or-flight response is insidious because it is a neurophysiological response that circumvents rational thought. It begins in the amygdala—the sensory hub of the brain.

The amygdala interprets the threat from sensory input and alerts the cerebellum (your autonomic brain) of the threat. The cerebellum triggers the release of neurochemicals and hormones, including adrenaline, testosterone, and cortisol, into your bloodstream to prepare you to either stand your ground and fight or run.

Your heart rate accelerates, skin flushes, and pupils dilate. You lose peripheral vision, your stomach tightens, blood vessels constrict, digestion slows down, and you begin shaking.

To prepare your body to defend itself, oxygen- and glucose-rich blood floods into your muscles. However, since there is only so much to go around, blood is moved from nonessential organs and into your muscles.

One of these nonessential organs from which blood is drawn is your neocortex—the rational, logical center of the brain. It turns out, from an evolutionary standpoint, that thinking through your options is not an asset when dealing with threats. You need to move quickly to stay alive.

In the clutches of fight-or-fight, you can't think; you struggle for words, and you feel out of control. Your mind reels, palms sweat, stomach tightens, and muscles become tense. As blood drains from your neocortex, your cognitive capacity becomes that of a drunk primate. Then, like me, you click the wrong button and poof, you ended the meeting in the middle of the biggest presentation of your career.

The real secret to avoiding this response on video sales calls is simple: *practice and planning*. Since that horrible incident 10 years ago, I've sharpened and honed my virtual sales call skills by conducting hundreds of video calls. Along the way, I learned that the better I plan, the fewer mistakes I make, the fewer issues I face, and the more I am prepared for anything.

Be Prepared for Anything

In Chapter 14, we discussed why directors and producers of TV shows and movies go to such lengths to ensure that audio, lighting, framing, and sets are perfect. Doing so allows them to produce an experience that people enjoy and are willing to pay for.

We discussed that you are always on stage. Stakeholders are observing everything about your call—what you do and don't do. They make judgments about whether they like and trust you based on what they see and hear.

The fact is, with video calls, you are putting on a show. The details matter. The emotional experience you deliver matters. Therefore, you cannot wing it. You must be prepared.

Each time pilots prepare for a flight, they go through a checklist. Just peek into the cockpit of the next commercial flight you board prior to take-off. You will observe that the pilot and co-pilot have a physical book open and are going the through the checklist step by step.

These are professionals with thousands and thousands of hours of flight time. They go through that same checklist on every flight. They can recite it by heart. Yet, they still go through the checklist, the same way, every time. Why? Because if something goes wrong at 30,000 feet, the results can be catastrophic. So, it's better to identify problems while they are on the ground.

This is exactly why, at Sales Gravy, we have a checklist for video calls. It starts with *Turn the power on,* and *Plug the laptop into power.* Those first two steps might seem remedial and a blinding flash of the obvious, unless you were with me when my laptop shut down in the middle of a video sales call because I had not plugged it in and the battery died. Or, the time it was plugged into a power strip, but the strip had been inadvertently turned off and my battery died right in the middle of an important sales call with very busy executives.

There are no words to describe how embarrassing these situations are. Because the stakeholders could not see me, they had no idea what happened. If I had been there with them, I would have simply said, "Oops, my battery died; is there an outlet I can plug into?" Instead, as soon as my screen went dark, they were left to make up a narrative in their own heads about what happened.

It took me several minutes to get back into the meeting. By the time I got back in, the stakeholder group was gone. They had moved on to other things. I'd spent weeks working to get them together and blew it because of stupidity and a dead battery.

These are just a couple of examples of the many embarrassing incidents I've endured on video calls. Developing our *Video Sales Call Checklist* and having the *discipline* to go through the checklist prior to each video sales call changed everything. It eliminated 99 percent of issues that contributed to these embarrassing situations. These days, my calls go smoothly, I have more confidence, and my prospects and customers have a better experience.

Video Sales Call Checklist

When I say checklist, I mean a physical checklist that is printed and laminated. Before EVERY call, I go through each step on the checklist and use a dry erase marker to check through each item on the list. I've learned the hard way that it is a grave mistake to leave anything to chance on a video sales call.

Give yourself enough time between calls and before calls to run your checklist. You'll need at least 15 minutes to run through and check everything.

Power and Battery Backup

Power is everything. No power, no video sales call. I highly recommend investing in a backup power unit. These units double as surge protectors and have internal batteries that kick on in the event of a power outage so that your meeting is not interrupted.

- Check all cords and connections to ensure that your laptop or device is plugged into power.
- Check the power icon on your laptop or device to ensure that it is receiving power.
- If you are on a fiber internet connection that requires power, check your backup battery to be sure that it is fully charged and working.
- If possible, connect your Wi-Fi router to a backup battery source.
- Ensure that all batteries on devices, mics, cameras, and lights are fully charged. I find that it is a good idea to plug everything in the night before so that you have full charges at the beginning of the day. If you begin your day on empty, you'll be chasing your batteries all day.

Internet Connection and Backup

Like many people, you may live in an area where (1) speed and bandwidth go up and down depending on the day, (2) weather impacts speed, or (3) internet speed is poor all of the time. We run into problems in our office if too many people are uploading large files at the same time.

I highly recommend investing in a backup connection source like a mobile hotspot. Having a backup source has saved me on many occasions when my main broadband source went down.

- Use an ethernet connection when possible. Check that the ethernet cable is plugged in correctly and you have turned Wi-Fi off on your device.
- If you are using Wi-Fi, check your signal strength.
- Check your internet upload speed. If it is super slow, try restarting your router and restarting your computer or devices (allow plenty of time before your call for these resets).
- Turn Wi-Fi off on all devices that are not involved in the video call—this includes digital assistants like Google Home and Alexa. Make sure people in your household are not streaming video, playing games, or uploading files. Even small interruptions in audio and video caused by slow internet speeds can cause people to have a negative perception of you.[2] Don't take any chances.
- Pause uploads on all file sharing apps like DropBox, Google Drive, and OneDrive.
- Close your email application.
- Check your backup connection to be sure that it is fully charged, has a good signal, and that your computer or device sees it. Practice connecting to your backup source so that you can do it with one click if your main connection goes down. Check to be sure that your computer or device will connect to this source before your call.

Audio

You've learned that the most important technical element of your video call is audio.

- Check to be sure your mic is connected properly to your laptop, desktop computer, or camera.

- Check to be sure the correct microphone is selected on your video conferencing platform. *Tip:* If you cannot find your microphone in the videoconferencing microphone settings, it is not connected properly to your device.
- Test volume levels and make adjustments.
- Make sure your microphone is positioned correctly.
- Test output speakers or earphones to be sure you can hear the other party.
- Check batteries in microphones and earphones to ensure they are fully charged.

Lighting

Good lighting is the key to looking your best on screen.

- Check the position of your lights.
- Check brightness and temperature levels.
- Check power connections and backup batteries.
- Check for harsh glares and pull shades on windows to regulate natural light.
- If you are using a virtual backdrop with or without a green screen, check the lighting to ensure that you are not disappearing into the backdrop, discolored, or distorted. You'll need to give yourself plenty of time for this and check it on every call.

Camera

Check camera settings before every call. Give yourself plenty of time. Never leave this to chance. It is embarrassing when you must make camera adjustments in the middle of the call.

- Check to be sure your camera is connected properly to your laptop.
- Check to be sure the correct camera is selected on your videoconferencing platform. *Tip:* If you cannot find your camera in the videoconferencing video settings, it is not connected properly to your device.
- Check color temperature and focus. Be sure that the lighting is set properly so that you look natural and are not washed out.

- Check power connections and backup batteries.
- Check your camera position and framing so that the camera is at eye-level, your hands and torso are visible, and you are aligned appropriately on the vertical and horizontal axis with no distortion.

Backdrop

Your backdrop is your set. It sends a powerful message. Be sure that it is the message you want to convey.

- Check your backdrop to be sure that everything is in place and it looks good in the video frame. In an active working space, it is not uncommon for your backdrop to be disturbed or moved. If you don't have a permanent backdrop or you have to move it to another area, check it in the frame before your video call.
- Check to be sure that your backdrop is properly lit and there are no distracting glares or shadows.
- If your backdrop includes a TV, smartboard, or other interactive whiteboard, make sure that it is turned on and the correct image is on screen.
- If your backdrop includes a whiteboard, make sure that it is erased and clean or has the message you wish to convey.
- If you are using a virtual background replacement, log into your videoconferencing platform and check to be sure you have the correct background image loaded. When I use virtual backdrops, I'll often build my prospect's logo into the background. I've made the embarrassing mistake of launching a meeting at the last minute with another company's logo behind me.

Platform Settings

Check your videoconferencing platform settings before your call begins. Just because everything was working on your last call, do not assume that it will work on the next call.

- Check to ensure your app is updated to the latest version.
- Check audio source.

- Check video source and virtual background source if you are using that option.
- Check to be sure you are connecting to the right meeting ID—nothing like you and your stakeholders being in different meeting rooms (I have that T-shirt).
- Check meeting recording settings, make sure you are recording, and note where that recording will be stored—nothing like forgetting to push record or losing the video after the fact. I've set my platform to default to record to keep this from happening.
- Check the video quality settings.
- Check to be sure chat is set to *activated* or *deactivated*, depending on your intentions.
- If you are using a password to grant access, be sure you know how to move participants from the waiting room into the meeting.
- Check and practice screen sharing to be sure that you have your windows arranged correctly to make the transition from video interface to screen sharing seamlessly.
- Check the join meeting settings to be sure that people can see and hear you and you can see and hear them when you join.

This is important, so pay attention. If you join a meeting on your prospect or customer's platform, go to that platform at least 15 minutes BEFORE your meeting starts to download any required apps and check audio and camera compatibility settings. Trust me on this; you will likely need to make adjustments, and you do not want to be making those adjustments when the call starts.

Background Noise and Distractions

Background noise like pets barking and alerts from your phone can make you seem unprofessional. Distractions steal your attention, causing you to break eye-contact, stop listening, and lose your train of thought.

- Whether you are in the office or at home, make sure everyone around you knows that you are on a sales call and that they need to be quiet. A sign on your door at home or at your office is also a good idea. I purchased a QUIET light (like you might find in a studio) and had it installed over the door of my office. When it is on, people know to be quiet and not disturb me.

- If you are making a video sales call from a hotel, put the DO NOT DISTURB sign on your door and call the front desk to tell them that you are not to be disturbed.
- Isolate pets in an area of your home so that they don't distract you with barking or jump into your video sales call set.
- Mute all devices, put them in do-not-disturb mode, and move them away from your line of sight.
- If you are expecting a delivery, put a note on your doorbell asking the delivery person not to use it. If you have a smart doorbell, mute the sound.

Computer Desktop

Many, many people have been deeply embarrassed by inadvertently sharing the wrong desktop window on a video call or having to dig through the clutter on their desktop to find the correct file to share.

- Close all windows on your computer except the videoconferencing app and visuals you plan to share on the call.
- Put your computer or laptop in do-not-disturb mode.
- Practice the motion of choosing the correct window and sharing your screen several times so that you can do it seamlessly.
- It is never a bad idea to restart your computer prior to calls. It will run faster, and updates will process before you join your call.

Sweat the Small Stuff

On video sales calls, you are on stage, and on stage the details matter. You need to sweat the small stuff.

- Review your pre-call plan.
- Know your objective and targeted next step.
- Review the agenda and check to be sure you have a copy in front of you. I like to send it out ahead of time and post it in chat.

- Prepare for small talk. Someone will be late or need to restart their computer, or perhaps the stakeholders on the call are happy to chit-chat for a moment. Make sure you are ready to engage in pre-meeting small talk.
- Review the questions you plan to ask your stakeholders. It's a good idea to keep them in front of you.
- Check to be sure you know the names of every person who will be on the call. I find it helpful to grab pictures of everyone who will be on the call from LinkedIn and paste them onto a single document with their name and title underneath their headshots. I print this out and keep it in front of me. It helps me welcome people by name when they join the call.
- Check to be sure you have the resources you plan to share on screen ready to go.
- Check to be sure you have a pen, notepad, and water at your fingertips.
- Go to the bathroom. It is hard to concentrate with a full bladder.

I like to keep a white board behind me on my virtual sales call set for brainstorming with stakeholders, capturing ideas, or as a parking lot for red herrings. It keeps the meeting on track, makes it easy to summarize and check to be sure I captured everything, and creates a great visual effect.

Physical Appearance

I once did an entire video call with my shirt collar on the outside of my jacket—like John Travolta in *Saturday Night Fever*. I didn't notice it until watched the replay video. Another embarrassing moment because I failed to check. Before you start the video sales call, check your hair, teeth, nose, face, and clothing.

Always Be Video Ready.

18 | Video Messaging

The incoming data on the influence of video on buying behaviors is incontrovertible. Three quarters of buyers state that they made a buying decision after watching a video.[1] We consume video online at an ever-accelerating pace. Video accounts for 75 percent of internet traffic and is projected to rise to 82 percent in the near future.[2]

As a content marketing tool, video has moved from cutting edge to essential. So much so that I started my own video production company called Knowledge Studios to provide services to Sales Gravy and our customers.

Video is so powerful that I could write another entire book on video sales and marketing strategies. Rather than overwhelming you, though, I'm going to focus specifically on video messaging and the actions that you can take right now to deploy video messaging in your virtual selling arsenal.

Video Messaging Is No Joke

Where video marketing, like most content marketing strategies, is a one-to-many lead generation and brand building tool, video messaging is one-to-one. It's personal. Each video message is unique; made by you, for one prospect or stakeholder.

Video messaging is a powerful medium that gets results. In one study, SalesLoft found that personalized videos delivered a 75 percent close rate. Their conclusion, "You don't have to be in the sales game very long to know that a 75 percent close rate is no joke."[3]

In another case study, HubSpot saw a 400 percent increase in email prospecting conversion when those emails included a personalized video.[4] Likewise, Hippovideo.io has demonstrated that video messaging can reduce the sales cycle by as much as 40 percent.[5]

As a virtual selling tool, video messaging is unparalleled. No other asynchronous channel can rival its results. Yet, it is just beginning to come into its own. Early adopters stand to generate tremendous results by blending video messages in their business development sales processes.

It's not unlike the story I told you earlier about how I adopted PowerPoint when it first came onto the market. Because few people had experienced it, I was able to wow stakeholders, clobber competitors, and close many more deals than my peers. Hence why now is the time to dive in headfirst into video messaging.

Tapping into the Law of Reciprocity

Academic studies prove that people love and crave content that is personalized for them.[6] But you already know this because you are human, and you do, too. The most insatiable human need and craving is to feel important, appreciated, significant. We all want to know that we matter.

A video that was made *just for you* makes you feel this way, which is one of the key reasons why personalized videos are such a powerful and compelling communication channel.

Because the need for significance is so insatiable, when you make someone feel important, you give them the greatest gift that you can give another person. The beautiful thing about gifts is, when you give one it compels the other person to *feel* the need to reciprocate.

Robert B. Cialdini, author of *Influence*, says, "One of the most potent of the weapons of influence around us is the rule for reciprocation. The rule says that we should try to repay, in kind, what another person has provided us."[7] This feeling of obligation, the need to reciprocate, is baked deep into human psychology.

In layman's terms, the law of reciprocity simply explains that when you give a stakeholder a gift—like a personalized video message—it triggers a subconscious feeling of obligation. This feeling increases the probability that they will agree to meet with you (prospecting), advance to the next step on the buying journey (sales), and give you more business (account management).

Video Messaging Is Versatile

Though most salespeople and leaders view video messaging primarily as a prospecting tool, what I love most about video messaging is its versatility. Video messaging may be leveraged throughout the entirety of the business development, sales, and account management journeys (Figure 18.1).

You've learned that your stakeholders' emotional experience while working with you is the most consistent predictor of outcome of any other variable. At every stage of the buying journey, video messaging, used well, helps you deliver a positive emotional experience.

Figure 18.1   The Virtual Selling Journey

Prospecting

Personalized video messages attached to an email or a direct message exponentially improve open rates, click-throughs, and call to action conversions. Video messages help you break through the noise, stand out, and grab attention. They help you put a face to a name and build familiarity. When video messaging is integrated into well-designed prospecting sequences, the results are phenomenal.

It is important to note that creating video messages takes time. Depending on your level of competency with shooting the video and doing basic editing, it can take 3–15 minutes per message. Therefore, to be effective and remain productive, you'll want to focus your efforts on select groups of targeted, high-potential prospects.

Invites

Personalized videos are a perfect vehicle for inviting prospects to webinars and online events, open houses, seminars, conferences, and face-to-face meetings at trade shows. It's easy. Just smile into the camera, bridge to the *value* (what's in it for them) of attending the event or coming by your booth, and tell them how much you look forward to seeing them.

Confirming Appointments

No-shows suck. They steal your thunder and impact your attitude, especially when you've been pursuing an opportunity for a long time and you finally landed an appointment.

A short, personalized video message sent after an appointment is booked with a new prospect can cut no-shows in half. The video message turns you into a real person, shows your enthusiasm, and creates a sense of obligation—making it much harder for your prospect to ditch the meeting. In situations in which the prospect legitimately can't make the meeting, they'll be much more likely to politely reschedule.

Follow-Up after Sales Meetings and Advancing the Deal

Sending personalized video messages to your stakeholders after discovery meetings, demos, and presentations demonstrates your professionalism, builds trust, and anchors relationships. You continue to build familiarity (the more people see you, the more they like you); and, most importantly, these messages keep deals from stalling in the pipeline.

Leverage follow-up messages to let stakeholders know how much you appreciate the time they gave you, restate what you discovered and remind them of next step agreements and the date and time of your next meeting. For example:

> Hi Anna (smile and wave hello), thank you very much for spending time with me today and teaching me about your current payroll processing workflow. I'm looking forward to getting the information on your current benefits plan tomorrow. Once I have that I'll put together a proposal that we can review at our next meeting on Tuesday the 2nd. Have a great weekend, I'll see you next week [smile and wave good-bye].

Education, Insight, and Micro-Demos

Short video messages are a nonintrusive way to tell your story and provide insights to stakeholders during the buying journey. These videos are often shared by stakeholders with others inside their organization. This helps you extend your reach and influence.

This morning a group of stakeholders was meeting to discuss my proposal for a virtual sales training program. Last night I shot a short behind-the-scenes video of our virtual training set and sent it to our coach in the account via text message. Their meeting was at 9:00 am. At 10:30 I received a text back from him saying how impressed everyone in the meeting was with our setup.

Micro-demos are short, easy-to-consume personalized video demos of your software (screen recordings), products, and services. They help educate and keep stakeholders engaged during the discovery phase of the sales process. I recently made a big purchase from a rep who helped to educate me on his product's full functionality in a series of short videos that he texted to me over the course of a week. His videos made it much easier for me to decide to buy from him.

Many video messaging distribution tools allow you to track open rate, shares, and watch time. The data you gather from micro-demo videos can also give you important insight into stakeholder engagement. Based on the video analytics you can adjust your strategy and approach to ensure your opportunity continues to advance.

Influencing Decision–Making

When stakeholders are making decisions about who they are going to buy from, a short video expressing your interest in doing business with them, recapping and highlighting your business case, and specifically how you are going to help them makes an impact—thus, improving your win probability.

My salespeople leverage videos like this regularly. Near the end of the sales process, either right before the final presentation and proposal, or right afterwards, they will get me to send a personalized video to their stakeholders. It works. Over the past three years, our close rate on accounts that get these videos is 94 percent.

This is an excellent way to leverage your leadership team. Back when all of my sales calls were face-to-face, I would drag leaders like my group vice president to closing meetings. When he was there, we almost always sealed the deal.

Video allows you to do the same thing with even more opportunities. My salespeople make it easy for me. They create a short script that includes the name (or names) of the stakeholders and three bullet points that they want me to cover. We review it together. Then, they hold the camera, and say, "Action!" All I need to do is smile and get my lines right.

Account Management, Customer Appreciation, and Retention

This is easy. Jump in front of the camera and shoot a quick, personalized video for the key stakeholders in your accounts. A short message that says thank you, have a nice weekend, enjoy your vacation, happy birthday (or happy anything), goes a long, long way. These messages anchor your relationships and create loyalty, and you'll be amazed at how often they lead to a conversation about giving you more business.

Account Handoffs

From time to time you'll need to introduce your contact or stake-holders to another person on your team. It could be a handoff to an account manager, sales engineer, customer success rep, service manager, etc. These relationship handoffs can be awkward for you and uncomfortable for your customers. To make it easier on them, shoot a short video with the person you are introducing and let them know that they are in good hands.

Shooting Video Messages Is Wickedly Easy

For all of the reasons we've already discussed, the first step to lever-aging video messaging is getting past your aversion to being on camera. Let me assure you that the more video messages you create, the easier it will get.

Stop thinking about it and push "record." Let go of your perfectionism. Especially with video prospecting, you'll need to sacrifice quality for quantity. Most of these videos will be viewed once. They don't need to be absolutely perfect. So, loosen up and have fun with it.

Short, Spontaneous, and Authentic

Video messages should be short. Thirty to 60 seconds is optimal. With video messages, follow the three BEs:

- Be brief.
- Be bright.
- Be gone.

You want your video messages to be authentic and feel spontaneous. This doesn't mean that you should just wing it.

It doesn't mean that you should be sloppy. You need to be thoughtful about your message and process.

It does mean that elaborate video production is unnecessary. In fact, it can hurt you when the video looks and feels too scripted. This makes shooting video messages easy because you can shoot them anywhere, anytime, with almost any backdrop.

Almost Any Backdrop

Always look behind you before you shoot and always check what's behind you on video before you hit "send." Though just about any backdrop is acceptable for video messages, it is important that you avoid backdrops that may damage your company or personal brand or reveal proprietary company information.

I like to shoot video messages when I'm traveling. I'll make a list of prospects and customers to whom I want to send messages before I leave. Then I shoot my videos with cool landmarks as my backdrop. These messages always get the most responses. When I'm alone I ask strangers to hold my phone and shoot the video so that I can get a better frame. I've never had anyone refuse.

When I'm not traveling, I have a studio at my office called "The Club House." It has an interesting backdrop with a 65-inch flat-screen monitor, and I put my customer's logo on the that screen.

Camera and Framing

The beautiful thing about shooting video messages is that you have an excellent camera for this in your pocket right now. Just whip out that smart phone and start shooting. Likewise, you can simply turn on your webcam and record a video message. It really is that easy. From time to time, I'll also use my GoPro—especially when I'm traveling.

Framing is still important. Follow the framing guidelines from Chapter 14. Make sure your torso is visible, that you are making eye contact, that the vertical and horizontal axis lines are symmetrical.

If you are shooting with your phone, use a tripod that allows you to step back from the camera. I carry a portable one with me all the time. It has legs that grip so I can always find something to attached it to, which allows me to place the camera at eye-level.

If I am with another person, though, I get them to hold my phone and shoot the video. While shooting, I ask them to very slowly and smoothly move the camera horizontally back and forth. This slight movement adds dimension to my video, which grabs attention. It is a form of pattern painting. If you look closely, you'll notice similar movements in movies and TV shows.

Lights

As you learned in Chapter 14, lighting matters. The camera needs light to capture a good picture. Most spaces indoors and outdoors will have enough light for a good picture. Webcams, though, often require supplemental lighting such as an LED ring light for a good picture.

Always avoid shooting with bright windows or the sun behind you because you'll end up in "witness protection." Avoid bright windows or the sun directly in front of you, because when the light is too bright it will wash you out.

Audio

For video messages, the microphone on your phone or webcam will do the trick. Certainly, if you have a setup with a professional microphone, you should use it. I do when I'm in my studio. It's just not necessary for these types of short-and-sweet messages.

The microphone on your camera is so good that it will isolate your voice against background noise even in busy offices, airports, and streets. You just want to avoid really loud noises, like a car honking, that can distract from your message. Always, always, always avoid rooms that generate big echoes.

Editing

Should you record your video into a direct messaging app like LinkedIn, you won't have the luxury of editing your video. If you record on your phone or webcam, though, it is a good idea to do some minimal editing to enhance the quality of your message. The basics of editing video messages include:

- Clipping the beginning and end to remove the typical fumbling around as you turn record on or off.
- Adding your company logo to the lower right-hand corner.
- Cutting out long pauses and mistakes.
- Add captions. This can take a few minutes, but if you are good enough to do it quickly, it will get more of your messages viewed because the receiver won't need to turn their sound on to "hear" your message.
- Add personalized graphic overlays like "Hi, Jeb!"

There is a simple editing tool on your phone and any number of mobile and desktop apps that make quickly editing your video messages easy. With editing, the more you practice and get a workflow down, the faster you'll get. I've included a list of these video editing apps at: https://www.salesgravy.com/vskit

Micro-Demos

Micro-demos are the exception to the rules above. These videos will be longer—typically two to three minutes. When you are shooting micro-demos, editing and production matter. You are showing off your product or service. It is important that you shine. Take time to plan your message and follow the rules you learned in Chapters 14 and 15 to create micro-demos that pop and grab attention.

Sending Video Messages

There are multiple options for sending video messages, including email, text, and direct messaging. You may simply upload your message to a free Vimeo or YouTube account and send a private link in an email, text, or direct message.

A best practice when sending video messages via email is to include the word "Video" in your subject line. For example: "Video Inside" or "Jeb, I made a video for you." This has proven to significantly improve email open rates.

Direct messaging apps, including basic text messaging, LinkedIn, Facebook Messenger, WhatsApp, WeChat, Instagram, and Twitter, allow you to record and send personalized video messages embedded right in the direct message.

There are also dozens of platforms built specifically for sending video sales messages that allow you to embed your video (often with a GIF thumbnail) directly into email. These platforms may be stand-alone or integrated into your CRM.

Video messaging platforms such as Hippo and Vidyard have the added benefit of pushing prospects to personalized webpages and providing engagement data on whether your video was watched, how long it was watched, if it was shared, and who it was shared with. I've included links to some of the most popular video messaging platforms at: https://www.salesgravy.com/vskit

Crafting Compelling Personalized Video Messages

Last week, I received a video message from a sales rep via email. The first 15 seconds were awesome. It was personalized, authentic, and about me. I thought to myself, "Wow this is good! I'm going to give her a call."

Then, she ruined it with a generic pitch. It was as if she didn't feel that the message was complete until she gave me her 30-second elevator speech. It was an instant turnoff. Instead of engaging, I clicked Delete!

Nobody likes a pitch. Not you, not me, not your prospects and customers. If you are no more than a talking marketing brochure, your video message will land cold. Save your elevator pitch for elevators, preferably when you are in one alone.

Video messaging is not about pitching, it's about connecting at the emotional level. Where other asynchronous communication channels like email, text, and direct messaging are flat, save for the random emoji, video gives your personalized message dimension. It helps you create a one-of-a-kind emotional experience.

On video, stakeholders can see your body language and facial expressions and can hear your voice tone. It allows you to demonstrate empathy. When prospecting, video messaging transforms you from a faceless stranger into a real, authentic human being.

Video messages also build familiarity. The more stakeholders see you, the more they like you. The more they like you, the higher the probability that they will do business with you.

First and foremost, video messaging is about authenticity. Smile, have fun, and be yourself. Be sincere, kind, and engaging. Be human. No different than if you were sending a message to a friend.

The quest for "authenticity" however, does not mean that you can step over the line of professional communication. Last month a sales rep sent me a video prospecting message that began with, "Jeb, my man." Total turnoff. I felt disrespected. Delete!

Be careful. Authenticity without regard for your audience is arrogance. You message and tone must flex to the person you are messaging and where they are on the buying journey.

Four-Step Video Prospecting Message Framework

We all want those magic words that roll off our tongue like sugar, grab a prospect's attention, and reel them in. The bad news is, there are no magic words. The good news is, a proven four-step framework allows you to craft impactful video prospecting messages that compel people to engage (Figure 18.2).

1. Hook
2. Relate
3. Bridge
4. Call to action (CTA)

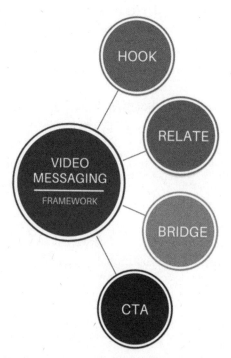

Figure 18.2   Four-Step Video Messaging Framework

Hook

The hook is for grabbing your stakeholders' attention and compelling them to keep watching. In our crazy-busy world where everyone is in a state of near-constant stress and information overload, this is a challenge. What's more, you have just a couple of seconds to do it.

The good news is that it is super easy to hook them. The secret? Say the most beautiful word in the world to them: *their name.*

But there is a challenge. Many prospects will begin playing your video before they turn on the audio. Therefore, you must hook them with what *they see* and with what *you say.*

An easy way to do this is to use a small, handheld white board (or another visual device/graphic overlay). Write their name on it and hold it up at the beginning of the video message. That way they can *see* that the video is personalized to them even if they don't hear you say their name. Just smile and wave while holding your sign and say:

Hi, Julian.

Relate

Your generic pitch is not personal, it's noise. It adds no value and creates instant resistance. To your prospect, your pitch translates to, "I would love to waste an hour of your life to talk about me." Trust me on this, people are not going to engage with you for a kitchen-sink features dump or to learn more about your company being "number one of this" or the "biggest of that."

Do not pitch. Relate. Remember, the entire point of video messaging and what makes this such a powerful communication tool is that it is personalized. Step into a stakeholder's shoes, be empathetic, and relate to their situation. For example, you might say:

> Hi Julian [smile and wave hello]. Thank you for watching this short message I made just for you. I can't even imagine how challenging it must be in your situation with so many maintenance projects on your plate.

Bridge

The bridge connects the dots between their problems or issues and how you can help them. A basic and important truth is prospects engage with you for their reasons, not yours. Therefore, you must articulate the value of complying with your call to action in the context of what is most important and of interest to them. It might sound like this:

> Hi, Julian [smile and wave hello]. Thank you for watching this short message that I made just for you. I can't even imagine how challenging it must be in your situation with so many maintenance projects on your plate. It's got to be incredibly frustrating. This is exactly why we should talk. I help multi-location property managers like you with a tool that eliminates the need to waste time chasing down engineers and contractors for updates.

Call to Action

At the end of your message, you need a call to action. Otherwise, what's the point? You might ask them to:

- Call you.
- Respond to your email, direct message, or reply to your video on a personalized page.
- Click on your calendar link and choose a time to meet with you or agree to a specific time you've offered.

- Click on a link or button and go to a resource.
- Sign up for a webinar.
- Connect you with someone else in their organization.

Be sure that your CTA is clear and confident. Say it verbally. If it makes sense, make it visual as well. Hold up a graphic with your ask or use a caption or graphic overlay. A best practice is to say their name again and wave goodbye.

Hi Julian [smile and wave hello]. Thank you for watching this short message that I made just for you. I can't even imagine how challenging it must be in your situation with so many maintenance projects on your plate. It's got to be incredibly frustrating. This is exactly why we should talk. I help multi-location property managers like you with a tool that eliminates the need to waste time chasing down engineers and contractors for updates. How about we get together on Thursday for a short call so I can learn a little more about your situation to see if this will be a fit? I have 2:00 open, or you can click on my calendar link right below this video and pick a time that works better for you. Thank you for watching my video, Julian. I can't wait to meet you [smile and wave goodbye].

PART IV

Telephone

19

Pick Up
the Damn Phone

During the early days of the coronavirus pandemic, the *New York Times* ran an article about how people were suddenly rediscovering the "humble phone."[1] In one article, the *Guardian* announced the "return of the phone," going on to describe how people were rediscovering that "a call can offer real closeness.[2]

On LinkedIn, there was an endless stream of social media posts extolling salespeople to "make the telephone your new best friend." Even the "phone-is-dead" evangelists seemed to have a change of heart and were encouraging salespeople to "phone a customer."

What was most disappointing about these admonitions to "rediscover the humble telephone" is that it illustrated just how far we had fallen as a profession. Rather than picking up the phone and talking to people, sales professionals everywhere—even inside sales reps—had replaced this beautiful, synchronous sales communication tool with asynchronous communication channels.

The sales profession's aversion to talking with people had become so dire that over the past five years, at least half of Sales Gravy's training and consulting engagements have been focused on one thing: teaching and compelling salespeople to *pick up the damn phone.*

The problem with getting salespeople to use the phone is so prevalent that powerful and sophisticated, omnichannel sales engagement engines, including VanillaSoft, HubSpot Sales Pro, Outreach, and SalesLoft, have become little more than expensive ways for salespeople to send thousands of automated emails cloaked under the guise of sales activity.

The Workhorse of Virtual Selling

Ever since Alexander Graham Bell uttered the first words on the first phone over 140 years ago, "Mr. Watson—come here—I want to see you," the telephone has been the workhorse of virtual selling. The telephone has always been and will continue to be the most powerful virtual selling tool.

I'll bet my book royalty check that there is one next to you right now. People sleep with their phones, eat with their phones, and are more likely to lose their car keys and wallet than their phone. Though it is probably used more for texting, posting selfies, and watching cat videos, if you dial a number, in an instant, you can be in a sales conversation.

So, I'm going to say this one more time, slowly, for the folks in the back of the room who are still not tracking. There is no other tool that will connect you to people faster, deliver better results, fill your pipe more effectively, and help you cover more ground in less time than the phone.

Salespeople who ignore the phone sub-optimize their productivity and cheat themselves out of cold hard cash. The humble telephone is the most versatile virtual selling tool. Period.

When in Doubt, Pick Up the Phone

If you are one of the many salespeople who are quick to say, "My customers like it better when I use email," I've got a message for you. The "my customers like it better when I use email" trope is primarily a bullshit story that YOU keep telling yourself to justify why YOU are not talking with people.

This lazy excuse is why so many salespeople have devolved into asynchronous sellers. Trust me, if you keep this behavior up, the robots are coming for you.

I am not casting aspersions at email as a communication channel. There are plenty of situations when email is the most appropriate communication channel. What I'm trying to get through to you is that when you default to an asynchronous communication channel like email, because emotionally it's easier for you to keep people at arms-length, human connections begin breaking.

There is also the hit to productivity. In so many cases, one short phone conversation can replace five or more emails and the frustrating back and forth that comes with them. When there is a misunderstanding, before you reach for your keyboard to blindly send another email, stop and pick up the phone.

Over my many years in business, I've found that the phone is the quickest and most effective way to easily solve problems and complete innumerous sales tasks that require human to human connection.

This is exactly why I live by a simple sales mantra: *When in doubt, pick up the phone.*

- Got a customer service issue? *Pick up the phone.*
- Have a misunderstanding? *Pick up the phone.*
- Want to stay in touch and keep your relationships anchored? *Pick up the phone.*
- Need a reference or a referral? *Pick up the phone.*
- Have a question? *Pick up the phone.*
- Need to follow up? *Pick up the phone.*
- Deal stalled? *Pick up the phone.*

- Need to qualify an opportunity or identify a buying window? *Pick up the phone.*
- Empty pipeline? *Put down the cat video and pick up the damn phone!*

Closing Transactional and Short-Cycle Sales

For closing transactional and short-cycle, one- to two-call deals, the phone is an unparalleled virtual selling channel. With these low-risk, fast-moving opportunities, momentum is your friend and time, your enemy. There is no other sales tool that keeps the ball rolling like the phone.

I should note, though, that in a comprehensive study of more than 100,000 sales meetings, Gong.io revealed that 41 percent of deals were closed when inside sales reps combined phone conversations with video sales calls.[3] Just one more proof source that illustrates the power of *blending*.

Likewise, when you sell to a customer base that is on the move and works from mobile devices, the phone blended with text messaging, video messaging, virtual presentation tools, and digital sales tools like DocuSign is a powerful combination. Sales success with this segment of prospects is all about maintaining momentum while making it easy for your customer to do business with you.

Account Management

You don't send me flowers, you don't sing me love songs, you hardly talk to me anymore. Barbra Streisand and Neil Diamond sang these words in their iconic love song "You Don't Bring Me Flowers," where two lovers, who have drifted apart, describe the feeling of being taken for granted.

A brutal truth that you discount at your own peril is that almost 70 percent of customers are lost because of neglect. Not prices, not products, not the economy, not aggressive competitors.

Neglect! They feel the sting of being taken for granted. If you have ever been taken for granted (and I bet you have), you know that it makes you feel unimportant, small, and resentful, which can lead to the feeling of contempt.

Resentment and contempt are the two most powerful negative emotions in the pantheon of human emotions. They are the gangrene of relationships, festering below the surface, often unspoken, slowly rotting away the connections that bind people together until the relationship is destroyed.

Resentment can be so emotionally debilitating that once it is triggered, communication and cooperation are often severed, creating a downward spiral that is not easily reversed. In this untenable situation, marred by distrust and lack of transparency, it becomes almost impossible to save the relationship.

Neglect happens slowly. It creeps up on customer relationships. Salespeople delude themselves into believing that if their customers are not complaining, they must be happy. So, they spend all of their time putting out fires and dealing with squeaky wheels, while ignoring accounts that don't raise their hand. Wrapped up in this warm blanket of delusion, salespeople swing the door open and invite competitors in.

Aggressive competitors don't miss an opportunity to displace salespeople who neglect their customers. This is exactly why you must never lose sight of the long-term consequences of neglecting customer relationships.

Relationships matter and must be protected against an onslaught of competitors that relentlessly pound on the door. When you fail to proactively manage your customer relationships, those competitors slip through and encourage buyers to consider other options.

You must not take any relationship for granted. Assume that every customer and every relationship is at risk.

I'm not saying this is easy. One of the hardest things to do is keep your fingers on the pulse of your customer base.

Quarterly business reviews and other formal meetings are time consuming. You probably have a large account base and you can't possibly meet with everyone. Every single day you are putting out fires and dealing with immediate customer service issues.

The good news is the one secret to defending accounts is completely in your control. It's simple. *Pay attention to your customers.* A simple, regular, inexpensive phone call check-in can make all the difference.

- *How are you doing?*
- *What can I do to help you?*
- *I have an idea for you.*
- *Have a great weekend.*
- *Thank you for your business.*

Regular telephone contact ensures that you are top of mind with customers. Hearing your voice lets them know that you care. It doesn't need to be anything particularly special. You don't need a reason to tell your customers that you appreciate them.

So, pick up the phone and say "hello." It doesn't cost a thing to pay attention to your customers.

Qualifying and Discovery

Certainly, there is a massive amount of qualifying information available through internet and social media searches. Companies like ZoomInfo also offer a trove of data on the opportunities you are pursuing. Nevertheless, there is information and insight that you can only get from talking with people. Likewise, information you pull from online sources will need to be verified.

This is where the phone comes into play. With the phone you can reach deep inside of organizations and speak to people who may have no say in the decision, but have insider information that can help you.

For example: One of my customers was working on a huge enterprise-level account. Prior to engaging the C-level executive who was the decision maker on the project, the sales rep spent several weeks calling into the bottom of the organization and speaking to frontline users of her competitor's software system.

With the information she gathered, she was able to qualify that her competitor was failing to meet the needs of the organization and taking them for granted. She also developed valuable and relevant insight that helped her score a meeting with the decision maker.

Discovery is the heart of the sales process. When you do deep discovery, it allows you to build a powerful business case that increases the probability that you close the deal. Deep discovery, though, takes time. It requires that you interview and talk with a wide array of stakeholders inside your prospect's organization. The telephone makes it time-efficient and cost-effective to conduct these discovery calls.

With complex and enterprise-level deals, you'll need to get beyond the traditional "decision makers" to gather the information you'll need to build your case. Sadly, most salespeople are too lazy or clueless to take the time to get high, wide, and deep with discovery. Ultra-high performing sales professionals, on the other hand, leave nothing to chance when building their business case. They actively work to identify and talk with each person who has a "stake" in the outcome of the deal.

There are five types of stakeholders you'll typically interview during discovery: **B**uyers, **A**mplifiers, **S**eekers, **I**nfluencers, and **C**oaches—**BASIC** (Figure 19.1).

1. *Buyers* are the decision makers. These are the people with the ultimate authority to say yes or no.
2. *Amplifiers* are typically lower-level people who will either use or be impacted by your product or service. Leveraged well, they can show you the real state of things, become advocates for change, and amplify the message, problem, pain, or need up through the organization.

Figure 19.1   The Five Stakeholders

3. *Seekers* are stakeholders sent to look for information early in the buying process.
4. *Influencers* are stakeholders that play an active role in the buying process and have a say in the decision-making process. In complex and enterprise-level sales, you will spend most of your time with influencers.
5. *Coaches* are insiders who are willing to advocate for you, help you with insider information, and remove barriers.

In every deal, the stakeholders have a list. This list includes their personal success criteria, hopes, wishes, wants, needs, desired business outcomes, metrics that matter, must-haves, deal-breakers, and core motivations. Knowing this list allows you to build a stronger business case that locks out competitors as alternatives to you.

There is a bonus for taking the time to interview stakeholders during discovery. They'll appreciate that you took time to listen to them. So much so that they often become allies and advocates who actively work to help you win the deal.

Outbound Prospecting

When it comes to outbound prospecting, the telephone is the most powerful weapon in your sales arsenal. Nothing can connect you to more prospects, in less time, and do it more effectively than the telephone. Because the phone is the most important outbound prospecting tool, we'll spend the next five chapters taking a deeper dive into telephone prospecting techniques.

20 | Telephone
Prospecting

Back in January while delivering a two-day Fanatical Prospecting Bootcamp for 200 healthcare sales professionals, we ran live telephone prospecting blocks. The exercise was simple. I asked them to make 15 outbound dials in 15 minutes with the goal of setting one appointment.

Prior to the event, we'd asked the company's leadership team to give each sales professional a list of targeted prospects and let them know that we would be running live phone blocks at the event. We did not want this to be a surprise.

Following a training module on the Five-Step Telephone Prospecting Framework, I gave the instructions. *"Grab your phones. You have 15 minutes to make 15 dials and set one appointment. Go!"*

Stunned. That was the look on the faces staring back at me.

Stunned as in, "Are you shitting me?" stunned.

Stunned as in, "This has got to be a joke," stunned.

Stunned as in, "You're not really serious," stunned.

Stunned as in, "You mean, you actually want us to call people?" stunned.

A hand went up. "Yes?" I asked.

"Um, Jeb, I don't think you understand. Nobody answers the phone in the medical industry. The only way to prospect is face-to-face." There was a collective nod of the heads. The room erupted in pushback and more arguments for why making these calls was a mistake and a waste of time.

The thing is, I'm unmovable. Teflon. No excuses stick. Plus, I had the blessing of the leadership team to push the sales reps to make the calls. The company's leaders were well aware of the inefficiencies of prospecting by foot and how it was holding the organization back.

So, I smiled politely and, in a kind, but firm tone of voice said, "That's OK. We're going to give it a try anyway. You have 15 minutes to make 15 dials and set one appointment. Go!"

One by one, they reluctantly began calling. It's always magical watching it happen. Boom, someone on the left side of the room set an appointment. A fist pump on the right. In the middle, I heard, "Oh my God, that was amazing."

I shuffled over and asked what happened. Maria, the rep, shook her head in disbelief. "I've been trying to meet with that doctor for three years with no luck. I just spoke to him and arranged a meeting for next week. That was crazy."

All across the room it was happening. One after another, the reps were having conversations, gathering information, and setting appointments. The leaders in the back of the room were beside themselves.

In that first 15-minute phone block the reps set 93 appointments. In the previous week of prospecting by foot (face-to-face) the group had only set 27 appointments. Stop for a moment and take this in. Consider the staggering productivity gap between eight hours a day of driving around, knocking on doors, for a full week (40 hours), versus 15 minutes of virtual prospecting by phone.

A top-five insurance company said that the single biggest challenge facing their new agents was telephone prospecting. Their words: "We are having such a hard time getting them to just pick up the phone and talk with people."

When I arrived on the morning of the training, one of the leaders pulled me aside and said, "I hope we haven't put you in a bad spot. We didn't spend time discussing the new reality in our industry, but no one answers the phone anymore. I realize you are going to do live phone blocks, but I wouldn't expect too much out of them."

We did three live phone blocks that day using targeted lists the agents brought with them. Over the course of the day, we saw a whopping 51 percent contact rate—actual live prospects answering their phones—generated by 19 agents who made 1,311 outbound dials.

At the end of the day, I showed the leader the numbers. He was speechless. "I don't understand how you got those results. Everybody tells me that people don't answer the phone anymore."

"Who is telling you that?" I asked.

"The agents," he responded.

"The same people that you say won't make calls?" I asked.

He slowly nodded his head as the weight of this realization sank in.

Ninety military recruiters stared at me in disbelief. I'd just given them the order. "You have 15 minutes to make 15 dials and set one appointment." Trust me when I say this: When a group of noncommissioned officers in the United States military, most of whom have been in combat, stare you down, it can be intimidating. Teflon begins to crack.

They argued that teenagers don't answer the phone. That it was too early to call. That it was the wrong day to call. Excuse after excuse, until I finally had enough.

I stood there, side-by-side with their Command Sergeant Major who was backing me up, and gave the order again. "You have 15 minutes to make 15 dials and set one appointment. Go!"

Fifteen minutes later, heads were shaking. The soldiers had set 133 appointments—more than the entire battalion had set in the last 30 days. It turns out that even teenagers answer the phone.

I want to be absolutely crystal clear that these stories are not anomalies. My team of master trainers has a front-row seat to these eye-opening, transformational moments every day as we work with sales organizations. We get these results everywhere we go, with every group, across every industry.

Telephone prospecting works. It's fast, efficient, and effective. All you need to do is pick up the damn phone.

Nobody Answers a Phone That Doesn't Ring

For thousands of salespeople, picking up the phone and calling a prospect is the most stressful part of their life. Many of these reluctant salespeople stare at the phone, secretly hoping that it will disappear. They procrastinate, get ducks in a row, and work to ensure that everything is perfect before they dial. Any excuse—and I mean any excuse—to do something else takes priority.

They work over their leaders, too. Whining that no one answers the phone anymore. Arguing that it is a waste of time. Complaining that people don't like to be contacted by phone.

The myth that the phone no longer works because people don't answer, is just that, a myth. All of our real-world evidence flies directly in the face of the myth that gets repeated over and over again that the telephone has a low success rate.

The statistics don't lie. We see between a 15 percent and 80 percent contact rate prospecting by phone, depending on the industry, product, and role level of the contact. For example, in the business services segment, contact rates are consistently between 25 and 40 percent. This, by the way, is far higher than response rates with email and direct messaging.

It gets better. We have stats on phone prospecting going back to the early 1990s. There are clear trends that contact rates via phone have actually risen by around five percentage points. There are three reasons more people are answering their phones:

1. *Phones are anchored to people, not desks.* It is common for prospects to answer their mobile phone when you call them—either because their mobile line is their only line or because their office line rolls over to their mobile line.
2. *No one is calling.* Because so much sales communication has shifted to email, direct messaging, and texting, phones are not ringing nearly as much as in the past. Because of this, salespeople who call stand out and get through.
3. *Email and direct messaging fatigue.* People are getting burned out on impersonal, irrelevant (and often automated) prospecting emails and direct messages. Email and social inboxes are being flooded with crap. Prospects are hungry for something different—a live, authentic human being.

Think about it. If the phone did not work, why are there so many tele-prospecting companies springing up across the globe—and thriving? Companies are spending tens of thousands of dollars on outsourcers who use the phone to prospect because there is no other way to keep the pipe full.

Nobody Likes It; Get Over It

In the heat of the global pandemic when it became impossible to prospect in-person, legions of field sales reps were paralyzed. Pipelines quickly depleted. Rather than picking up the phone and calling, they stared at it. The excuse, "I'm way better in person." From this myopic viewpoint, in-person was the only way to prospect.

From the very beginning of this book, I have stipulated that face-to-face is a more effective way to build emotional connections, relationships, and trust. Except for one activity—outbound prospecting. And just to be sure, I'm not just picking on field reps. There are thousands and thousands of inside sales development reps that argue that they are "way better on email." Both groups are dead wrong.

If you are a field rep, one of the reasons you have a job is that in-person selling gives your company a competitive edge. You are supposed to be better face-to-face. Nevertheless, as we've discussed, face-to-face sales calls, blended appropriately with virtual sales calls, makes you more agile, increases your productivity, and gives you a competitive edge.

Substituting prospecting by foot with prospecting by phone gives you an instant productivity boost. In sales, time is money, and you can cover far more ground, qualify more opportunities, and set more appointments in a one-hour targeted phone block than in an entire day of driving around in your territory and prospecting with your feet.

Think about it this way: How many prospects could you qualify or set appointments with face-to-face in an eight-hour period? Even on the busiest city street, 30 would be a stretch. In most territories, with travel time and parking, it would be closer to 10. If it is hot, raining, snowing, or freezing outside, the numbers go down further.

How about one hour on the phone, with a list of targeted prospects? How many phone calls could you make? Averaging one to two minutes per call, you could make 25 to 50 calls. Therefore, if you are touching twice as many prospects in about a tenth of the time, in a climate-controlled environment, which do you think will yield better results?

The answer is an obvious no-brainer. *Pick up the damn phone.*

21

Five-Step Telephone Prospecting Framework

I'm not going to sugarcoat it. Telephone prospecting is the most despised activity in sales. Calling and interrupting invisible strangers is uncomfortable. You are going to get rejected a lot more on the phone because, statistically, you will generate more real-time interactions with prospects than through any other prospecting channel.

Still, the telephone is more effective than any asynchronous communication channel including email, direct messaging, and social media. Because, when you are actually speaking to another human being, there is a higher probability that you'll set appointments, make sales, and gather qualifying information.

Sadly, many salespeople find it awkward to use the phone for prospecting because they:

- Fear calling invisible strangers.
- Don't know what to say, say stupid things, or use awkward phone scripts that generate resistance and rejection.

181

- Don't have an easy-to-execute telephone prospecting framework that actually works.
- Don't know how to handle objections.
- Are afraid of rejection.

However, if you desire bigger commission checks and to stand tall on top of your team's ranking report, you've got to accept that telephone prospecting sucks and get over it.

When You Fail to Interrupt, You Fail

When you pick up the phone and call a prospect and they are not expecting your call, you are an interruption.

In a perfect world, salespeople would not interrupt prospects, and prospects would be happy that they were not being interrupted. It would be a lovely utopia where buyers and sellers sat in circles and sang "Kumbaya." A world where qualified buyers reached out and contacted salespeople at just the right time and no one had to make an outbound prospecting call ever again.

But that's a fantasy. If you want the peace of mind of a full pipeline, if you want sustained success in your sales career, if you want to maximize your income, then you've got to interrupt prospects.

Unless you are a pure inbound sales rep, if you wait for your prospect to interrupt you, you will fail. Why? Because the number-one reason for failure in sales is an empty pipeline, and the number-one reason salespeople have empty pipelines is that they fail to pick up the phone.

It could be a prospect that filled out one of your web forms or downloaded your latest white paper. Maybe they connected with you online. It could be an old customer you are trying to reactivate, or a prospect in your defined database, a list you pulled from ZoomInfo, or someone you met at a trade show.

No matter the circumstance—warm, hot, cold—prospecting has always been about the willingness on the part of the salesperson to interrupt. Relentless interrupting is fundamental to building robust sales pipelines. No matter your prospecting approach, if you don't interrupt relentlessly, your pipeline will be anemic. When you fail to interrupt, you fail.

Don't Overcomplicate It

Few things in sales have been more overcomplicated than the simple telephone prospecting call. Efficient and effective telephone prospecting should get you to yes, no, or maybe as fast as possible, in the least intrusive way, using a relaxed, confident, professional tone that reduces resistance. That way you get the yesses on the table fast and deal with objections directly without the painful dance around the bush.

Consider how you feel when your workday is interrupted by someone calling you unannounced. It can make you feel irritated, angry, or resentful, because in most cases, the call comes when you are in the middle of something else.

Let's step into your shoes. What would you want?

Your first response is probably, "I wouldn't want to get the call in the first place." I'll give you that. No one wants to be interrupted, not me, not you, not your prospect—even if the call is something we welcome.

But let's get back to reality. Salespeople who don't interrupt prospects have skinny kids. As a salesperson, you've got a choice to make: Interrupt or start a new career at your local coffee shop making minimum wage.

So, if you're going to get interrupted, what would you want? You would want the caller to get right to the point and get off the phone quickly so you could get back to posting cat videos on YouTube.

Now try standing in your prospects' shoes. They are people just like you who resent having their day interrupted by an unscheduled caller. Therefore, since interrupting people is your job, to be respectful, the call should be quick and to the point so that you achieve your objective and your prospect can get back to what they were doing.

To do this effectively, your call must be structured so that you get to the point fast and sound like an authentic professional rather than a scripted robot or a stereotype of the cheesy sales guy so often portrayed in movies.

You need a framework that is consistent and repeatable. Frameworks make you agile, freeing you to focus on your message rather than the time-consuming effort of rethinking your process each time. They give you a set of rails to run on that flex to changing context.

This structure takes pressure off of you and your prospect. Because you are not winging it each time you call, you won't have to worry about what to say. Shorter, more impactful calls mean you get more prospecting done, in less time, with better outcomes.

Five-Step Telephone Prospecting Framework

Telephone prospecting should be professional and straight to the point. There is no reason to overcomplicate it with cheeseball scripts that piss off prospects, create resistance, and make you look foolish.

Here is an example:

> *Hi, Julie, this is Jeb Blount with Sales Gravy. The reason I'm calling is to set an appointment with you. Because, I just read an article online that said your company is going to add 200 new sales positions over the next year, and our onboarding system has been proven to get new salespeople selling fast by cutting ramp-up time in half. I want to learn more about you and your unique situation to see if our program might be a fit. How about we meet Wednesday afternoon around 3:00 p.m.?*

Let's take a closer look at the elements of the Five-Step Telephone Prospecting Framework (Figure 21.1):

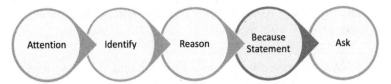

Figure 21.1   The Five-Step Telephone Prospecting Framework

Step 1: Attention. Get their attention by using the sweetest word in the world to them, their name.

Step 2: Identify. Tell them your name and name of your company.

Step 3: Reason. Tell them what you want.

Step 4: Because. Give them a compelling reason to meet with you.

Step 5: Ask. With relaxed, assertive confidence, ask for what you want.

Here is another example:

Hi Ian, this is Jeb Blount with Acme Restaurant Supply. The reason for my call is to set an appointment with you. Because, you are building a new restaurant over on the 44 bypass and I want to learn more about your process for purchasing kitchen equipment. I realize I'm calling a little bit early in the game; however, I've found that when we get our design team working with your team before you make critical decisions about kitchen layout, you'll have more options and can often save money on construction costs and labor with a more efficient and streamlined kitchen layout. How about we schedule a short video call tomorrow at 2:00 p.m. so I can learn more about you and your process?

Here is another example where my objective is to qualify and move them directly into a sales conversation:

Hi, Corrina, this is Jeb Blount from HubSpot. The reason I'm calling is to grab a few minutes of your time because you downloaded our white paper on creating more effective landing pages for lead generation. I work with a number of marketing executives like you who've been struggling to bring in enough quality leads to meet their growth objectives. I've got a few best practices that my clients are using to generate more and better leads that I'll be happy to share with you. I've got time right now or tomorrow morning at 10:00 a.m. what works best for you?

When you use this framework, you'll find that you stumble over your words less and achieve your objective more often.

One important point about this technique. There are no pauses. The moment you pause, you lose control of the call. As soon as my prospect answers the phone, I walk through the five-step framework without stopping. My goal is to respect their time by getting to the point and getting an answer—yes, no, or maybe—fast.

Get Their Attention

Once your prospect answers the phone, you have a split second to grab their attention. The easiest, fastest way to get someone's attention is to use the most beautiful word in the world to them—their name.

Anywhere, anytime, when you say another person's name, they will sit up and look up. For that split second you have their attention. The same dynamic is at play when telephone prospecting, and it is important to use this to your advantage. Just say: "Hi, Julie."

Another important point: Notice that I didn't ask Julie, "How are you doing?"

There is a reason for this. When you interrupt a prospect's day, you get resistance. This resistance hits a peak as soon as they realize that you are a salesperson and that they made a big mistake by answering their phone.

This realization happens right after you say something like, "Hi, this is Stephen from the widget company. How are you today?" Then you pause.

That's when your prospect's instinct to get off the phone and back to whatever they were doing kicks in. They immediately hit you with a reflex response like "I'm not interested," or ask, "Who is this?"

Your prospect was going about her morning happily when her phone rang, interrupting her day. Then she realized her mistake as soon as you said, "How are you doing?" Suddenly her get-away-from-this-salesperson-fast mechanism kicked in.

Then you paused, giving her the opportunity to hit you with an objection and a stern tone of voice. That's how your prospect is doing, and that's how you lose control of the call.

Don't ask, "How are you doing?" and don't pause or leave any awkward silence. Say their name and keep moving.

Identify Yourself

Get right down to business. Say your prospect's name, then tell her who you are and the reason you called. Transparency has two benefits:

1. It demonstrates that you are a professional and that you have respect for their time—save the idle chitchat until you have established a real relationship.
2. By telling them who you are and why you are calling, you reduce their stress because people are more comfortable when they know what to expect.

The one thing that I know to be true is that prospects are people just like you. They don't want to be tricked, they don't want to be manipulated, and they don't want to be interrupted. What they want is to be treated with respect. The best way you can show your respect is to be truthful, relevant, and to the point.

Because Statement

When you ask people to do something for you, like give up their time, they are more likely to do so when you give them a reason—or a because. The *because* connects the dots between what you want and why they should give it to you. You've interrupted their day, told them why you are calling, and now you must give them a reason to give up more of their precious time to you.

The person you are calling could not care less about your product, service, or features. They don't care about what you want or what you would "love" or "like" to do. They don't care about your desires, your quota, or that you are "going to be over in their area."

They only care about what is relevant to their problems. They will agree to meet with you for their reasons, not yours. This is why message matters. What you say and how you say it will either generate resistance and objections or it will pull the wall down and open the door to a yes.

Avoid saying things like:

- "I want to talk to you about my product."
- "I'd love to get together with you to show you what we have to offer."
- "I want to tell you about our new service."

These statements are all about you, and the words *talk, tell,* and *show* send a subtle message that what you really want to do is pitch. I assure you the last thing your prospect wants or has time for is you talking at them.

Instead, use phrases that indicate you could be a solution for their problem:

- Learn more about you and your business.
- Share some insights that have helped my other clients.
- Share some best practices that other companies in your industry are using to . . .
- Gain an understanding of your unique situation.
- See how we might fit.

Use emotional words that resonate:

- Flexibility
- Options
- Peace of mind

- Save
- Frustrated
- Concerned
- Stressed
- Waste
- Time
- Money

These statements and words are all about them. Prospects want to feel that you get them and their problems, or are at least are trying to get them, before they'll agree to give up their time for you. We'll take a deeper dive into crafting effective because statements in the next chapter.

Ask for What You Want and Shut Up

The most important step is asking for what you want.

- If you are qualifying, ask for the information you need.
- If you want an appointment, ask for a day and time.
- If you want to engage in a sales conversation, ask an open-ended question that gets them talking.

Your goal is to get to yes, no, or maybe, fast. Don't waste any time here. Don't talk in circles. Don't use passive, limp language and phrases like "maybe if it would be OK and if you are not too busy, we could kinda maybe get together for a few minutes, what do you think?"

Ask with relaxed, assertive, and confidence. Ask and assume. Then shut up. The single biggest mistake salespeople make on prospecting calls is they keep talking instead of giving their prospect the opportunity to respond to their request. This increases resistance, creates objections, and gives your prospect an easy way out.

Shut up and let your prospect respond. Will there be objections when you ask for what you want? Absolutely. This is reality—in sales, there are always objections. However, because you wasted no time getting to the objection, you will have more time to respond, which, in turn, will give you a better chance of achieving your objective.

We're going to dive headfirst into techniques for tuning around prospecting objections in Chapter 23. What I want to impress upon you, though, is just how many prospects will say yes when you are straightforward, confident, and assume through your words and tone of voice that they're going to say yes.

22 | Developing Effective Because Statements

Robert Cialdini, author of *Influence*, writes that, "A well-known principle of human behavior says that when we ask someone to do us a favor, we will be more successful if we provide a reason. People simply like to have reasons for what they do."

When prospecting, if you give your prospect a *good enough* reason (from their perspective) to meet with you, they'll say yes. Good enough is the name of the game. Because statements are like horseshoes and hand grenades, they don't need to be perfect—just *good enough* to convert your prospecting call into an appointment, sales call, or qualifying information.

The Power of *Because*

In a landmark study on human behavior, psychologist Ellen Langer and a team of researchers from Harvard demonstrated how using the word *because* compels people to comply with your requests.[1] Langer and her team of researchers attempted to cut in line in front of people waiting for access to photocopiers.

She discovered that when the researcher politely asked to jump in front of the person waiting for the copier without giving a reason—*"Excuse me, I have five pages. May I use the copier?"*—the subject would say yes about 60 percent of the time. However, when the researcher qualified the request with a valid reason—*"because I'm in a hurry"*—the subject said yes, on average, 94 percent of the time.

Then things got interesting. When the researcher gave a non-sensical reason like, *"Excuse me, I have five pages. May I use the copier? Because I have to make copies,"* the subject still said yes 93 percent of the time.

It was a stunning finding. It turned out that just saying the word *because*—giving a reason—was more important for gaining compliance than the reason itself. The study proved that when people are given a reason they are more likely to comply with a request.

Now, I want to be absolutely clear that I am not advising you to make up nonsense and use that while prospecting. What I am saying, though, is that simple, straightforward *because* statements—giving relevant reasons to meet with you—work like magic.

For example, just saying, "I'd like 15 minutes of your time because I want to learn more about you and your company," works surprisingly well with owners of small businesses.

The Secret to Crafting Powerful *Because* Statements

The real secret to crafting *because* statements that reduce resistance and convert prospecting calls into meetings is never forgetting a simple but powerful premise:

People make decisions based on emotion first and then justify with logic. In other words, they feel, then they think.

This is why pitching logic—features—doesn't work. Trust me. Your prospects abhor a pitch. They do not want to hear your elevator speech or 30-second commercial. This, by the way, is why you get so much resistance with those long scripts your marketing department writes for you.

Instead, they want to feel that you get them and their problems (emotional and logical), or are at least trying to get them, before they'll agree to give up their time to meet with you. Make your message relevant and offer them value:

- *Emotional value.* You connect directly with them at the emotional level. This can simply be expressing a desire to learn more about them. Business owners, in particular, love to talk about themselves. It can also mean relating to painful emotions like stress, worry, insecurity, distrust, anxiety, fear, frustration, and anger OR offering them peace of mind, security, options, lower stress, less worry, or hope.
- *Insight (curiosity) value.* You offer information that gives them special knowledge, power, a competitive advantage, or leverage over other people. Most prospects worry about maintaining their competitive edge—either as a company or an individual. They're anxious that there may be something in the marketplace that they are not privy to. They want to know about future trends. Unknowns are disconcerting—especially if a competitor has a best practice, information, system, or process that they don't.
- *Tangible (logic) value.* People value hands-on demos, trials, free stuff, pilots, exclusive access, data, and case studies.

What You Bring to the Table

An effective because statement should build a bridge from the issues your prospect is facing and how you might help them—*using their language, not yours.* Speaking their language is the key because it causes them to feel that you get them. Everyone desires to be understood.

Start the process by answering a basic question, "People choose (or call) our company (or me) when?" Analyze your product and service delivery strengths and weaknesses. Review your competitive advantages and the value you bring to the marketplace. Look for commonalities among your best customers. Why are they so loyal to you? Take a close look at the deals you are closing and gain a deeper understanding of trigger events that open buying windows.

Stand in Their Shoes

Next, stand in your prospect's shoes. Never forget that people meet with you for their reasons, not yours. Use your God-given empathy to sense their emotions and to consider what might be important to them or what they might be going through. Consider how you might feel in their situation. Focus on the emotions:

- What would cause you stress? When do you feel stress?
- What makes you worry? When do you worry? Why do you worry?
- What creates anxiety? When do you feel anxiety?
- How do you feel when you run out of time for important things?
- How do you feel when you don't have enough money to accomplish your goals? When does this happen?
- How do you feel when you don't have enough resources to accomplish your goals? When does this happen?
- How do you feel when you don't have the knowledge to accomplish your goals? When does this happen?
- How do you feel when you fail to accomplish your goals?
- When do you get overwhelmed, and how does it feel?
- What impacts your peace of mind or sense of security?
- How would it feel to have limited options?
- What is causing you to feel frustrated or stuck?
- What makes you mad?
- What causes you to feel distrust?
- What causes you fear?
- What causes you anguish?

- How do you feel when _____ happens?
- What might you want to know?
- What unknown would make you worry?
- What information would you fear getting into your competitors' hands?
- What might a competitor be doing that would make you want to do it, too?
- What information would you believe might give you a winning edge?
- What would cause you to be curious?
- What might be stealing your time, money, or resources?

Use the answers to these questions to build because statements that are about your prospect rather than you. For example:

> *Because so many business owners in your position are stressed out over remaining compliant with the new payroll rules, we've developed a system that is guaranteed to eliminate fines.*

Targeting Because Statements

Building effective because statements is hard work. To do it right, you have to think. You must test and hone your messages.

When you have a large prospect base and high activity expectations, there is no time to stop and build a personalized because statement for every prospect. Taking time to research each prospect and building a unique because statement before every call would make no sense. To remain efficient, you need to craft because statements that may be used with multiple prospects.

With a large prospect base, you won't have deep and detailed information about the specific issues, problems, or concerns of each individual prospect. It's unlikely that the information in your CRM (if there even is any) is accurate. Therefore, to build effective because statements you'll need to infer problems based on economic trends or your knowledge of what other businesses are experiencing in the same industry, geographical area, market segment, or with a certain competitor's product.

Start with segmenting your prospect database into large groups of similar prospects—company size, revenue potential, decision-maker roles, industry verticals, product or service applications, competitor accounts, and so on. Then build several because statements for each segment. Over time, you'll naturally iterate and refine your message as you engage in more conversations with these prospects. Here is an example:

> Hi, Candace, this is Jeb Blount from Sales Gravy. The reason I am calling is to grab a few minutes on your calendar. BECAUSE I find that so many leaders like you are frustrated with how long it takes to get new salespeople ramped up to full productivity. Our new learning system has been proven to cut onboarding time in half for new sales reps and get them selling fast. How about we get together for a short meeting so I can learn more about you and see whether it makes sense to schedule a demo? I have 2:00 p.m. on Thursday open.

You'll notice I implied Candace is frustrated that it is taking too long to get her new salespeople up to speed and selling. I don't know for sure that this is her issue, but because most companies that are hiring salespeople have this problem, there is a good chance she has this problem, too.

Stop now and practice crafting because statements for each of your major prospect types or segments in the format shown in Table 22.1.

Table 22.1 Craft Because Statements

Prospect Type/Segment	Because Statement

Personalizing Because Statements

When the stakes are high, though, you'll want to craft a personalized because statement specific to the account and person you are calling. Personalized because statements require research and a concerted effort to get the message right. In some cases, you may only get one shot to engage a C-level executive at an enterprise account, so you need to be relevant and give them a compelling reason to set an appointment with you.

Personalizing because statements for individual stakeholders is time consuming. However, with high-value opportunities, the investment is risk/reward positive.

Begin with defining the objective of your prospecting touch. This will help you remain focused and relevant:

- Are you attempting to get more information to further qualify the opportunity and the buying window?
- Are you seeking an introduction to another person?
- Do you want to set up an initial meeting?

Next, research:

- Set up Google alerts to have information about the company or individual sent directly to your inbox.
- Review notes and history in your CRM.
- Browse the company/division/location through online searches, website, and press releases.
- Check out company and individual pages on LinkedIn, Twitter, Facebook, and YouTube.
- Make notes of jargon, core values, awards, trigger events, initiatives, changes, and problems that you can solve.
- Research industry trends and read the most recent trade articles.

Then, craft your message to demonstrate that you can relate to their unique situation and solve specific problems they are facing, using *their* language.

An example:

> *Hi, Windsor, this is Jeb Blount from Sales Gravy. The reason I am calling is to set an appointment with you. I read in* Fast Company *that you are adding another hundred sales reps. I've worked with a number of companies in your industry to reduce ramp-up time for new reps. At Xjam Software, for example, we cut ramp-up time for their new reps by 50 percent. While I don't know if our solution will be a fit in your unique situation, I've got some ideas and best practices I've seen work well for companies like yours and thought you might be interested in learning more about them. How about we get together for a short meeting on Thursday at 2:00?*

Stop now and craft personalized because statements as in Table 22.2 for your top five dream or conquest accounts.

Table 22.2 Crafting Because Statements

Prospect	Because Statement

23 | Getting Past Telephone Prospecting Objections

The sad truth is many salespeople, start their sales day with the intention of getting on the phone and engaging new prospects. Instead, they waste prime prospecting time piddling around, avoiding the inevitable.

Finally, as they reluctantly dial the first number their palms sweat and heart pounds while they secretly pray that no one will answer.

"Hello, how can I help you?" The voice on the other line sounds cold.

Nervous, the salesperson stumbles over their call script and then BAM! They get hit with "Look, we're happy with our current vendor!"

Their mind goes blank and a wave of embarrassment rolls over them as their weak attempt to overcome the objection is rebuffed and the prospect hangs up. And with this, their motivation for telephone prospecting evaporates.

To avoid making any more calls, they "research," fiddle around on LinkedIn, dig through the CRM, and check email—anything but dial another number. Then justify their lack of activity to the boss with being overwhelmed with admin work or being "so much better in person."

Of all sales objections, prospecting objections are the most severe. They're often harsh and cold, and at times, flat-out rejection. This is why so many salespeople treat telephone prospecting like the plague and allow avoiding it to damage both their careers and chances for income advancement.

There is a simple reason why telephone prospecting is so emotionally difficult and why it generates such harsh rejection: Prospecting is interrupting. You don't enjoy being interrupted. Neither do your prospects, and they are not shy about letting you know it.

The Five-Step Telephone Prospecting Framework, along with effective because statements, is designed to make interrupting more effective and reduce resistance. But, no matter how good you are, you are going to get prospecting objections.

Prospecting Objections Can Be Anticipated in Advance

When I ask salespeople how many potential telephone prospecting objections can be thrown at them, the most common answer is, "It's infinite."

Sadly, this is how most salespeople think. They approach each prospecting objection as if it is a unique, random event and thus wing it on every call. Winging it on prospecting calls is a big mistake because it is almost impossible to control the emotional response to rejection without a plan.

The truth is, there are a finite number of ways a prospect will tell you no. In fact, there are common sets of objections in every industry and usually three to five that make up 80 percent or more of the prospecting objections you'll face.

When I ask salespeople to list all the possible prospecting objections they can think of, they rarely get past 15. When I ask them to list the ones they hear most often, it's rarely more than five. The most common prospecting objections include:

- We're happy or all set.
- I'm not interested.
- Don't have the budget.
- We're under contract.
- I'm not the right person.
- I need to speak to someone else before . . .
- I'm too busy.
- Just send information.
- Overwhelmed—too many things going on.
- We used your company before, and it didn't work out.
- We do this in-house.
- We don't work with outside vendors.
- One of your reps called me last week, and I already said no.
- We tried this product/service before, and it didn't work out.
- Just looking/checking you out (inbound leads).

Prospects don't always use these exact words. For example, instead of saying, "We're happy," they may say, "We've been with your competitor for years, and they do a good job for us." The words are different, but the intent is the same—we're happy.

Making a list of the most common objections you encounter during prospecting interactions is the first step toward learning to anticipate objections and crafting effective responses. Take a moment right now and use Table 23.1 to list all the prospecting objections you get on calls. Then rank them from most frequent to least frequent.

Table 23.1 List Common Prospecting Objections

Prospecting Objection	Rank Based on Frequency

Planning for Prospecting Objections

You are going to get prospecting objections, and they will trigger your disruptive emotions. But since virtually every prospecting objection can be anticipated, you can plan responses in advance. Knowing exactly what to say allows you to both gain control of your emotions and disrupt your prospects' thought pattern and flip the script.

To master and become effective at turning around prospecting objections, you simply need to:

1. Identify all the potential objections (see Table 23.1) unique to your industry, product, geography, service, current market conditions, and customer verticals.
2. Leverage the *Three-Step Telephone Prospecting Objection Turnaround Framework* to develop simple, repeatable scripts that you say without having to think—allowing you to remain relaxed, assertive, and confident.

Why have a repeatable practiced script for prospecting objections? In Chapter 17, we explored the fight-or-flight response and how social threats like rejection make it very difficult to think on your feet. It's exactly why you stumble over your words and say things you regret when you try to wing it with prospecting objections.

In emotionally tense situations, scripts free your mind, releasing you of the burden of worrying about what to say and putting you in complete control of the situation. A practiced script makes your voice intonation, speaking-style, and flow sound confident, relaxed, authentic, and professional—even when your emotions are raging beneath the surface.

Scripts work especially well with prospecting objections because you tend to get the same ones again and again. To observe the power of scripts, just watch a movie. The dialogue between the actors is scripted. Otherwise, it wouldn't be entertaining.

Just notice the difference when a politician is speaking off script in a confrontation with reporters as opposed to giving a speech with the aid of a teleprompter. On stage, the politician is incredibly convincing. But without a script, he stumbles on his words and makes many of the same mistakes salespeople make when winging it on prospecting calls.

The worry for most salespeople, though, is "I won't sound like myself when I use a script." This is a legitimate concern. Authenticity matters. Which is why actors, politicians and top sales professionals rehearse and practice until the script sounds natural and becomes their voice.

The good news is, you already have the habit of saying certain things in certain ways on prospecting calls. So, begin with analyzing what you are already doing. Then formalize what is working into a script that can be repeated with success, time and again.

Take a moment now to write down your five most frequent prospecting objections and how you currently respond to them (Table 23.2). Consider what is working and what is not working. Look for patterns in your messages. Make note of the messages that make you feel and sound the most authentic.

**Table 23.2 Write Down How You Respond
to Prospecting Objections Now**

Top Five Objections	How You Respond Now

The Three-Step Telephone Prospecting Objection Turnaround Framework (LDA)

You learned in an earlier chapter that a framework acts as a guide to give you structure but flexes to context. Frameworks give you agility, in the heat of the moment, to shift your message to the unique situation and prospect. With prospecting objections, you'll deploy a simple but powerful three-step framework:

1. Ledge
2. Disrupt
3. Ask

Once you master this framework, you'll gain the confidence to deftly handle any prospecting objection that gets thrown at you. (see Figure 23.1).

Figure 23.1 Three-Step Telephone Prospecting Objection Turnaround Framework

Ledge

When you get hit with a prospecting objection, the fight-or-flight response kicks in, triggering a flood of disruptive emotions. The secret to rising above these emotions is giving your rational brain a chance to catch up and take control. In fast-moving situations like with telephone prospecting objections, to effectively deal with these disruptive emotions, you need only a millisecond for your logical brain to wake up and tell the emotional brain to stand down. This allows you to regain your poise and control of the conversation.

In her book *Emotional Alchemy*, Tara Bennett-Goleman calls this the "magic quarter second"[1] that allows you to keep the disruptive emotions you feel from controlling your subsequent response and behavior. The most effective technique for activating the magic quarter-second is called a *ledge*.

A ledge is a memorized, automatic response that does not require you to think. It gives your logical brain the moment it needs to catch up, rise above disruptive emotions, and gain control. Because prospecting objections tend to evoke strong emotional responses, the ledge technique is a critical part of the turnaround framework.

Examples of ledge statements include:

- That's exactly why I called.
- I thought you might say that.
- Other people said the same thing before they learned . . .
- I figured you might say that.
- That's fantastic.
- That makes sense.
- That's OK.

Disrupt

Your prospect has been conditioned from hundreds, if not thousands, of prospecting calls. When they hit you with an objection, they have an expectation for what you will most likely do next.

When your behaviors match their expectations, no thinking is required; they just reflexively react.

You've learned that your prospect's brain (specifically the amygdala) ignores patterns and is pulled toward anomalies—different, unexpected, bright, shiny things. The secret to turning around your prospect's objection, therefore, is delivering a statement or question that disrupts the expected pattern.

Pattern painting—doing the unexpected—is how you flip your prospect's script, turn them around, and pull them toward you. Here are some examples:

When they say they're happy, instead of arguing that you can make them happier if they just give you a chance, respond with something that is completely unexpected:

> *Awesome. If you're getting great prices and service, you should never think about changing. All I want is a few minutes of your time to learn more about you and see if we are even a fit. At a minimum, I'll give you a competitive quote that will help you keep those other guys honest.*

When they say they're busy, instead of arguing that you will only take a little bit of their time, disrupt their pattern by agreeing with them:

> *That's exactly why I called; I figured you would be, and all I want is to find a time that's more convenient for you.*

When they say, "Just send me some information," you can call their bluff and force engagement, or bring the real objection to the surface with:

> *That's fantastic! I'm happy to hear that you are interested in learning more. But, since we have so much information, the last thing I want to do, as busy you are, is completely overwhelm you. Can you tell me specifically what information you'd like to see?*

When they say, "I'm not interested," respond with:

That makes sense. Most people aren't the first time I call, and that's exactly why we should meet.

It is also important to avoid using words that only salespeople use. As soon as you do, you play right into their expectations. Overused phrases like "Reaching out," "I just wanted to," "That's great," and "I understand" make you sound just like every other sales rep and turn you into an easy-to-ignore pattern.

Ask

To get what you want, you must ask for what you want. You may deliver the perfect disruptive turnaround, but if you don't ask again, you won't get the outcome you desire.

The ask step is where most prospecting objection turnarounds fall apart. The salesperson hesitates and waits for the prospect to do the work for them. Trust me, they won't.

You must control your emotions and ask again—assumptively and assertively, without hesitation, directly following your turn-around script. About half of the time, they'll throw out another objection—one that tends to be closer to the truth. Be prepared to turn it around and ask again.

What you should never do, though, is fight. It isn't worth it. When you get two objections and still can't turn your prospect around, graciously move on and come back to them another day. As they say, there are plenty of fish in the sea.

Putting It All Together

It is essential that you avoid overcomplicating this process. You need turnaround scripts that work for you and sound natural coming from your lips. They need to make you sound authentic, real, and confident. Keep them simple so that they are easy for you to remember and repeat. Turnaround scripts don't need to be perfect, and they won't work every time, but you need scripts that give you the highest probability of getting a yes.

Here are some examples:

Prospect: "We used you before and had a bad experience."

Sales Rep: "Nancy, that's exactly why I called, because I want to grab a few minutes of your time to learn exactly what happened. How about we get together next Wednesday at 3:00?"

Prospect: "We're not interested."

Sales Rep: "You know, that's what a lot of my clients said until they learned how much I could save them. Look, we don't even know if my service is a good fit for you, but wouldn't it make sense to get together anyway and find out? How about Friday at 2:00?"

Prospect: "There's no way we can afford you."

Sales Rep: "That's exactly the same thing my other clients said until they learned how affordable we are. All I want is an opportunity to get to know you a little better and show you how we have helped so many other businesses in your same situation reduce and manage risk without increasing expenses. How about I come by on Tuesday at 11:30?"

Prospect: "We do this in-house."

Sales Rep: "That's perfect, because most of my clients have in-house programs. We complement what they are already doing and make it even better. Since we don't know if this would even be a good fit for you, why don't we get together and I'll show you how I help my other clients in your industry, and we can make a decision from there whether or not it makes sense to keep talking. I'm free Monday at 2:00."

Now it's time to build your own scripts. Using Table 23.3, start with your five most common prospecting objections. Write down a ledge and construct a disrupt statement. Once you complete the first pass, walk away from it for a day, and then come and do it again. You'll find that this process gives your brain a chance to adjust to the messaging process and will help you iterate your scripts and make them better.

Table 23.3 Build a Turnaround Script

Common Prospecting Objections	Ledge	Disrupt

24 | Leaving Effective Voicemail Messages

When you prospect by phone the majority of your calls are going to go to voicemail. That's a fact. But far too often sales professionals feel that leaving a voicemail message is a waste of time. It can feel like you are sending those messages into a big black hole because so many voicemail messages never get returned.

This is exactly why the most frequent question I get about voicemail is not *how* to leave an effective voicemail message, but *should* I leave a voicemail? Frankly, if you aren't asking this question, you're not human.

In my experience, there are two camps on this. One that says you should never leave a voicemail and another that says you should always leave a voicemail. Both are wrong. Leaving effective voice-mail messages is important because:

- People do listen to and return voicemail messages.
- A series of voicemail messages, over time, educates and builds familiarity.
- It tells your prospect that you care enough to be persistent, and you are not going away.

If you never leave a voicemail, you will never get a callback. You signal to your prospect that you don't you care enough to pursue them, you abdicate your responsibility to educate your prospect, and you hinder your efforts to build familiarity. Since getting a callback is a very good thing, it doesn't make sense to *never* leave a voicemail.

There are some circumstances, though, where it might not make sense to leave a voicemail. For example, if you are dialing a completely cold list of prospects and your goal is to make as many dials as possible while connecting with as many prospects as possible in the shortest possible time, voicemail will slow you down. It can take 30–60 seconds to leave a voicemail, causing you to spend a significant amount of your phone block, leaving voicemail messages for completely cold, unqualified prospects.

However, on most prospecting calls, you should leave a voice-mail. We've analyzed data on how many prospecting touches it takes to get a prospect to engage across a diverse set of sources and industries. The data tell us that prospecting is rarely a one and done activity. It takes persistence and many touches to get sales engagement. Consider these numbers:

- 1 to 3 touches to reengage an inactive customer
- 1 to 5 touches to engage a prospect who is in the buying window and is familiar with you and your brand
- 3 to 10 touches to engage a prospect who has a high degree of familiarity with you or your brand but is not in the buying window

- 5 to 12 touches to engage a warm inbound lead
- 5 to 20 touches to engage a prospect who has some familiarity with you and your brand
- 20 to 50 touches to engage a cold prospect who does not know you or your brand

Keep in mind that these are averages across a wide statistical distribution. Depending on your brand recognition, geographic location, prospecting channel, product, service, sales cycle, and industry vertical, you may find that these numbers shift in or out of your favor.

The point, however, is not the numbers. It is the story these numbers tell us. It takes multiple touches to get prospects to engage, and that means that to be successful you will need to master multiple prospecting channels including phone, email, direct messaging, video messaging, text messaging, social media, and voicemail.

A Commitment to Persistence

Richard left 71 voicemail messages asking for an appointment. He sent 18 emails. He stalked me on LinkedIn.

He managed to get me to answer the phone on at least three occasions. But I brushed him off each time. He also called, and wrote, and connected on social media with each of the key stakeholders in my organization.

For five months, Richard asked and asked and asked for an opportunity to demonstrate his software solution. And for five months, he got nowhere—until he finally caught me at the right time. It was in May, five months after his first attempt to set an appointment.

When I answered the phone, I recognized his voice. I almost brushed him off again, but since I didn't have anything else scheduled and he'd been so persistent, I felt a subconscious obligation to give him a chance.

Richard wasted no time getting me to agree to a demo. His SaaS solution was impressive, and it solved one of our training delivery problems.

Less than an hour later, he asked for my commitment to buy. Before I knew it, he had my credit card and Sales Gravy was his newest customer. Had he not persistently left all of those voicemail messages, this sale would not have happened.

Author and sales trainer Anthony Iannarino says it best: "Your commitment to persistence and multiple touches establishes a couple things. First, it says that you are not going to go away, that you intend to keep calling. Second, it acknowledges that you believe it is your responsibility to call them, rather than waiting for them to call you."

Three Objectives of Voicemail

There are three objectives with voicemail:

1. *Educate.* This is typically accomplished by leaving a series of short voicemail messages that provide valuable insight and information to help your prospect learn more about the challenges and problems your product or service helps them overcome or solve.
2. *Build familiarity.* When prospects don't know you, it's much harder to get a return call. But you can build familiarity over time with sequenced and repeated prospecting touches. The more a prospect hears and sees your name, the more familiar you become to them and the more likely they are to engage. This is one of the core reasons persistence pays off.

    Familiarity as a prospecting objective requires a long-term focus because it is improved through the cumulative impact of ongoing prospecting activity. This is why savvy sales professionals create prospecting sequences and pursuit plans that cross-leverage virtual communication channels. Voicemail plays a key role in these sequences.

3. *Get a response.* This means your message compels the prospect to respond. A response is ideal because when they call you back, conversion rates soar.

There are three reasons, within your control, why voicemails don't get a response:

1. *Long-winded.* Somewhere in the middle of the rambling, the prospect hits "delete."
2. *Nothing relevant or interesting.* The message does not motivate the prospect to want to call back.
3. *Difficult.* You say your number too fast or only once so the prospect must replay the message to get the information they need to call you back. They usually don't waste the time.

If you are honest with yourself, these are the same reasons you don't return voicemail messages.

Five-Step Voicemail Message Framework

This leads us to the formula for getting more of your messages returned. To be effective, voicemail messages must be short, to the point, and easy to return. They must give your prospect a compelling reason to call you back.

The key to putting short, easy, and compelling into practice is leveraging the Five-Step Voicemail Message Framework (Figure 24.1). Sales professionals who adopt this framework double their response rate.

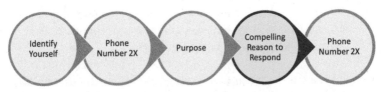

Figure 24.1   Five-Step Voicemail Message Framework

Step 1: Identify yourself. Say who you are and the company you are with up front. This makes you sound professional and credible.

Step 2: Provide your phone number twice. Give your contact information up front and say it twice—slowly and clearly. People can't call back if they don't have your number.

Step 3: State your purpose. Say what prompted you to call and/or specifically what you want.

Step 4: Give a compelling reason to call back. Motivate them to call you back by sparking their curiosity; or, if your objective is primarily to educate, provide compelling insight.

Step 5: Repeat your phone number twice and identify yourself. Give your contact information again, slowly and clearly. Before you end your message, repeat your name and company.

It sounds like this:

Hi, Rick, this is Jeb Blount from Sales Gravy. My phone number is 1-888-360-2249, that's 1-888-360-2249. The reason I am calling is, you downloaded our white paper on virtual selling, and I want to learn more about your situation and what triggered you to seek out this information. I also have some free training resources on telephone prospecting that I'd like to give you for your sales team. Give me a call back at 1-888-360-2249, that's 1-888-360-2249. This is Jeb Blount from Sales Gravy.

Steps One and Two Start your voicemail message by confidently identifying yourself and your company. Then leave your phone number twice—slowly and clearly. This makes you sound professional and transparent, which increases the probability that the prospect will keep listening. Say:

Hi, Rick, this is Jeb Blount from Sales Gravy. My phone number is 1-888-360-2249, that's 1-888-360-2249.

There are three reasons for leaving your phone number up front twice. First, it makes it clear that you want them to call you back and makes it easy for them to do so.

Second, because so many voicemail messages are transcribed automatically on mobile phones or via email-based applications, your phone number is featured prominently up front, making it easier for the prospect to just click on your number and call you back.

Finally, after they hear your name and company, they might not need to listen to the rest of your message. If you work for a well-known brand, the prospect has an immediate need, or you've built enough familiarity through a multitouch prospecting sequence, they may skip the rest of the message and call you right back.

Step Three   In step three, you will state why or what prompted your call and specifically what you want. Say:

> *I'm calling to schedule time on your calendar.*
> *The purpose of my call is to schedule a demo.*
> *I'm calling because Susie over at ABC company said that you and I should talk.*
> *The reason for my call is, you downloaded our white paper on cold calling, and I want to learn more about your situation and what triggered you to seek out this information.*

This transparency is both respectful and professional. Being prepared with a specific request helps keep your message succinct and to the point and avoid rambling. Keeping the reason short and sweet sends the message that you don't intend to waste their time.

Step Four   Prospects call back and engage when you give them a compelling reason to do so. Keep voicemail messages, brief, simple, direct, and relevant. Be authentic, human, and engaging.

Consider how you might be able to relate to your prospect's unique situation and how you can express what's in it for them to call you back in a concise message. Compelling can be:

- Something that sparks curiosity.
- Exclusive offers.

- Scarcity.
- Special or limited-time offers.
- Knowledge, insight, or information.
- Solution to a problem.
- Saying that you were referred by someone they know.

It can be as simple as:

I also have some free training resources on telephone prospecting that I'd like to give you for your sales team.

Boring voicemail messages about your company, product, or service don't work. Avoid overcomplicating things and sounding like a talking marketing brochure. Stand in your prospect's shoes. Look at things through their eyes. Build your message around what might be important to them. This is how you get a callback.

If you have thousands of potential prospects to call, taking time to research and build a unique voicemail message for each prospect makes little sense. It is a better use of your time to build a series of targeted messages based on common problems and trends in their particular industry, or your knowledge of what other businesses are experiencing in the same geographical area or market segment.

Targeted voicemail messages work best with large groups of similar prospects, decision-maker roles, industry verticals, or product or service applications. They are most appropriate when you have little information and the cost/benefit of doing the research isn't worth it.

However, when you are leaving messages for high-value opportunities and stakeholders like C-Level executives, you'll want to craft a personalized voicemail. This type of voicemail message will require research and effort because your message must be specific and relevant to that individual.

To research your prospect and develop targeted, personalized messages:

- Set up Google alerts to have information about the company or individual sent directly to your inbox.
- Review notes and history in your CRM.
- Research the company through online searches, visiting their website, press releases, and company pages on LinkedIn and Facebook.
- Visit their social media profile pages.
- Review blog and social media posts for jargon, core values, PR, awards, trigger events, initiatives, trends and problems that you can solve.
- Research industry trends and read the most recent trade articles.

Crafting voicemail messages that are personalized to a single prospect is time consuming. However, when there is much at stake, or if you only get one shot at a C-level executive, you'll want to make your message count.

Salespeople can sometimes be tempted to say or do things that trick prospects into returning calls. Don't do it. Don't be disingenuous, don't be cheesy, and don't attempt to trick your prospect into calling you back by being cryptic about your intentions or insinuating something that isn't true.

There is nothing more irritating to a buyer than a salesperson who is not honest and transparent about their intentions. Nothing will destroy your credibility and break trust faster. You are a sales professional so be professional. Be direct and transparent about who you are and what you want.

Step Five   Leave your number again twice. Speak slowly and clearly. Remind them of your name and company. Say:

> *Give me a call back at 1-888-360-2249, that's 1-888-360-2249. This is Jeb Blount from Sales Gravy.*

You may also choose to leave your email if it is simple and easy to understand.

> *Give me a call back at 1-888-360-2249, that's 1-888-360-2249. Or my email address is jeb@salesgravy.com, that's jeb@salesgravy.com. This is Jeb Blount from Sales Gravy.*

You leave your contact information for a second time at the end because, if your message compelled them to want to call you back, they won't have to replay the message. This increases the probability that you'll get the callback.

I am aware that it feels awkward to say your phone number four times on the same voicemail message. I assure you, though, that this technique works and will result in many more callbacks. Just remember that your objective is to make it easy and pleasurable for them to call you back, not more comfortable for you.

The One Thing You Must Never Do on a Voicemail Message

On voicemail you have mere seconds to get your prospect's attention. In those precious few moments, what you say and how you say it matters. Your voice tone must be confident, bright, professional, and enthusiastic. One of the truths about human behavior is that people tend to respond in kind. If you want prospects to be enthusiastic about meeting you, be enthusiastic about meeting them.

One of the challenges with leaving voicemail is maintaining a positive tone of voice while leaving many voicemail messages during a call block. As you slog through one voicemail after another, you can begin to sound bored or like a detached robot. It's also natural to begin speeding through messages.

For this reason, it is important that you maintain awareness of your tone of voice, inflection, and pace. Even though you may be leaving many voicemail messages, your prospect is only going to hear your message once. Therefore, on each message, you must be your best. A confident, enthusiastic tone of voice and relaxed pace will compel prospects to call you back like nothing else.

When you leave multiple voicemail messages for a prospect who is not calling you back, it's natural to become frustrated. When this happens, salespeople sometimes make the mistake of calling the prospect out for not calling them back. They say things like,

> *I've left a couple voicemails for you already.*
> *I left a message for you last week.*
> *This is my third voicemail message.*

Along with this, their voice tone changes. They can become whiny and unlikable.

Imagine for a moment that a friend called and left a voicemail that you didn't return. Then a few days later, they left you another voicemail calling you out for not calling back. How would you feel? If you are human, you'd feel bad and then get angry at your friend for making you feel bad.

This is exactly how prospects react when you call them out by telling them that they didn't call you back. They get mad and don't like you. And when they don't like you, they won't engage. Therefore, you should never, ever leave a message indicating that you've left other messages that were not returned.

Voicemail Block Productivity Hack

One of the core goals with virtual selling is to get more done, in less time, with better outcomes. An easy productivity hack with voicemail that will help you toward this goal, is to schedule a dedicated voicemail call block.

With a voicemail block, your objective is to leave voicemail rather than set appointments. For example, if you called a list of 30 prospects during your morning call block and only connected with seven of them, later that afternoon, schedule a voicemail block with the remaining 23. Since voicemail is asynchronous communication, it may be left at any time of day and outside of prime prospecting hours.

A best practice is to build lists of similar prospects so that you are leaving the same basic message for each prospect. This makes you much more efficient because you are not switching back and forth between different voicemail messages.

You'll find that scheduled voicemail blocks allow you to concentrate your focus and leave many more voicemails, in a shorter period of time, than you can during your morning call block. This also makes your morning call block more effective because you'll make more calls and speak to more people during prime calling time when you aren't leaving voicemails on each call.

PART V

Texting, Email, Direct Messaging, and Chat

25 | Blending Text Messaging into Account Management and Down-Pipeline Communication

I love text messaging. As a virtual communication tool, it's fast, efficient, less formal than email, and allows for arm's-length, nonintrusive synchronous communication that still feels personal.

Text messaging is extremely versatile. You can attach videos, images, voice messages, and links to articles and resources. And, when the person you are texting is not available, texting shifts from synchronous to asynchronous communication.

I primarily use text for account management, customer service, nurturing relationships, and advancing pipeline opportunities. Secondarily, I prospect with text, present offers with text, negotiate with text, and close deals with text.

There are two reasons why text messaging is such a powerful virtual sales tool:

1. *It's mobile.* Text messaging is integrated into the mobile and wearable devices that are attached to us 24/7. These are the primary communications devices in our lives and businesses. Everyone has a mobile phone, and for Apple users, text is integrated across all devices and desktops.
2. *It's a priority.* One of the key reasons why text messages work so well is that most people feel compelled to read and/or respond to them immediately.

Blending Text into Account Management Activity

It's for these reasons that text messaging is the perfect virtual communication channel to blend into account management and down-pipeline activity. Text messages are an easy way to do the following:

- Check in and let your customers know you care.
- Send account updates and data.
- Send insight and educational resources.
- Keep them apprised of shipments and order information.
- Schedule appointments.
- Check their pulse.
- Send offers and specials.
- Spark conversations that lead to additional opportunities.
- Be proactive with solving issues.

The key to blending text into your account management process is twofold. First, account management texts should not be random. Build this communication channel into your account management plan and be intentional and systematic.

Second, do not allow text to become an easy way out of meeting with you customers by phone, video, and in-person.

I recently ended a several-year relationship with one of my vendors because my account manager was just "texting it in." We'd always used text as a way to stay in touch. I appreciated being able to communicate with him and quickly get questions asked or problems solved. I'd even purchased several items via text.

A year earlier, though, text became his primary channel. Where we used to talk, now he never called. He was no longer blending texting into his account management process; texting had *become* his account management process. If he had an upsell or special offer, he sent it via text. When it was time to restock, he sent a text. Soon, I started to feel that he was taking me for granted, like he felt he no longer needed to make an effort to retain my business.

This is the dark side of text messaging. It's fast and easy, but it is not a substitute for talking with people and investing in relationships. Interpersonal communication is a combination of words, voice tone, body language, and facial expression. Since stakeholders cannot associate the words in your text messages with the context of your voice tone and facial expressions, they assign their own meaning, which can lead to miscommunication, or, in my case, resentment.

Sadly, for my account manager, one of his competitors called me. She invested in the relationship. I gave her a little of my business, and she did a great job. As the business relationship bloomed, I gave her more and more of my business. Soon she had it all.

And my old account manager? He has still not called. But I did get a text message from him this morning asking how I was doing. All I can do is SMH.

Responsive Customer Service

Issues come up with customers. They may leave you a voicemail, send an email, or call into your customer service center. Often, these issues arise at an inopportune time when you are busy with another customer or project.

Customers don't expect you to be perfect, but they do expect you to be responsive. Business relationships rarely get damaged when things go wrong. The damage occurs when customers are left in the dark, waiting on a response. Trust me, their minds always focus on the worst possible scenarios.

There are two important ways to leverage text for managing customer service issues:

1. *Response.* A simple and timely text message letting your customer know that you are aware of the issue, that you are following up, and when they can expect to hear from you is worth its weight in gold. This simple act of responsiveness tells people you care and engenders massive customer loyalty.
2. *Updates.* Text is a fantastic tool for keeping customers apprised of the ongoing process toward resolution. This gives them peace of mind that you and your team are working on it and keeps them from calling every five minutes to check on the situation, allowing you to stay focused on the problem. But, beware, text is not a substitute for picking up the phone and letting people hear your voice.

Checking Stakeholder Temperature after Video Sales Conversations

As you've learned, a big challenge with video and telephone sales calls is the inability to see the entire picture and gauge reaction. A simple text message is an easy way to both anchor virtual conversations and check a stakeholder's temperature and engagement. I'll send something like:

Janice – It was so nice to meet you this morning. Thank you for spending time with me. I look forward to getting together again on Wednesday for our demo. – Jeb

Likewise, purposeful text messages can also help you keep deals moving through your pipeline and remain top of mind with the stakeholder group. I often send links to relevant articles and resources.

If I get a positive response, I know I'm on the right track. If there are emojis, we hit it out of the park. However, if I get no response, it tells me that there may be a problem and allows me to rethink my approach or strategy.

Video Message Tip: Don't forget that you can substitute a text-based message with a video message. Sometimes seeing your face and hearing your voice makes all the difference.

26 | Text Messaging for Prospecting

When using text for prospecting, the probability of your text message converting—compelling your prospect to take action—increases exponentially if:

- The prospect is familiar with you.
- Your text comes after contact through another channel.

Familiarity is everything with text. Text messaging is the go-to medium for communication with family, friends, and coworkers and a haven on our phones that is typically not touched by spam or outside influence. The people we text with are most often people we know—even when it is business.

We can all relate. Almost everyone recoils when they get a text from someone they don't know. We don't want our text inbox to be invaded by strangers or filled with junk and spam. For this reason, text is not an effective vehicle for pure cold outreach.

People are averse to getting random text messages from people they don't know—especially salespeople. Therefore, you'll want to use text messaging with a targeted list of prospects that have at least some familiarity with you.

The most effective way to leverage text with a targeted list is to integrate it into a prospecting sequence, rather than using it as standalone channel.

For example: Voicemail > Email > LinkedIn > Text

According to a study conducted by Velocify that covered 3.5 million lead records from more than 400 companies, a text message sent alone converts at 4.8 percent. That same message, sent after a phone contact, increases conversion by 112.6 percent.[1] Your text message is most likely to convert when it follows a voicemail, email, social media interaction, or a positive in-person networking interaction.

Follow Up after Networking Events and Trade Shows

Text messages are excellent vehicles for setting appointments following face-to-face interactions at networking events, trade shows, conferences, and other situations where you've had a positive encounter with a potential customer.

Many of those encounters end with a vague promise to get together sometime in the future. Yet, most of those promises are never fulfilled because you get busy and fail to follow up; or, your follow-up gets lost in the noise of the other person's overflowing inbox.

Text messaging is a much easier, faster way to get through the noise, get their attention, and set a meeting. Since almost everyone includes a mobile phone number on business cards these days, it's easier than ever to text a quick follow-up thank-you message and ask for the next step. Here's what you do:

1. During your conversation, when the vague agreement is made to meet sometime in the future, casually say, "Sounds good. I'll text you and we can set up a video or phone call to discuss the next step." (It is highly unlikely they'll protest if your conversation has been positive.)

2. As soon as you walk away from the conversation, send a personalized connection request on LinkedIn using the LinkedIn app on your phone. This anchors your name so they'll remember you, and once they become a first-level connection, you may direct message them with text, voice, and video messages.

3. Within 24 hours of the event, send a text message thanking them for the conversation and request a meeting. Personalize it with information you gleaned from your conversation.

4. If you don't get a response, try sending your text again a day later. In many cases, they will not recognize your phone number and may ignore your initial attempt.

5. If your second attempt fails, shift to the phone and email to make contact. It serves no purpose to potentially create ill will by continuing to text.

6. Always send a handwritten note or personalized card within a week of the event via snail mail—this will make you stand out from the crowd and anchor the relationship with a positive emotional experience. I recommend using OutboundCards.com for personalized snail mail.

Nurture High-Value Prospects

Text messaging can play an integral role in nurturing prospects:

- With whom you have a relationship but are not yet in the buying window.
- That have deferred making a buying decision.

- That decided at some point to purchase from your competitor (closed/lost).
- That are inactive customers you want to win back.

With these prospects, a well-placed, value-added text message is an easy way to remain top of mind without seeming too pushy, eager, or intrusive.

With high-value prospects like this, my objective is simple: Stay top of mind so that when the time is right, they engage.

Often, I send links to relevant articles, videos, podcasts, and resources that are relevant to them, their situation, and their industry. When I send these text messages, I almost always get a text back with a "thank you." The most enthusiastic responses are when I send them news about their competitors.

My strategy is to stay top of mind and nurture the relationship without wearing out my welcome. I send no more than one text a month (usually, just twice a quarter), unless I have a particularly juicy bit of information. I want my text messages to be both valuable and appreciated, so that when things change, they feel an obligation to give me a shot at their business.

Use Text Following Trigger Events

A trigger event is a disruption in the status quo that may compel your prospect to act. When you become aware of a trigger event, it creates an opportunity to reach out to your prospect via text messaging.

Text messaging works with trigger events because trigger events create urgency to act and text messages are perceived as more urgent. Be warned, though, that the law of familiarity is at play in a big way with trigger-event text messages. Make sure the prospect knows who you are before sending this type of message.

I've found a soft approach with trigger events works best. It requires a bit of patience and creativity. The key is becoming a resource by adding value and leveraging that into a deeper conversation.

I simply text over a link to an article that references the trigger event and ask how they are doing. If the trigger event is impacting them, it usually leads to a deeper conversation.

Seven Rules for Structuring Effective Text Prospecting Messages

For your text message to be effective, you need to engage your prospect and get them to take action in a blink of an eye. Packing your message into a small space requires you to be thoughtful, creative, and focused. There are seven rules for effective text messages:

1. *Identify yourself.* Never take for granted that your prospect (or even a customer) has your information saved on their phone. In most cases they don't and won't recognize your number. As a best practice, include your name and company at the top of the message.
2. *Message matters.* What you say and how you say it carries impact. Be very careful that your tone is not misinterpreted in a negative way. Use complete sentences to avoid sounding abrupt, harsh, sarcastic, or flippant.
3. *Be direct—be brief.* Say exactly what you mean in clear, precise, well-written sentences using good grammar and spelling. Remember that this is a professional message. Keep the message to one to four short sentences, or less than 250 characters, when possible. Avoid rambling, run-on sentences. Only use emojis with customers whom you know well.
4. *Avoid abbreviations.* Avoid using abbreviations on text messages to prospects. Abbreviations like LOL, OMG, WTF, SMH, and others don't come off as professional, and the person on the other end might not understand what you mean. Likewise, avoid acronyms and slang.
5. *Use transparent links.* People are extremely suspicious of shortened hyperlinks. When you send URLs to prospects that link to articles or other resources, send the entire URL so they know where they are clicking.

6. *Before clicking "send"—pause and read it again.* Make this your rule when it comes to text messages (and, frankly, all written communication).

7. *Do not text while driving*—PUT THE SMARTPHONE DOWN!

27 | Email Essentials

There is a funny thing about email. Almost since Ray Tomlinson sent the first email in 1971 and it subsequently took over our lives, experts have been prognosticating its death.[1] Social media was supposed to kill email, millennials were the executioner's noose, collaboration engines like Slack would make it roadkill, and text was going to put a nail in its coffin.

Yet, it lives. Email is always on—at work and in our nonwork lives. We check it before bed. We check it when we wake up. New emails take the place of old in a never-ending, always-on, overwhelming cascade. We complain viciously about the waterfall of email we receive, all the while adding to the torrent by sending out still more.

Nearly 300 billion email messages are sent and received each day.[2] Governments work to regulate it. Spam filters try to filter it. Hackers attempt to hack it. But, despite all the measures to control it, just like physically mailing something, you can send an email to anyone if you know their email address. And so, it continues on.

As a virtual selling channel, email is way overused. It is the asynchronous seller's primary form of communication. Email is the perfect channel for avoiding human interaction and keeping people at arms-length.

Email is cold, one-dimensional, and often leads to misunderstanding. Far too many account managers and customer service professionals have replaced the telephone with email, causing great damage to customer relationships and lost revenue.

Still, email works hard for sales professionals. Under the right circumstances, email:

- Generates leads.
- Engages prospects.
- Sets appointments.
- Qualifies opportunities.
- Gathers information and does discovery.
- Follows up and advances deals.
- Takes orders.
- Negotiates.
- Gets purchase orders and contracts signed.

In some respects, email is like the delivery truck of virtual selling, carrying packages and information from one address to the next. It's one of the most efficient transportation devices for data, images, documents, and videos, for seven important reasons:

1. *It's fast.* You can pop out an email or respond to one in a split second.
2. *It's slow.* It gives you space to think carefully about your message. Of course, it allows receivers to take their time responding to you, too.
3. *It can be scheduled.* You can decide when your email is delivered.
4. *It's always on.* Email follows you everywhere. From your smart phone, you can email from anywhere at any time.

5. *It's private.* It's very difficult for people to eavesdrop on an email conversation unless they are looking over your shoulder while you are writing it.

6. *No eye contact is required.* You can multitask when communicating via email.

7. *You can retain emotional detachment.* It also gives you the emotional distance to handle situations that might be much more difficult in person. For example, when negotiating, it allows you to remain emotionally detached.

Four Types of Sales Emails

For sales professionals, there are four main types of emails that you will send (excluding those that are internal to your organization):

1. Bulk marketing
2. Prospecting
3. Sales
4. Account management

In the next chapter, we'll do a deep dive into rules and frameworks for crafting effective prospecting emails. First, though, we'll discuss why mastering basic email communication is a crucial virtual selling skill set for sales professionals.

Sales emails are primarily for keeping opportunities advancing through the pipeline. They are sent to stakeholders that are engaged in the sales process for follow-up, discovery, clarifying data after discovery calls, setting next steps, introducing yourself to other stakeholders, sending information, and negotiating.

Account management emails are sent in the regular course of doing business with your customers. Especially with emotionally uncomfortable conversations and customer services issues, these emails can be the greatest cause of miscommunication and damaged relationships.

In the normal course of business, we send hundreds of emails to stakeholders in our managed accounts and pipeline opportunities each month. So much so that we don't always consider the impact of those messages.

We send so much email that you'd think that by now we'd have mastered it as a virtual sales channel and this chapter would be unnecessary. Sadly, this isn't always the case. Sales professionals still make egregious errors with email that damage credibility, trust, and their reputation.

A big part of this problem is a misunderstanding that the rapid communication style that is acceptable with texting and social media is not OK with email. The focus of this chapter is to remind you of the etiquette, tactics, and techniques that will improve email communication, bolster your reputation, and build trust.

To Email or Not to Email

For all the previously stated reasons, email is an essential virtual communication tool. Used appropriately it can help you get a lot done fast. Used inappropriately, it can cause miscommunication, confusion, add to your workload and get you into deep trouble.

As I've said on more than one occasion, email is overused. Salespeople and account managers are far more likely to default to an email rather than just picking up the damn phone. This then begs the question: *To email or not to email?*

Written Communication Is Not Private Communication

Always assume that anything you write will be shared with other people. Treat it like a permanent record. Trust me on this; there is nothing like sitting in a deposition and having the opposing attorney stick an email, that you don't even remember writing, in your face and ask you about the contents—totally out of context.

Lawyers use email communication as weapons. As will the procurement teams in your accounts during contract renewal negotiations.

- Never send an email that you would be uncomfortable with others reading.
- Don't send emails that say anything negative about another person.
- Never, ever use profanity.
- Avoid sarcasm and other forms of humor. It does not translate well in writing and can easily be pulled out of context.

Email is not private communication. Always keep emails formal, emotionally neutral, and professional, and you will never go wrong.

When to Use Email Communication

It is appropriate to use email communication for these purposes:

- The content of your email does not require an immediate response or is not urgent.
- Following up after a sales call with a letter of understanding on action items and expected next steps.
- Sending calendar invites and confirming appointments with stakeholders.
- Expressing appreciation or congratulating someone on an accomplishment.
- Sending information to multiple people at one time.
- The person you are writing is difficult to reach by phone.
- Sending attachments, data, video messages, and other media.
- You need to cover your ass (CYA).
- You need to keep a written record of the correspondence.

When Email Communication Is Inappropriate

There are times that email is not the right tool. Sometimes it doesn't work well; other times, it is flat-out inappropriate. Here are some examples:

- You need to express complex ideas that cannot be winnowed down to a short email.

- Something is hard to explain in writing or there is context that you need to provide which requires a story.
- Your message is confidential, and you don't want it to be shared with other people.
- You are dealing with emotionally charged issues that are better diffused with a phone or video call.
- You would be unwilling to say what you are writing in person.
- You wouldn't want your mom to read it.
- You are angry.
- There is a possibility that your tone and message could be misconstrued.
- A quick phone call can solve the problem.

Remember the mantra: *When in doubt, pick up the phone.*

Subject Lines

I have an overflowing email box. It isn't unusual for me to get 1,000 new emails every day. When I'm working with a sales rep to purchase a new service or product, I sometimes need to search my inbox for an email they sent me about an action I must take.

I find it absolutely maddening when, because of a subject line issue, it takes twice as long to find what I need. This reflects poorly on that person and causes me to have bad experience with them and their brand. I'm constantly amazed at how little thought sales-people put into writing effective subject lines.

Subject lines that are vague or do not accurately match the content of the email are one of my major pet peeves. On sales and account management emails, the subject line matters. Think of it like an article headline on your favorite news app.

It needs to be clear, direct, specific, and congruent with the content of the email. If it is not, you'll frustrate the reader. The receiver should know exactly what the email is about by reading the subject line. This, by the way, should be your litmus test.

New Thread = New Subject

There is one very important rule with subject lines. When there is a new thread on an email chain, you need a new subject line.

It happens all of the time. In the middle of an email chain someone starts a conversation about an unrelated issue. Yet the subject line of the original email lives on.

This is confusing and makes it extremely difficult to search your inbox to find the correct email thread. As soon as there is a new thread, change the subject line to reflect the new conversation—even if you did not initiate it.

In similar form, don't be lazy and hit reply to an old message because an email address you needed was on that message. Be professional and compose a new message.

Formal Business Writing

When you send email messages that contain typos and grammatical errors, it can damage your credibility and trust. This is especially true when you are sending these missives to executive-level decision makers and influencers. Poorly written emails hurt your reputation.

If you struggle with writing and grammar, slow down when writing email messages and give yourself plenty of time to proofread. It is easy to make big mistakes when you are moving too fast. Beware of auto spell check, especially when composing email messages on your mobile device. It can and will embarrass you at exactly the wrong time.

One of my favorite writing tools is Grammarly. This free app plugs into your email client and Google Chrome. Grammarly guides you when writing email, direct messages, and even social media posts. The more you use it, the better writer you will become.

You might even consider taking a course on business writing. Writing well is that important! Grammar, punctuation, and spelling matter. Research shows that people tend to view you as less intelligent, trustworthy, and conscientious when your emails contain such errors.[3]

Skip the Emojis

Because email is formal communication, skip the emojis. It has become natural and normal to add these little images to text messages and social media posts as a means to express emotion. Yet, research has shown that adding emojis to email communication hurts your reputation.[4]

Readability

It is a sad fact of modern life, which is dominated by texting and social media, that attention spans have shrunk to that of mosquitos. We no longer have the patience, desire, or mental capacity to deal with long-winded, difficult to consume email messages.

People are overwhelmed with incoming communication. Remember our conversation earlier about cognitive overload? If your message requires the reader's brain to work harder because your email is difficult to read, the probability increases that they will not read it. If they do read, it is likely that in this state, they will not take action.

For this reason, it is important to make emails readable. When you do so, you are much more likely to grab and keep their attention. Follow these guidelines:

- Use no more than three paragraphs.
- Keep emails to 250 words or less (100 words or less with direct messages). You want your reader to be able to read and absorb your message in 30–60 seconds.
- Break your message into short paragraphs and leave white space between paragraphs.
- Write in short sentences.

- Express ideas and lists in easy-to-consume bullet points.
- Use bolded headings to separate important ideas.
- Bold important dates, numbers, and terms.

Clarity and Brevity

A good email should be clear, concise, and brief. Use direct rather than passive language. As you proofread and edit your messages, make it your goal to reduce the number of words. Step into the shoes of the reader:

- Will they understand your message?
- Will your message lead to your desired outcome?

Emails that are disorganized, complex, and ramble cause confusion. Confusion leads to miscommunication. This, in turn, causes a massive waste of time as you and the reader email back and forth to straighten out the misunderstanding. To ensure that your email message is clear, follow these five rules:

1. The subject line should be congruent with the content of the email.
2. Clearly state the purpose and objective of your email in the first paragraph.
3. Provide context. Don't assume that the reader has all of the information. Especially when you are asking questions or for a decision, provide a frame of reference to make it easy for the recipient to give you an answer. Attach data, documents, images, and videos that provide context.
4. Keep emails to one issue. People are much more likely to act when you keep it simple.
5. Clearly and succinctly state your desired outcome. Tell the reader exactly what you want them to do and when.

When it comes to email, you will never go wrong with the three *BE*s: Be Brief, Be Bright, Be Gone.

Check Your Tone and Mind Your Manners

Written communication is easily misconstrued because visual and audio cues like voice inflection, facial expressions, gestures, and body language are not there to support your words. The wrong choice of words, phrases, and even punctuation can confuse your message and may offend the other party.

It is easy to be respectful. No slang, no "bro," "brother," "my man," "what's up," or shorthand like LOL, WTF, SMH, etc. Always, always, always maintain the highest level of respect. As I, too often, must point out to salespeople who forget the basics of respect: *Don't bro me until you know me.*

Message matters. The words you use matter. The easiest way to avoid this kind of misunderstanding is to mind your manners. Strike a polite tone. Say please and thank you. Be nice. Be likeable. Always use a kind salutation at the conclusion of your email:

- Sincerely
- Warm regards
- Thank you
- Thank you for your time
- Thank you in advance
- I truly appreciate your help
- Cheers

It doesn't cost a thing to be nice.

Email Signature

Don't allow your email signature to be an afterthought. It is a reflection of your personal and company brand. It's also functional. I make several phone calls a day just by clicking on the phone number in an email sender's signature. Here are some best practices for building an effective email signature line:

- *Headshot.* Puts a face with a name.
- *Name and title.* Tells people who you are.
- *Company name and logo.* Builds brand recognition and gives you credibility.
- *Calendar link.* Allows people to easily book appointments with you.
- *Office and mobile phone.* Makes it easy to call you back.
- *Mailing address.* Makes you legitimate.
- *LinkedIn profile link and other relevant social profiles.* Builds your network connections.
- *Link to a resource landing page, press release, etc.* Generates leads.
- *Video in your signature to introduce yourself (use a moving GIF image).* Makes you human.
- *Use fonts and colors that are consistent with your brand.*
- Ensures that your signature looks good on both desktop and mobile devices.

The marketing departments of most large companies have standard signature templates, so check there first. If you work for a small company without this resource, you'll find expanded email signature recommendations along with a tool that will help you build a professional email signature at https://www.salesgravy.com/vskit

Pause Before You Press "Send"

Before you press send, pause and proofread everything. Read it once. Read it twice. Check your fonts, colors, attachments, and hyperlinks. Print the really important emails and proof the hard copy. Consider asking a colleague or friend to proof it as well. If the email is important, walk away from it for a while, then proof again. It is incredible what you'll find when you give your brain a rest.

If you or your email are emotionally charged, sleep on it. You'll be glad you did. Time and space have a wonderful way of helping you gain perspective and change your tone. A best practice with emails like this, and for that matter all emails, is to add the email addresses in the *TO* and *CC* fields last. It's like a safety switch on a gun. It will keep you from making the embarrassing mistake of sending an email before intended.

It is also important that you check the CC fields. This can save you huge embarrassment when you meant to click *reply* to one individual but mistakenly clicked *reply all*.

Likewise, check what is below your freshly written email before you forward to another person. Bad things happen when you use the forward feature to send an attachment but leave in parts of the email string that you did not intend for the recipient to read.

I am the typo king. I'm quite sure you may have found a few of my mistakes while reading this book. Hence, I end this chapter with humble advice from a man who has made the terrible mistake of not pausing before pushing "send" and launching a typo-spelling-grammatical-error-laden email to a customer. It is a lesson you want to avoid learning the hard way.

Pause before you push "send."

28 | Four Cardinal Rules of Email Prospecting

Email prospecting that is leveraged poorly irritates prospects and damages your company brand. Done wrong, it wastes your time and makes you look like a chump. Leveraged intelligently, especially in sequences with other prospecting channels, email gets results.

Over the next two chapters we are going to take a deep dive into email prospecting techniques and messages. First, though, it is important that we distinguish between bulk email marketing and one-to-one email prospecting.

Bulk Email Marketing

Bulk email is *one-to-many* communication sent *en masse*, to many people at a time. It is a generic shotgun approach typically focused on direct offers and lead generation via the vehicle of newsletters, announcements, and educational messages.

Bulk email is primarily the domain of marketing professionals. The majority of salespeople should NOT be sending bulk email. Because of the compliance rules with bulk email and the damage caused by poorly thought-out mass email, I don't even allow my own sales professionals to send bulk email.

The art and science of bulk marketing email is an entire book unto itself. Because of this, I'm not going to do a deep dive. However, for some sales roles it is a foundational marketing tool and you ignore it at your peril.

If you are an entrepreneur, business owner, or in an independent sales role like a real estate agent, insurance agent, or financial advisor, and your livelihood depends on generating inbound leads, you'll need to focus on and master bulk email marketing. It is very much the cornerstone of many effective marketing campaigns.

List Building

Mastering bulk email begins and ends with list building. Build your lists organically, do not buy them. Buying lists is the fastest way to get your email account blacklisted and get you kicked off of your email service provider platform.

Make list building an integral part of your daily workflow. When I first started Sales Gravy back in 2006, we had 12 people on our email marketing list. Today that number is 1.4 million. List building is a daily grind. It takes a long time to accumulate a large list but much longer if you don't make it a priority.

Platform

You must send bulk email from an email service provider (ESP). A good platform will give you tools and templates for your bulk emails, provide analytics, allow you to hone your messaging with A/B testing, and keep you compliant.

Value and Consistency

If you ignore your audience, they will ignore you. It is important that you regularly—at least once per week—email your list. Just as important is offering value so that your audience looks forward to getting your emails. This keeps them engaged so that when the time is right, you'll have the opportunity to convert them into customers.

Prospecting Email

Most sales professionals send prospecting emails in one form or another. Prospecting emails are focused on engaging prospects and setting up meetings or sales calls. These emails contain a direct call to action. There are two types of prospecting emails: personalized and targeted.

Personalized

Personalized prospecting emails are written specifically for and are sent to a single stakeholder. These messages require a significant time investment to write and are typically reserved for high-stakes situations and high-level decision makers.

Targeted

Targeted prospecting emails are *one-to-many* messages that are sent in a *one-to-one* format. The message is tailored to a targeted list of prospects that have been segmented based on similar attributes, including:

- Industry vertical
- Geography
- Decision-maker role

- Challenges
- Purchasing behavior
- Competitor affiliation
- Specific needs, problems, or opportunities

Because the messaging in these emails is targeted to a segment rather than written to a single prospect, it will hit the mark with some prospects and miss with others. The key to success is crafting messages that have a high probability of connecting with the majority of the prospects you are targeting and cause them to feel that you wrote the email specifically for them.

Using Platforms

Prospecting emails are meant to be sent one-to-one. You may accomplish this by sending one message at a time from your company email platform. This, however, can be time consuming.

A better way is to leverage a sales engagement platform like HubSpot Sales Pro (https://crm.salesgravy.com) or VanillaSoft. These tools allow you to easily schedule and send emails to a targeted list of prospects with minimal effort and still create a one-to-one personalized feel.

Effective email prospecting requires thoughtfulness and effort to get the message right. The data these tools provide also make your email prospecting efforts more effective because you can test and measure response rates. This helps you hone and perfect your message for a particular market vertical or group of similar prospects.

No matter which platform you choose, however, small mistakes can keep your email from getting delivered, opened, or converted. In this chapter we are going to explore the four cardinal rules of email prospecting that, when followed, will make your email prospecting efforts more effective.

Rule #1: Your Email Must Get Delivered

For anything to happen, your email must first make it into your prospect's email inbox. If not, sending it was a total waste of time and effort.

Most companies and individuals have filters that either block or move "spam" emails to a junk folder. There is no perfect science to staying completely clear of spam filters. However, there are things you can do to increase the probability that your email will get delivered. This is not a comprehensive list—rather, it's a list of the most obvious and important tactics.

Prospecting Email Is One-to-One

It is one email from your address sent to one individual, one email at a time. This alone should help you clear 90 percent of spam hurdles. Sending bulk email (to multiple people) from your personal email address is the easiest, fastest way to get blacklisted, get blocked, and look like a total imbecile. Only send bulk marketing email using an email service provider platform.

Don't Target Too Many People in the Same Company at One Time

Spam filters look to see how many messages you're sending at a time. This is primarily designed to catch bulk emailers who are sending to large lists. However, if you are sending email to multiple prospects in the same company, it pays to drip these emails in at different times of the day rather than sending them all at once.

Don't Send Too Many Emails to the Same Person

This may seem counterintuitive, but with email, too much persistence can hurt you. If you become annoying, the recipient of your email may mark it as spam. This may not only block you from their inbox; with some systems, it could get you blacklisted across the entire enterprise.

Avoid Attaching Images

Because hackers and spammers embed malware in images, many email programs mark emails with images as spam or block images until permission is given to download. Your best bet on prospecting emails is to avoid sending images. The exception to this rule is when sending video messages; a thumbnail of your video (especially a GIF image with movement) will result in more click-throughs to your video message.

Minimize Hyperlinks

The primary tool of hackers is the hyperlink. You click on it and the hacker inserts malware on your computer and steals your information. Because of this, people are super suspicious of hyperlinks embedded in emails.

- Avoid embedding the URL in text.
- Include the entire URL for complete transparency.
- Avoid shortened URLs that obscure the website address. Some experts will advise that long URLs junk up your message. This is a valid point. In some cases, you may need to use a shortened URL. Just know that you may lose click-throughs.
- Limit the total number of URLs to as few as possible.

Avoid Attachments

Hackers have become adept at using attachments to infect computers with malware, hack websites, and infiltrate networks. Because of this danger, spam filters may grab your email if it contains attachments. Your best bet is to avoid sending direct attachments in prospecting emails. If you want your prospect to download a resource, include a link to a page where they can get the resource.

Skip Spammy Words and Phrases

What you say and how you say it can trigger spam filters. For example, using ALL CAPS in a subject line, adding lots of exclamation points, or using words like "FREE Offer," or "Buy Now," and even symbols like $$$$ or !!!! can light up spam filters like a Christmas tree.

There are hundreds of words and phrases that, used by themselves or in conjunction with other words, can send your email directly to spam. The point is, you must be careful and thoughtful about the words and symbols you use and how you phrase those words—especially in your email subject line. The best thing to do is step into the spammer's shoes—look at the annoying spam you get and then do the opposite.

There are far too many spam words and phrases to list in this space. I've included some resources on spam words at https://www .salesgravy.com/vskit

Scrub Bounces

Many spam filters will begin blocking your emails if you send multiple emails to addresses that no longer exist. This usually happens when the person you are trying to contact has left the company or you have a bad email address. When you get a bounce, view it as an opportunity to gather better information.

First, update the contact in your CRM and remove the email address so you won't mistakenly send to that address again. Next, check LinkedIn, a data provider like ZoomInfo, or do a Google search to find out if that contact is still at the company.

- If not, remove the contact from your CRM or update their record to reflect their new company.
- If yes, get to work by phone or online finding an accurate email address.

Be Careful with Sensitive Industries

Use extra caution when contacting sensitive industries like financial institutions, defense contractors, healthcare, and government entities. Hackers are relentlessly trying to infiltrate these organizations to steal data, and as a result, there are strict firewalls in place. With these groups, I recommend using text only with no links, attachments, or images.

Rule #2: Your Email Must Get Opened

The average office worked receives 90 emails per day.[1] That's a lot. The decision makers that you seek to engage, however, get more than double that amount.

According to the *Harvard Business Review*, the average business executive gets 200-plus emails a day.[2] Now add direct messaging, text messaging, internal instant messaging, and the chatter on tools like Slack, and there is simply no way they can possibly get to it all.

In this state of extreme overwhelm, stakeholders cope with inboxes that are set to "infinite refill" the same way you do: *Scan and Triage*.

They, like you, must make instant, split-second decisions to open, delete, or save for later. In this paradigm, to get opened, your prospecting email must stand out from all of the noise and be compelling enough to entice a click.

Familiarity Gets Your Email Opened

Imagine that you are scanning your inbox. An email from a person you recognize catches your eye. What is the your most probable next action?

The more familiar your prospect is with your name, brand, or company, the more likely they are to open your email. This is why leveraging the phone, direct messaging, and social channels prior to sending an email can increase the chances of getting your emails opened.

For example, you might call and leave a voicemail, ping them on LinkedIn, and follow that up with an email (or vice versa). This "triple threat" increases familiarity and leverages your persistence across multiple channels.

This is why prospecting sequences work. When you leave an effective voicemail, send a direct message, connect on LinkedIn, or like, comment, share (LCS) something your prospect posted on social media, it makes you more familiar. Then, when they see your name and email address in their inbox, your email will get more than a cursory glance.

Your Subject Line Must Scream "Open Me"

The subject line, however, can be the most important key to getting your email opened. Sadly, though, most prospecting email subject lines neither stand out nor are compelling. Most, in fact, scream "Delete me!"

Too Long. Data from many sources across the sales ecosystem prove that shorter subject lines outperform longer subject lines by wide margins. Frankly, it's intuitive. A long subject line requires your prospect's brain to work harder. That extra effort in the context of split-second decisions about the value of an email gets you deleted.

Nor do long subject lines play well on mobile. It's estimated that 50 percent or more of emails get opened on a mobile device. With the limited screen size, you get but a glimpse of the email subject line. If you think about your own behavior on your mobile phone, you are even quicker to delete a message there. More than 50 characters in your subject line and the open rate goes down exponentially.

Solution: Keep email prospecting subject lines super short— three to six words or 40 to 50 characters, including spaces.

Remember—less is more. It's important to note that, when your email is carrying a video message, data from Vidyard indicates that subject lines with the word "Video" are eight times more likely to be opened.[3]

Questions. Virtually every major study conducted on the efficacy of different types of email subject lines concludes that subject lines in the form of a question quickly doom your email to the delete-button death-roll. Though there may be a time and place for using a question in your email subject line, in most cases you should step away from the question mark.

Solution: Use action words and directive statements instead of questions. List-based subject lines that include a testimonial like "3 Reasons Why ABC Chose Us" are especially powerful, as are referral subject lines like "Jeb Blount Said We Should Talk" and statement-based subject lines like "Biggest Trend in Commercial Real Estate."

Impersonal. Generic, impersonal subject lines are boring. When you are attempting to engage hard-to-reach executives, a failure to connect will send you straight to the trash. Think about it. Every salesperson in your industry is trying to connect with the highest-value prospects in your market. These executives are inundated with requests for appointments. You will never break through this noise and get their attention with cheesy, impersonal subject lines.

Solution: Connect your subject line to an issue your prospect is facing—especially if it is emotional or stressful. Compliment them on a recent accomplishment or something that you know makes them feel proud. For example, the easiest, fastest way to get me to open your email is a subject line that reads: "I'm a big fan of your books."

We are all self-centered and almost always focused on our own problems, issues, accomplishments, and ego. So, play the odds, and make your subject line about your prospect. It's really easy to do if you take a little extra time to research the recipient of your prospecting email.

No One-Size-Fits-All Solution

The brutal reality, though, is there is no secret formula for creating the perfect email subject line every time. What works in one situation may not work in another. Advice that works in one industry vertical may not be applicable within your industry or prospect base. This is why experimentation and testing are the real secrets to success with subject lines.

Yet most salespeople don't test. Instead, they create subject lines on the fly and then send their emails into a black hole, hoping that they'll get a response. This is like throwing darts at a target while blindfolded and hoping you hit a bull's-eye, without any feedback to let you know if your aim is true.

Testing helps you zero in on which subject lines get the most opens. You'll often find patterns that lead to subject lines that work phenomenally well with certain prospect groups, job titles, geographic areas, and business problems.

With this information, you'll be able to focus on the words and phrases that get the best response, and your emails will stand out and get opened while those your competitor sends are relegated to the "delete" folder.

Rule #3: Your Email Must Convert

Far too many sales professionals have abandoned thoughtful email prospecting for sending pure spam. They send generic email templates that are copied and pasted, randomly sent to a large swath of prospects regardless of relevance and with no research. This lazy, thoughtless behavior damages your personal and company brands and gets you blocked.

Developing prospecting emails that convert is hard work. Thought and intention are required to craft relevant messages that connect emotionally and move prospects to take action.

This doesn't mean that every email you send must be built from scratch. Certainly, within specific industry verticals, markets, and decision-maker roles, there will be enough common ground and patterns that you'll be able to develop templates that can be customized for targeted lists allowing you to deliver more prospecting email touches in a shorter period of time.

Even with a customizable template, though, to be effective, you must conduct research so the email looks and feels unique to the recipient. It will fall on deaf ears if the recipient doesn't feel that the message was crafted specifically for them.

This investment of your precious and limited time is why it is imperative that your prospecting emails convert to the following:

- Appointment
- Video message view
- Qualifying information
- Introduction to a decision maker
- Forward to other influencers
- Download of documents
- Webinar registration
- Purchase

If your email doesn't compel the recipient to take action, your time and effort were wasted. This is why investing the time to get your message right is critical.

Rule #4: Your Email Must Be Compliant

From Europe's GDPR, to the USAs CAN-SPAM, and Canada's CASL, governments have sought to regulate email messages with an eye on protecting privacy. Most of these laws were passed in response to the huge amount of SPAM being sent to email inboxes. None of them have managed to stop the overwhelming flow of SPAM.

Some of these rules are tightly enforced; others are not. Many email related regulations apply primarily B2C and bulk email marketing while providing more leeway for B2B sales communication. With all rules, there is gray area.

There are also strict rules for what you can write (words you use) and send in emails for highly regulated industries like financial services and banking. Violating these regulations can result in your company paying massive fines.

Your company may interpret these rules differently from other companies. If you work for a large organization, the sensitivity to compliance will be much higher than if you work for a small company. The one thing you can count on is that the regulation will continue to expand, and the rules will always change.

The bottom line is, it is your responsibility to become familiar with regulations and your company's rules for email so that you remain compliant.

29

Four-Step Email Prospecting Framework

Because I am a business owner and decision maker, I get blasted by prospecting emails and direct messages from every direction—on my work email, LinkedIn, Instagram, Twitter, Facebook Messenger, and WhatsApp. I receive dozens each week that are laughable—embarrassments to the salespeople who sent them and their companies.

The objective when crafting a prospecting email is to compel the reader to take action. You don't have to look far to see that "compelling" is rare when it comes to prospecting emails. The vast majority of prospecting emails are awful.

I'm baffled at how often salespeople who took the time to send an email to me did no research. Like the email I received from a rep at a large sales training company pitching me on buying sales training for my sales training company, or the rep asking for a meeting to discuss safety products for my engineering team, or the rep who wants to meet to discuss how his company can help me turn my books into training programs. Seriously, a 20-second review of my LinkedIn profile or website would have saved them the bother.

Bad emails destroy your brand equity, credibility, and image. It stuns me that so many companies allow their salespeople to disseminate this crap. Worse, the majority of sales organizations spend no time teaching their salespeople how to write effective prospecting emails. The worst emails are:

- Important-sounding pitches using incomprehensible jargon—a lot of words with no meaning.
- Feature-focused product dumps.
- Cheerleaders who shout about their big, bad, award-winning company.
- The ones that get my name wrong—seriously, it is Jeb: three letters.
- The long ones that cause eyes to glaze over.
- The ones that are not relevant.

I delete 99.9 percent of them.

Relevance and Authenticity

Every once in a while, though, I'll get a brilliant email that makes me stop in my tracks. This golden email connects with me, makes sense, is relevant, and compels me to respond. The sender took time to research and plan.

I received an email like this from a rep this past fall. It was well written, personalized, specific to my situation, and it totally connected. She asked for a meeting and I said yes. I've spent over $100,000 with her company so far.

Before you write the first word of a prospecting email, consider your audience. Tailor the message to your prospect. Prospects are people—not robots—so your prospecting email should be authentic and personal.

The message you craft must be strong enough to compel the recipient to take action. It must demonstrate that you get them and their problems and be relevant to their situation. The most effective way to tailor your message to the person you are writing is to step into their shoes and ask some basic questions:

- What will get their attention?
- What's important to them?
- What will cause them to give you what you are asking for?

The key here is taking time to do some basic research to get to know your prospect. Use that information as the foundation on which you construct your message.

Four-Step Email Prospecting Framework

The Four-Step Email Prospecting Framework mirrors the video messaging framework (see Figure 29.1):

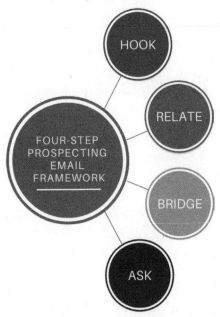

Figure 29.1   Four-Step Email Prospecting Framework

1. *Hook.* Get their attention with a compelling subject line and opening sentence/statement.
2. *Relate.* Demonstrate that you get them and their problem. Show empathy and authenticity.
3. *Bridge.* Connect the dots between their problem and how you can help them. Explain the WIIFM (what's in it for them).
4. *Ask.* Be clear and straightforward about the action you want them to take, and make it easy for them to do so.

Here is an example of a prospecting email addressed to a COO of a bank. It leverages the four-step framework:

Subject: COO—The Toughest Job in the Bank

Lawrence,

Ernst & Young recently reported that the COO has the toughest role in the C-suite.

The COOs I work with tell me that the increasing complexity of the banking environment has made their job harder and more stressful than ever.

I help COOs like you reduce stress by mitigating collateral risk and minimizing regulatory surprises.

While I don't know if we are a good fit for your bank, why don't we schedule a short call to help me learn more about your unique challenges? From there we can decide if it makes sense to set up a deeper conversation.

How about next Thursday at 3:00 p.m.?

Dave Adair

Senior Account Executive

JunoSystems

Let's compare this to a prospecting email I received this morning that totally bombed:

Subject: IT Solutions
Dear Jeb,

My name is Sandler Gleason and I work with MainLogic IT of Richmond, Va. We're an award-winning IT solutions provider.

We work to keep you secure, up-to-date, and backed-up, <u>without</u> <u>breaking the bank</u>. *Whether it is*

- *Desktop Virtualization*
- *Cloud Services*
- *Mobile Device Management*
- *Network Security*
- *Data Backup*
- *Unified Communication*
- *VoIP*
- *or simply de-hassling your IT team, we can help.*

We're an INC 5000 fastest growing company and I know we can help you. I'd love to learn more about you and any projects you are working on.

Best,
Sandler

Disclaimer*: If you don't want to receive email from us please reply to us by putting "Unsubscribe" in the subject line.*

Can you see the difference between these two email messages? Let's break this down into each of the four parts.

Hook

You have about three seconds to grab your prospect's attention. To hook them. In that three seconds, your subject line must compel them to open the email, and the first sentence must entice them to keep reading. Kendra Lee, author of *The Sales Magnet*, calls this the "glimpse factor."

Prospects choose to read your email for their reasons, not yours—their unique situation and interests. Therefore, the best way to hook them is to make your subject line relevant and the opening sentence about them.

Let's review the subject line and opening sentence of the email that bombed (name and company changed to protect the guilty):

Subject: IT Solutions

Dear Jeb,

My name is Sandler Gleason and I work with MainLogic IT of Richmond, Va. We're an award-winning IT solutions provider.

First, the subject line has no relevance to me. What does "IT Solutions" even mean? I run a sales training firm. Also, never use "Hi" or "Hello" or "Dear" or any other salutation in front of your prospect's name. No one in business does that except salespeople. "Hi _____" says, "I'm a sales rep, please delete me."

Next, how does the fact that Sandler is in Richmond, VA interest me in the least bit? My office is in Georgia. How is his name relevant to me? Why would that grab my attention? Besides, his name is in his email signature.

Finally, "*We're an award winning IT solutions provider.*" So what? Who cares? This is not relevant.

Let's take a look at our model email:

Subject: COO—The Toughest Job in the Bank

Lawrence,

Ernst & Young recently reported that the COO has the toughest role in the C-suite.

This email is being sent to a bank COO. The subject line uses the acronym "COO" and the word "bank". It implies that the COO has the toughest job in the bank. That is compelling because it plays on emotions. We all believe we have the toughest job in our company.

Next, we address our prospect professionally, as if he were a colleague.

Finally, the opening sentence is a great hook. Using a credible source, Ernst & Young, we hook the COO by stepping into his shoes and demonstrating that we get him (the toughest role in the C-suite).

Relate

Effective messages connect with the recipient on an emotional level. The reason is simple: People make decisions based on emotion. The easiest way to connect with your prospect emotionally is to demonstrate that you get them and their problems—that you can relate to their struggles and issues.

Here is Sandler's attempt to relate:

We work to keep you secure, up-to-date, and backed-up, <u>without breaking the bank</u>. Whether it is

- *Desktop Virtualization*
- *Cloud Services*
- *Mobile Device Management*
- *Network Security*
- *Data Backup*
- *Unified Communication*
- *VoIP*
- *or simply de-hassling your IT team, we can help.*

How does this relate to me or any of my problems? Notice that this paragraph is just a kitchen sink features dump. It's akin to throwing mud against the wall to see if any of it sticks. My reaction: YAWN.

Conversely, in our model email, Dave makes the effort to relate. Of course, since he is not himself a COO, nor has ever been a COO, it would be disingenuous to say that he understands Lawrence's situation. So instead, he uses his relationships with other COOs to demonstrate that he can relate.

The COOs I work with tell me that the increasing complexity of the banking environment has made their job harder and more stressful than ever.

Bridge

Since people do things for their reasons, not yours, you must answer their most pressing question: "If I give you what you want—my time—what's in it for me?" If you are unable to answer WIIFM with value that exceeds the cost of your prospect giving up their time, your email will not convert.

This is where your research pays off. When you know a specific issue that your prospect is facing in their business, you should bridge directly to that issue and how you might be able to solve it. When you are unsure of a specific issue, bridge to issues that are common to your prospect's role, situation, or industry.

Here is our buddy Sandler's attempt at bridging to WIIFM:

We're an INC 5000 fastest growing company and I know we can help you.

Again, so what? How is this important to me? He toots his horn but gives me no reason to waste my time with him.

Dave, on the other hand, ties his subject line, opening sentence, and relate statement together with a bridge that connects the dots between Lawrence's issue—stress—and solutions that reduce stress. He answers Lawrence's WIIFM question.

Most importantly, he speaks Lawrence's language—the language of COOs: minimizing risk and surprises. By speaking Lawrence's language, he continues to relate and demonstrate that he gets him and his problems.

> *I help COOs like you reduce stress by mitigating collateral risk and minimizing regulatory surprises.*

Ask

To get what you want, ask for what you want, and make it easy for your prospect to act.

Sandler:

> *I'd love to learn more about you and any projects you are working on.*

Sandler goes fishing. He says what he would love to do (every salespeople says the same thing). I read between the lines, *"I would love to hear the sound of my own voice as I pitch you on all of our wonderful features and tell you how great we are."*

Then he leaves it up to me to ask him for a time to meet. How does this make any sense? I don't want to waste my time with a pitch and I'm sure as hell not going to do his job for him.

Here's how Dave asks:

While I don't know if we are a good fit for your bank, why don't we schedule a short call to help me learn more about your unique challenges? From there we can decide if it makes sense to set up a deeper conversation.

How about next Thursday at 3:00 p.m.?

Dave disrupts expectations. He tells Lawrence up front that he might not be a good fit for his bank. That is exactly the opposite of what Lawrence would expect of a salesperson. Unlike pitching that pushes prospects away, disrupting expectations pulls prospects toward you.

Then Dave continues and sends a subtle but powerful message. He says he wants to "learn". This pulls Lawrence in deeper because everyone wants to be heard. We love to tell our story to people who are willing to listen.

Dave caps things off with the phrase "your unique challenges." This makes Lawrence feel important because everyone believes that their situation is unique. Finally, Dave lowers risk by implying that if it doesn't make sense, he's not going to push things.

Then he asks assumptively ("How about") for a meeting and offers a day and time, which takes the burden off of Lawrence to make that decision.

Practice, Practice, Practice

Writing effective prospecting email messages is not easy. The most difficult step is training yourself to stop thinking about your product or service and alternatively step into your prospect's shoes, relate to their situation, and learn to speak their language.

Develop the habit of researching prospects. Be aware of trigger events that open buying windows. You will struggle at first. Everybody does.

The key is practicing until effective, authentic emails roll off of your fingertips. The more you practice, the faster and more proficient you will become at writing prospecting emails that convert. Start now by crafting three email prospecting messages, based on Table 29.1:

Table 29.1 Template for Email Prospecting Messages

Prospect Name	Subject	Hook: First Sentence	Relate	Bridge	Ask

30 | Direct Messaging

Direct messaging is exploding. Almost 74 percent of smart phone users communicate through messaging apps. Drift calls it a sales mega-trend.[1] When you combine social media direct messaging—Twitter, Instagram, LinkedIn—with messaging apps including WhatsApp, Facebook Messenger, WeChat, and Viber there are more than four billion people using direct messaging.[2]

Direct messaging is like a Swiss army knife for virtual selling with many blades and tools:

- Video calls
- Phone calls
- Texting
- Video messaging
- Voicemail messaging
- Long-form email style messaging

Direct messaging has it all, combining every virtual communication channel we have discussed thus far. Direct messages can include video messages, audio messages, pictures, attachments, maps, calendars, and calendar invites. In the entire history of the world, there have never been this many ways to connect with other humans, in one sleek package.

In addition, with direct messaging apps like WhatsApp you can actually conduct sales transactions right within the app. Although these features are beyond the scope of the book, if you sell physical products, this will be something worth exploring.

Direct messaging is powerful for many of the same reasons as text messaging. It's mobile and is often treated as a priority. Direct messaging may serve as asynchronous communication—especially with social media direct messaging. Yet, it can easily shift to synchronous communication.

For example, I have many clients in other parts of the world that use WhatsApp as a primary communication tool. On WhatsApp and Facebook Messenger, I am constantly shifting from asynchronous to synchronous communication. It is not unusual to send a text/email-type message then several hours later get a response that turns into a text conversation, phone, or video call.

All the Rules Apply

Because direct messaging is a "virtual selling Swiss army knife" the rules that apply to video messaging, video calls, phone calls, texting, and email apply equally to direct messaging. Since direct messaging may either be part of social media platforms or share some of the features of social media platforms, you'll also want to consider how you might deploy social media strategies when working on direct messaging platforms.

Down Pipeline and Account Management

Like texting, direct messaging is most effective for communication with active pipeline opportunities, customer service, and account management:

- Advancing deals
- Post-call follow-up
- Discovery and gathering information
- Sending micro-demos
- Offering additional insight, data, and educational resources
- Customer updates
- Scheduling appointments
- Customer appreciation
- Cross-selling and upselling to existing accounts
- Handling customer service issues
- Answering questions
- Relationship nurturing

For account management and communicating with customers, direct messaging is a tremendous tool. It opens up a wide array of communication channels, helps you nurture and maintain relationships, keeps customers updated, and allows you to respond quickly to concerns, no matter where you are.

Down Pipeline

Direct messages help you cut through the noise of email when working with stakeholders in your pipeline opportunities. It's the perfect channel for follow-ups after meetings, additional discovery, sending meeting requests, providing additional insight and data, sending micro-demos, and staying top of mind with stakeholders.

One of the great benefits of direct messaging over email and telephone, is that direct messaging allows you to skip past gatekeepers, avoid the spam box, and with some apps, send messages to stakeholders even if you don't know their e-mail address or phone number. Our own surveys and experience at Sales Gravy suggest that post-sales call follow-ups via direct messages have a 40 percent higher engagement rate than through traditional email.

Prospecting

Each direct messaging app has rules and cultural norms of engagement for sending outbound prospecting messages to people who don't know you or to whom you are not connected. Unlike the phone and email, depending on the app, there are limits and rules that govern with whom you can connect and how those connections are initiated.

For prospecting on pure direct messaging platforms like WhatsApp, you should follow the same rules as prospecting via text messaging. You'll get the best results when you direct message prospects who know you and are familiar with you.

Since it is super easy for people to block you if you annoy them, it is important that you not only follow the rules but that you are thoughtful and relevant when prospecting. Purely cold prospecting outreach via direct messaging is likely to be treated as spam and get you reported and blocked.

The exception to this rule is LinkedIn, which is the primary go-to direct messaging platform for most B2B sales professionals. With LinkedIn, you may only send messages to your direct connections unless you purchase the paid version.

On LinkedIn, cold outreach is much more acceptable as long as your message is relevant. LinkedIn prospecting messages should follow the rules we've already reviewed for video messaging, voicemail, and email. However, with LinkedIn, it is easy to develop familiarity through social media activity prior to approaching a prospect. For this reason, few of your messages should be truly cold.

The Challenge with Direct Messaging

Because the direct messaging landscape is complex and constantly changing, this chapter is short. There is no possible way that I can dive into the features of and techniques for using each direct messaging platform. However, I have included some additional resources for direct messaging at https://www.salesgravy.com/vskit

The biggest challenge with direct messaging apps is that they are all different and constantly changing. There is no other way of saying this. It's a lot of damn work to keep up with these changes and effectively monitor conversations on multiple apps.

As an individual sales professional, there's no way you can effectively master them all, nor should you try. Instead, go where your prospects and customers are and make those your preferred platforms. For me, as an example, its (1) LinkedIn, (2) WhatsApp, (3) Facebook Messenger, and (4) WeChat.

Once you choose your preferred platforms, the only way to master them is to get hands-on and dedicate yourself to learning. Make it your mission to become an expert.

Remember the 3*A*s. This is how high TQ sellers integrate virtual selling technologies, like direct messaging, into their sales routine:

- *Adopt*: Adopt direct messaging and leverage it to achieve a game-changing competitive edge.
- *Adapt:* Adapt direct messaging to your unique sales process to gain more time for focusing on high-value human interactions and strategies.
- *Adept:* Blend direct messaging into your virtual selling process, and practice until you become adept at using it.

31 | Live Website Chat

I have no doubt that you encounter live chat boxes on many of the websites you now visit. You may also have a love/hate relationship with those little chat boxes, depending on your experience and preferences for communication. Most people hate it when they know they're talking to a robot and love it when they are engaging with a real human being who cares.

What may surprise you is that web chat has been around since the 1970s and evolving ever since.[1] Today, chat technology and innovation is exploding. The future of web chat is bright and promises to be robust. Recent innovations in web chat include:

- *CRM integrations.* Powerful applications that seamlessly connect chat to your CRM make chat interactions more personalized and improve customer experience.

- *Visitor intelligence.* Applications that provide immediate intelligence about website visitors that are not in your CRM help salespeople convert more leads into pipeline opportunities and sales.
- *Proactive chat.* AI powered chat engines that anticipate exactly when and how to proactively engage a web visitor in a conversation.
- *Omnichannel communication.* Chat is quickly shifting into an omnichannel communication platform that opens a gateway to voice and video calls with prospects and customers on the fly. One more reason to *always be video ready.*
- *Micro-sites.* Sales professionals have the ability to send prospects to these personalized web pages via video messages, direct messages, social media posts, and email and then engage prospects on those pages via reactive and proactive chat.
- *Chatbots.* Love them or hate them, AI powered chatbots that initiate and engage in low-level conversations continue to evolve.

What I can assure you is that live website chat is not going away.[2] Just the opposite. For most companies, it is now or will continue to be an essential communication tool. If you are a business owner or top-level executive and your company is not using chat, it is time to get in the game. As a sales professional, you need to quickly get comfortable interacting with prospects and customers on chat.

A Powerful Customer Experience Tool

Live chat is a powerful customer experience tool, making your website three-dimensional. It gives website visitors an easy means to ask questions and get problems solved quickly.

Poor chat experiences, on the other hand, leave a bad taste in customers' mouths. There are two main contributors to these bad experiences:

1. *People* who communicate poorly and fail to understand that chat is a human-to-human experience.

2. *Bad robots* that are unable to answer basic questions and create frustrating loops that are frankly comical.

Bad robots are a direct consequence of overhyped AI, the false expectation that robots can effectively engage people in complex conversations, and bad algorithms that fail to anticipate the questions people will ask and answers that are appropriate to those questions.

Bad robots are bad because people made them that way. Programming chatbots is complex work, and despite the promises, AI has yet to live up to its hype with chat. Robots are good at initiating conversations but terrible at conducting them. Likewise, hand-offs from robots to humans are often clunky and awkward.

What we have learned through our own experience at Sales Gravy is that people hate talking to robots.[3] We've found that when humans conduct chat conversations, customer experience improves along with chat outcomes.

A Powerful Sales Tool

My team at Sales Gravy first began working with clients to help them develop chat teams and improve chat communication back in 2012. Back then, chat technology wasn't nearly as good as it is now, and website visitors were not as accustomed and adept at using chat as they are today.

Of our clients who had deployed chat, all were using it exclusively for customer service—solving problems and answering questions. The customer service reps responsible for chat were often unable to see a sales opportunity on chat, even when it was glaring like a neon sign. Selling and converting leads on chat was an afterthought and sadly, in most cases, chat itself was treated as an afterthought.

We, like many others at the time, though,[4] saw the massive opportunity chat offered as a sales tool while shaking our heads at all the missed opportunities we found while reviewing our clients' chat logs. We encouraged them to place greater emphasis on chat within their organizations. Then we taught them how to leverage chat for selling.

In one of our early success stories, one of our clients went from generating zero sales on chat to ramping up to over a million dollars a month in less than two years. Others became adept at converting web visitors into appointments and closing transactional sales right in the chat browser. Over the past eight years, not a single one of our clients has failed to increase sales when they deployed chat into their virtual selling process.

It Takes Talent to Chat

Often, when working on chat sales acceleration projects with clients, we find that either the company's worst sales performers or their new hires are assigned to chat duty. Poor performers are assigned because it is easier to get them out of the way than fire them. New hires are assigned because there is a false belief that, on chat, they can do no harm.

In either case, they receive little coaching or attention. And, because few sales leaders are experienced with chat or adept at coaching chat-based sales skills, the poor performance on chat is further perpetuated. In this paradigm, chat performance lags the other sales channels, creating a sad, self-fulfilling, low-productivity prophecy.

Therefore, our first challenge is to convince leadership to assign their best and most talented salespeople to chat. We walk them through three reasons why:

1. *Inbound chat leads are HOT leads.* Prospects who engage in inbound chat are often ready to buy or ready to engage in a sales conversation. They are raising their hands. It's no different than if they were to call in by phone. It costs money to

make the phone ring just like it costs money to get prospects to visit your website. Wasting chat leads on poor performers is bad business.

2. *Chat is an inbound phone call without the audio.* Sales professionals who are talented at engaging prospects by phone are just as talented at engaging prospects on chat. Since chat is essentially a phone call without the audio, if a rep struggles to sell over the phone, they'll likely be even worse on chat.

3. *Converting chat conversations requires nuance.* There is an art to engaging someone on chat. It requires a unique combination of empathy, impulse control, and outcome drive to reel prospects in and convert the conversation into qualifying information, an appointment, an immediate phone or video call, or a sale. It requires both emotional intelligence and good sales instinct. Done well, it is a special art form. Done poorly, it's a trainwreck with a transcript.

The reason why you want your best people on chat is the same reason you don't give hot leads to bottom performers. Leads are valuable, and smart sales leaders give the best leads to the most talented salespeople because talent always finds a way to win.

Start Your Chat Engines

It's reasonable to wonder what in the world this chapter has to do with you. It may feel like chat is something far away or that it may not apply.

I get it. Very few salespeople have ever engaged in a web chat conversation. If your company does have a chat on its website, it is likely handled by a specialized team or assigned to inside sales.

Here's the deal and why you need to wake up to chat. Even if you are not engaging in interactive web chat now, brace yourself. It's coming your way. When it does, you better be ready!

To be clear, I am not implying in any way that you are going to become a full-time chat agent. Nor will chat become your primary virtual communication channel. Instead, as more and more sales organizations embrace chat, it is highly likely that you'll be spending at least some of your day engaging with prospects and customers on a chat engine.

Especially with micro-site technology that gives you your own personal chat-enabled landing pages, you'll find yourself engaging and chatting with the prospects that you drive to those pages through your outbound prospecting activity.

I regularly go toe-to-toe with sales professionals who flat-out refuse to acknowledge that chat has value as a sales tool. My salespeople did when we first brought chat to Sales Gravy.

That is, until they see that their fellow reps who are using chat get more leads, close more business, and make more money. This usually leads to a swift mindset shift. Today my sales reps spend at least some of their day on chat and, as a result, make a lot more money.

Still, you may think that you can get by without learning how to conduct effective live chat conversations. I want to remind you of something I said early in this book:

> *If you fail to rapidly adopt and assimilate omnichannel virtual selling into your business development, sales, and account management processes, you will either become extinct or be replaced by a robot. At a minimum you will sub-optimize your income and become less valuable to your employer.*

This is a brutal and absolute fact.

Deer in Headlights

Of all the virtual communication channels, even video, none seem to push sales professionals to emotional extremes like learning how to be effective with live web chat. I regularly observe otherwise-capable salespeople completely freeze and lose the ability to communicate when the chat box pops up and there is a live person on the other side.

Even though chat is just a conversation with another person, it seems to conjure up the deepest, darkest human fears. Perhaps it's dealing with an invisible stranger, perhaps it's the inability to read body language or voice inflection, perhaps it's having to translate words you say into sentences you write, perhaps it's a fear of saying the wrong thing and looking foolish, or perhaps it is the speed of chat conversations.

When I teach people to conduct effective, robust conversations on chat that convert into positive sales outcomes, I begin with an acknowledgment that live, interactive chat is a challenging skill to master. It takes time to get out of your own head and learn new skills. When you are new to chat and just learning:

- You'll feel self-conscious, insecure, and uncomfortable.
- It will be challenging to think on your feet, and you will make embarrassing mistakes.
- You'll be so focused on your response that you miss listening fully to the other person.
- You will say the wrong thing or answer the wrong question and piss people off.
- You will hesitate too long while you try to formulate the perfect response, and the person on the other side will abandon you.
- You will be both shocked at how mean people can be on chat and amazed at how gracious and kind others treat you.
- Because there is a transcript of each conversation, it is easy to see your mistakes, be overly self-critical, and beat yourself up.
- Because there is a transcript of each conversation, it is easy to learn from your mistakes and improve faster than with any other virtual communication channel.

The bottom line is, like with any new skill, learning to chat effectively takes time, repetition, and practice. The only way to learn is to get on the bike, start peddling, fall off, skin your knees, brush yourself off, and do it again.

Reactive versus Proactive Chat

There are two types of chat conversations:

1. *Inbound or reactive.* These conversations are initiated by the website visitor to ask questions, solve a problem, or make a purchase.
2. *Proactive.* These are conversations initiated by either the salesperson or a chatbot based on the website visitor's behavior pattern.

The sales motion for each type of chat conversation mirrors those of inbound and outbound sales calls. Inbound chat is a passive channel through which prospects engage you. Proactive chat is a disruptive channel through which approach, interrupt, and engage prospects who are exploring a page or information resource on your website.

The inbound call is almost always easier because the customer is raising their hand. The outbound call is harder because you are interrupting a stranger and must give them a compelling reason to engage. Let's first explore the reactive, inbound chat.

Inbound Chat Is Just a Conversation

Mastering inbound chat begins with getting comfortable with the fact that chat is just a conversation. It's not something special or different. It's just one human talking with another human.

Because you cannot see or hear the other person, you must listen deeply to the emotional cues hidden in the other person's words and conversation pace. Like all human conversations, if you treat other people like a transaction, they will treat you like a transaction. But if you treat them like a human, they will almost always respond in kind.

Make It Personal

Start all chat conversations by introducing yourself. Don't take for granted that just because your name is on the chat window, it means you are introduced. Many people are worried at the outset that they are dealing with a robot. You want to allay those fears as early in the conversation as possible. By introducing yourself, you personalize the conversation.

- *"My name is Jason, and it will be my pleasure to help you."*
- *"Good morning! I'm Jason. Thank you for the question."*
- *"By the way, I'm Jason."*

If they don't naturally share their name with you, then follow up your introduction with asking them for their name.

- *"Who do I have the pleasure of speaking to this morning?"*
- *"By the way, my name is Jason. May I get your name?"*

If they are already in your CRM, or a repeat visitor and you can see their name on screen, welcome them back by name.

Listen and Avoid Talking Over the Other Person

Very few things derail a chat conversation faster than the failure to listen. Salespeople don't listen on chat for the same reasons they don't listen in other synchronous conversations:

- Listening with the intent to respond rather than to understand.
- Thinking about what they plan to say next rather than being fully engaged.
- Assuming they know the answer before hearing the other person out.
- Moving too fast and failing to grasp what their customer is trying to express.

The key to effective listening while chatting is slowing down and *carefully* reading what the other person said. Absorb the entire message. Read the words and listen deeply to the message behind the words. This way, your responses are thoughtful, relevant, and demonstrate that you heard them.

When you don't understand what your customer means, don't make assumptions. Instead, take a moment and clarify before you respond.

The best clarifying questions are open-ended questions that encourage them to tell you more. Clarifying questions are a form of active listening that demonstrate that you care.

As they elaborate, sprinkle active listening cues into the conversation like *"I see,"* *"OK,"* or *"makes sense."* This signals that you are engaged and listening in the same manner as eye contact, body language, and verbal feedback on a video sales call.

When it makes sense, take a moment to summarize what they said before addressing their issue. Restating is a highly effective form of active listening.

When chatting, it is also easy to talk over the other person. When you start throwing out answers or pitching before they have finished their thoughts, it can cause them to feel that you are not listening. This can anger them and quickly erode trust. When you are spitting out canned responses rather than just listening, you come off like a cold, unfeeling robot.

On your chat platform you'll be able to see when the other person is typing a response. On some chat platforms you may even get a glimpse of what they are typing before they click send. Be patient. Allow them to fully express themselves before jumping in.

One way to avoid the bad habit of talking over the other person and to better understand what they are trying to express is to read the customer's chat out loud. This simple act has proven effective with formulating thoughtful responses.

Finally, consider the rules we discussed for email. When the issue is complex, and the response is longer than a simple paragraph, ask your customer to hop on the phone. It's incredible how many thank you notes we get from customers when their rep shifted from chat to the phone and helped them.

Frame Silence

When chatting, you must not forget that your customer has no idea what is happening in your environment. They don't know that you are juggling four different chats and a phone call. They are unaware that you are looking up an answer for them.

They don't know unless you tell them. Just like on video sales calls where you need to frame the reason why you are breaking eye contact to look at something out of the frame, on chat you must frame silence.

When you need to look up an answer, review their account, track down a resource etc, say so. *"Scott, please excuse me for just a moment while I look that up."* If it is taking longer than expected, jump back on chat and let them know.

Going dead silent in the middle of a chat with no explanation is akin to suddenly walking away from the phone in the middle of phone call with a customer. Your customer would ask, "Hello, hello, is anyone there?" And then, baffled by the sudden silence, hang up.

Answer Chats Immediately

Do not allow an inbound chat to go unanswered. Do not wait more than 10 seconds to answer a chat. Leaving chats unanswered is like burning money. If you are juggling multiple chats at a time, it is perfectly acceptable to say, *"Hi there, I'm Jeb, I'm helping another customer, may I get back to you in just a moment?"* We use this technique at Sales Gravy:

> *Thank you for reaching out to us. My name is Jason. I'm currently assisting another customer, but it shouldn't be too long before I can get back to you. In the meantime, can you let me know who I have the pleasure of assisting and how I may help you?*

It's simple, polite, and human. I've reviewed over 100 chat transcripts that used this approach. In 99 percent of the cases, the customer waited.

Make People Smile

Your customer's emotional experience while chatting with you is the most consistent predictor of outcome with any other variable. The words you use and how you structure those words matter. Punctuation, emojis, and sentence structure carry meaning.

Be polite, respectful, nice, and pleasant. Be professional, but not cold and stiff. You're a human. They're a human. So, loosen up, have fun, be authentic. It's OK to use a happy-face emoji or a "Haha."

According to a Forrester Survey, when you make people smile, they have a better experience.[5] When people feel good about chatting with you, you have a much higher probability of converting them into a lead or a sale. Smile while you chat, people will see it in your words and respond in kind.

Here is an example of a real reactive chat conversation from the Sales Gravy University website that resulted in a sale. I've changed the prospect's name and contact information. Notice how Jason engages and listens.

Chat on https://www.salesgravy.university
Conversation started on: Friday, May 22 at 17:40 (GMT+0)

[17:41]	Kevin Raymonds: Hi which course would you recommend for a start up service company, seeking a sales plan
[17:42]	*Jason has joined the conversation*
[17:42]	Jason: Hello Kevin! I'll be happy to help you?
[17:43]	Jason: Can you tell me a little more about the type of company and your target market?
[17:43]	Kevin Raymonds: Yes, we work with young adults in the music performance category to help them become more confident.
[17:44]	Jason: Wow, I love that. As a musician myself, I can see that would be exceptionally helpful.
[17:44]	Kevin Raymonds: Seeking to directly engage students of music studios

[17:44] Jason: Smart!

[17:44] Jason: Ok, so a few things come to mind.

[17:44] Jason: How many salespeople do you have?

[17:44] Kevin Raymonds: 1

[17:45] Jason: Perfect. Does that happen to be you?

[17:45] Kevin Raymonds: No, but I am seeking info to help that person. We're a startup.

[17:45] Jason: And this person will have an inside sales role?

[17:45] Kevin Raymonds: inside sales yes primarily email, and phone

[17:45] Jason: Ok, that's great.

[17:46] Jason: Will this role be primarily responsible for finding opportunities, or will they also be responsible for the whole sales process?

[17:47] Kevin Raymonds: We have a lead list of about 1,000 now and yes that individual will be responsible for everything

[17:47] Kevin Raymonds: and to grow the list

[17:47] Kevin Raymonds: we will add people as we gain sales

[17:48] Jason: Would you be open to a call? I think that I have a few ideas that will help you get rolling.

[17:49] Kevin Raymonds: Not right now, I can certainly arrange that at a later time next week

[17:49] Jason: No worries, I will give you a few ideas now. In case we get disconnected my I please get your email address?

[17:50] Kevin Raymonds: That would be fine here is my personal email kraymond@ virtualsellingchatexample.com

[17:50] Jason: There are multiple ways to consume courses, but in your case, I'd recommend the All-Access-Pass (AAP).

[17:50] Jason: Here comes a link. . .

[17:51]   Kevin Raymonds: Okay

[17:51]   Jason: https://www.salesgravy.university/pages/
               all-access-pass

[17:51]   Jason: You can buy a year up front or pay month
               to month. This gives you access to ALL of our
               courses AND our Virtual Instructor-led courses.

[17:51]   Kevin Raymonds: Is there a course in the all
               access you recommend?

[17:52]   Jason: Yes, I would start with four courses.

[17:52]   Jason: Give me a moment to assemble that
               list for you.

[17:52]   Kevin Raymonds: Okay terrific

[17:52]   Kevin Raymonds: Do you want to email that to me?

[17:53]   Jason: Of course. I can do that too.

[17:53]   Kevin Raymonds: Perfect!

[17:54]   Jason: I will assemble that list now and email you
               in the next five minutes.

[17:54]   Jason: I will also get you a discount code for the
               annual pass.

[17:54]   Kevin Raymonds: I will share this info with the
               person we would like to set up our Sales Plan

[17:54]   Jason: Awesome.

[17:54]   Jason: I look forward to talking with you more,
               Kevin. I hope you have a great weekend!

[17:55]   Kevin Raymonds: Okay Jason thanks so much

[17:55]   Jason: You're quite welcome, my friend.
               *[Kevin purchased an All Access Pass for his
               sales rep three hours later.]*

Proactive Chat

We know that buyers are doing far more research on their own
these days. When modern buyers have a problem they need to

solve, they do research. They jump from vendor website to vendor website, download resources, look for answers, and from time to time, fill out inbound marketing forms. Inbound marketing teams are constantly at work collecting these leads, doing basic qualification, and sending marketing qualified leads (MQLs) to their sales teams.

Salespeople then chase down these prospects by phone, email, and social media. But, there is often a long gap between the time a lead comes in and a lead gets called. During that gap, the prospect may have purchased from another company or cooled off.

Some research indicates that potential buyers with a defined need, if left on their own, will be somewhere between 50 percent and 70 percent of the way through the decision process before they proactively engage a company or salesperson. Therein lies the problem. If you wait until the prospect is this far down the road, the chances are good that a competitor will beat you to the deal.

Proactive chat helps you jump over all of these hurdles. Used effectively, it connects you with hot prospects in the early discovery phases of the buying process.

When you engage prospects who are moving into the buying process ahead of your competitors, you gain a decided competitive advantage because you have the opportunity to develop a relationship and influence and shape buying decisions. While your competitors sit around waiting for the prospect to call, burn effort chasing down MQLs, you are in the driver's seat accelerating the deal through the pipeline.

Wait, Wait, Wait, Now!

Think about it. A person who is reading an article on your website (or personalized micro-site), watching a video, or downloading a resource is there because of some level of interest in your product, a trigger event that has disrupted status quo, a problem they wish to solve, or an impending buying window. In other words, these are hot leads.

Most chat platforms provide detailed, real-time, insight into what page a visitor is on, what they are reading, watching or downloading, how they arrived on your website or micro-site, how long they've been there, and their browsing behavior. With these visitors, the name of the game is conversion. You must proactively bring up the chat box and ask a question that compels them to engage, before they bounce off of your site.

Proactive chat, though, is a lot like fishing. You have to be patient with nibbles and wait, wait, wait, until just the right moment to set the hook. You can't engage too soon or you'll scare them off, and you can't wait too long or they'll leave before you get a chance to connect.

One of the biggest challenge salespeople face on proactive chat is getting prospects to engage long enough to convert that connection into an appointment, qualifying information, or an immediate sales conversation. Once you ask a question and get them talking, you must be very careful not to move too fast and push them away. If you attempt to convert them too soon, they'll break the line and swim away.

Converting leads on proactive chat is about nuance. It's asking questions, engaging in a conversation, and developing rapport and trust before you reel them in.

Seven Steps to Converting Leads on Proactive Chat

1. *Be patient.* When a prospect hits your site, the easiest, fastest way to chase them off is to immediately open a chat window and start talking at them. Instead, you need to be patient. Give them time to get absorbed in the content. On chat, impulse control is a meta-skill. Impatient salespeople get crushed.
2. *Use a soft approach.* When you open the chat window, you have one shot to pull your prospect in and get them to engage. Mere seconds. If you approach them in an intrusive or blunt manner, they will at best ignore you and at worst bounce off of your site.

3. *Hook them.* Engagement is the name of the game. The best approach for hooking them is asking an easy and relevant open-ended question that draws them into a conversation.

4. *Humanize the experience.* What you say and how you say it matters. Chat is one-dimensional communication. Unlike verbal or visual communication, all you have are words. Nuance and meaning are gleaned from sentence structure, word choice, punctuation, and letter case. Ask relevant questions based on how they are interacting with your site and key words they are using for search. Choose empathetic words that humanize the experience of communicating with you.

5. *Ask provocative questions.* Once you have your prospect engaged, ask deeper, more provocative questions. Get them talking to learn about their situation and gather qualifying information.

6. *Provoke curiosity.* Curiosity is powerful. When you have additional insight, information, and resources that might help your prospect with their problem or situation, they will be more likely to move to the next step with you. You must become adept at provoking curiosity by bridging from their problem to your additional insight within the context of your conversation.

7. *Convert.* Your ultimate goal is to convert the chat engagement into an immediate sales conversation or appointment. Therefore, you must ask for the next step. If you fail to ask, the prospect will not do your job for you.

Here is an example of a real proactive chat from the Sales Gravy website that resulted in a sale. I've changed the prospect's name and contact information. Notice how Brooke follows the seven steps and converts for an appointment.

Chat on https://SalesGravy.com
Conversation started on: Thursday, April 16 at 19:53 (GMT+0)

[19:54]   Brooke: Thank you for checking out our Fanatical Prospecting Bootcamp. What do you have going on?

[19:54]   Scott: Hi

[19:55]   Scott: I'm interested in Sales Training.

[19:55]   Brooke: Hi Scott, my name is Brooke Holt and
               it's my pleasure to assist you.

[19:55]   Scott: Hi Brooke

[19:55]   Brooke: I understand you are interested in
               sales training.

[19:55]   Scott: yes

[19:56]   Brooke: Ok, awesome.

[19:56]   Brooke: What are some of your goals when it
               comes to training for yourself?

[19:56]   Scott: Learn how to increase sales volume by
               setting the right goals, KPIs and working
               with my CRM

[19:56]   Scott: HubSpot

[19:56]   Brooke: Ok, awesome. We use HubSpot
               and love it!

[19:56]   Brooke: What industry are you in?

[19:57]   Scott: Commercial real estate lending

[19:57]   Brooke: Got it. Are you making outbound calls
               to prospects or are you working inbound
               leads only?

[19:57]   Scott: outbound. . . outbound. . . outbound!

[19:57]   Scott: I'm working to increase inbound.

[19:58]   Brooke: Sounds like you and I are a lot alike ☺
               Let's schedule a call so I can learn more about
               your goals to better assist you?

[19:58]   Scott: LOL

[19:58]   Brooke: Let's schedule a call so I can learn more
               about you and your goals?

[19:58]   Scott: Here's my contact info – 777.999.1234
               and scott@virtualsellingchatexample.com

[19:58]   Brooke: Thank you. How about this afternoon
               at 3:00pm?

[19:59]   Scott: Sounds great!

[19:59]   Brooke: Awesome. I just sent a meeting invite.

[19:59]   Scott: Got it. I need to run to another meeting

[19:59]   Brooke: See you at 3. Go catch your meeting.

[19:59]   [*Brooke left the chat conversation and went on to close
               the deal two calls later.*]

Author's Note: A special thank you to Jason Eatmon for his invaluable contribution to the content in this this chapter and coaching the Sales Gravy chat team.

PART VI

Social Media

32 | Social Media Is an Essential Foundation for Virtual Selling

Not since Guttenberg invented the movable-type printing press has something had such a profound impact on society like social media. The influence of social media on our behaviors is inescapable. Millions of people are linked together on social media sites—constantly checking and updating their status.

For the sales profession, social media is the most important technological advancement since the telephone. LinkedIn has profoundly impacted the B2B sales profession. Similarly, Facebook, Instagram, YouTube, and Twitter are integral to successful B2C sales approaches.

Social Media Is Essential

I've endured my share of salespeople who whine that they are not comfortable on social media, don't know how to use it, think it is a waste of time, and mostly complain that they don't have time for it. If you are in this camp, then you need to wake up, and wake up fast.

There has never been a time in sales when so much information about so many buyers was this easy to access. And not just contact information, but context. Through the social channel, we gain glimpses into our prospects' motivations, desires, preferences, and triggers that drive buying behavior and open buying windows.

It is critical that you include social media in your virtual selling arsenal and work to become a master at leveraging the social channel. As a sales tool, it is essential. No matter what you are selling, social media is no longer optional.

To be blunt, it is stupid to ignore social media as a virtual selling channel. Pure sales malpractice. Eventually it will be a death sentence for your career.

Social Media Is Not a Panacea

On the other side of this equation, though, are the salespeople who drink social media like a religion. They reject all other forms of selling. In a twisted form of asynchronous selling, it allows them to drift on the periphery of human relationships, in the delusion that what they are doing equates to selling activities and human to human interaction.

Long ago, the social media evangelists pinned all of their hopes and dreams on social selling. They proclaimed that social selling was the one true path to sales salvation and pronounced all other forms of selling dead.

Some of these gurus built entire training organizations around this false promise—putting all of their eggs into the social selling basket. They came and went like the wind. Almost all of them failed. Even the self-proclaimed "Father of Social Selling" was forced to close his social selling company and get a job.

They never understood that social selling is inextricably woven into the fabric of virtual selling, but it is NOT virtual selling.

The Social Media Challenge

Social media will not solve all of your problems. It will not protect you from interrupting strangers and talking with people. It will not deliver an endless stream of leads into your pipeline. It's not like the movie *A Field of Dreams.* A LinkedIn profile and some social media posts will not fill your pipeline.

From time to time, though, I'll hire a new sales rep who will challenge me on this premise. They'll claim that they've learned how to eliminate cold calling (which means all calling) with a more powerful LinkedIn strategy. Their justification for going asynchronous is always the same, "No one answers the phone anymore."

So, I challenge them. They can deploy their LinkedIn strategy for a week while I'll talk with people on the phone. Here is a synopsis of one of my most recent social media challenges:

> At the end of the first day, the rep proudly beamed that his contact requests had been accepted by 16 people and that he'd done a lot of liking, commenting, and sharing. "I made some great connections!" he said proudly.
>
> "Awesome! How many appointments did you set?" I asked. That morning I'd made 47 dials, had 12 conversations, made one small e-learning sale, and set a discovery appointment.
>
> "You don't understand, Jeb. It doesn't work that way," he replied. "This takes time."
>
> We repeated this exercise for four more days. At the end of the week, I'd set eight appointments for initial meetings, closed four more deals, and added three new opportunities to my pipeline.
>
> He'd added 29 new connections, followed many company pages, posted content, liked content, and made a few friends. In the

process he'd made ZERO appointments, ZERO sales, added ZERO opportunities to the pipeline, and lost a $20 bet.

To be sure, I used social media, too. Three prospects called me back after I left video messages for them on InMails. I also sent connection requests to folks I set appointments with.

I leveraged LinkedIn to build more targeted lists and focus my *because* statements. I also gathered information on LinkedIn and used it to update the CRM. In other words, I *blended* social media into my prospecting effort rather than making it my exclusive channel.

The false social media promise has been that of a full pipeline, with minimal effort, and no rejection. If you decide to buy into this crap, you might want to keep your resume warm.

Social media will not solve your pipeline woes and provide an endless stream of inbound leads with little effort. It takes far more than a LinkedIn connection, likes, comments, and shares to move buyers to take action.

Social media is not a panacea. The social channel enhances, elevates, and sometimes accelerates your virtual selling efforts. But it is not a replacement for a complete system that fully leverages all virtual communication channels—synchronous and asynchronous—in concert to achieve your sales goals.

Social Media Platforms

The social media landscape changes rapidly—often on a dime. If you fail to pay attention, you'll quickly be left behind. For this reason, I am not doing a deep dive into the specific technical features of the major social media sites and tools. Because social media platforms are so feature rich, there is not enough room within the pages of this book to include them; and, even if I could, by the time this book was published, it would be out of date.

Instead, my focus with this section is to teach you a framework for leveraging social media platforms to build familiarity. For most salespeople, LinkedIn will be your primary social media platform. Therefore, much of my focus will be LinkedIn-centric. However, all of the concepts, techniques, and tactics that you learn may be applied to any social media channel.

33 | The Law of Familiarity and the Five Cs of Social Selling

Think of your favorite actors. You know their faces, vocal patterns, body language, and mannerisms. You are drawn to the movies and TV shows they star in. There is a comfort level with them that causes you to enjoy seeing them in almost any role.

If you saw them in public, you'd recognize them instantly. You'd be starstruck and feel compelled to walk up and express how big a fan you are or tell them about the impact they've had on your life. You'd be excited to ask for a selfie or get an autograph.

But, if you think back, it wasn't always like this. You didn't feel this level of connection the very first time you saw them on screen. You became a fan over time, after seeing them many times, in many different roles.

The more familiar they became to you, the more you liked them. At some point, they crossed your *familiarity threshold*. Only then did you put them on a pedestal and become a fan.

The Law of Familiarity

With social media, the name of the game is *familiarity*. The more familiar a prospect is with you, the more likely the person will be to engage. Familiarity is virtual selling lubrication. It takes the friction out of virtual communication and makes everything easier. For example, video calls are much more collaborative when stakeholders are familiar with you.

The lack of familiarity is why you get so many objections. When people don't know you, it's much harder for them to trust you.

Never in the human experience has it been easier for individuals to build familiarity. Point, shoot, write, click, and post—it's all at your fingertips. You can get your name and reputation out there fast and for very little cost.

To build familiarity, you must make a direct investment in improving the awareness of your name, expertise, and reputation. You must be present and consistently engaging on social media so that people see you often and, over time, become more comfortable with you. Engaging means posting valuable content along with liking, commenting, and sharing (LCS) on the posts of your targeted prospects and account stakeholders.

Familiarity leads to liking. In time, just as your favorite actor did with you, you'll cross the familiarity threshold with targeted prospects. When stakeholders begin to feel like they know you, virtual doors open, virtual meetings become easier, and opportunities advance.

The familiarity threshold is why the senior reps in your organization make selling look so easy. The years of investment they've made in building familiarity by meeting people in their territory have paid off.

With social media, though, you don't need years. If you are willing to make an investment of time, intellect, and energy, you can build familiarity and elevate your personal brand much faster. This investment begins and ends with the five Cs:

- Conversion
- Consistency

- Connection
- Curation
- Creation

Conversion

To be worthwhile, the time and effort your invest in social media needs to produce real, tangible results. Social media is a long-game play, but at some point, you must convert your social connections into value, in the form of leads, appointments, qualifying information, sales intelligence, closed deals, and account expansion and renewal.

Lead Generation

The very best outcome of the investment you make in social media is to entice prospects to contact you. An inbound lead is much easier to convert into an appointment, sale, or qualifying information than an outbound prospecting call.

Familiarity plays a key but passive role in inbound prospecting. When you are well known to prospects, from time to time, they will contact you as they move into the buying window for your product or service.

An active way to generate inbound leads is to directly share links to white papers, ebooks, and reports that require prospects to enter contact information to get the content. Likewise, sharing and publishing relevant content and posting thoughtful comments that position you as an expert can prompt prospects to contact you for more information.

Trigger-Event and Buying-Signal Monitoring

Trigger events are disruptions in the status quo that open potential buying windows. Buying signals are indications that a prospect may

be in or moving into a buying window. To be aware of these opportunities, you must monitor the social media stream.

Most social networks give you the ability to follow people
without being directly connected to them. When you follow targeted prospects, their announcements and posts will show up in
your news stream. LinkedIn and other tools (some free, some paid)
provide updates on the people you are following. You'll also want to
monitor hashtags and keywords that are relevant for your industry.
Signals to monitor include:

- A prospect asking for information or advice on purchasing a
  service or product you sell.
- Press releases about acquisitions, mergers, or expansion.
- Funding events.
- New product announcements.
- Job posts and headcount increases.
- Layoffs or headcount decreases.
- Promotions and job changes.
- Stakeholders in your current accounts moving to other com-
  panies.

Use trigger events and buying signals to develop targeted prospecting lists. Build familiarity by liking, commenting, and sharing
(LCS) the posts of these targeted prospects. Most importantly, when
the signal is hot, pick up the phone and call.

For example, if a key contact from an existing account moves
to another company, you should act quickly. Congratulate them on
LinkedIn, send a handwritten note, then call them. That person is
much more likely to do business with you, because they know and
trust you, than with someone they don't know. Take the initiative;
never assume that they will call you.

Research and Information Gathering

Social media is a smorgasbord of data. You can gather an impressive
amount of information about prospects that can be plugged into

your CRM, used to develop prospecting messages, and leveraged for stakeholder mapping and pre-call planning. LinkedIn (especially LinkedIn Navigator) offers powerful search capabilities that give you access to detailed information about prospects.

Outbound Prospecting

Social media is a powerful prospecting list-building tool—especially when paired with a data tool like ZoomInfo that gives you the contact information to go with the name, when that information is not available on their profile.

Build lists of people who:

- Have viewed your profile.
- Have liked, commented, or shared your posts.
- Have liked, commented, or shared the posts of other people on your team.
- Have liked, commented, or shared the posts of your competitors.
- Have liked, commented, or shared posts on industry news.
- Are in your groups.
- Follow you.
- Follow your company page.
- Follow your competitors' company pages.
- Are your direct connections and their connections.
- Are kicking off buying signals or responding to trigger events.

Once you have these lists, drop them into multi-touch prospecting sequences that include phone, email, video messaging, direct messaging, and social touches (LCS and profile visits).

I've included a list of tools for social media monitoring and search at https://www.salesgravy.com/vskit

Consistency

Every day, every day, every day. To be effective with social media, you must be active every single day. It is the cumulative impact of daily activity that builds familiarity. Consistency is crucial. A post here and a like there, randomly and infrequently, is like tossing a small pebble into the ocean and expecting it to generate a wave.

A big challenge you'll face is the ocean of content flooding social media platforms. This makes it difficult to stand out and get noticed. Social media platform algorithms, the hidden programs that determine whether or not your posts get seen, reward consistency. The more consistent your activity, the higher the probability that your posts get moved to the top of feeds, earning you more eyeballs.

What few social media evangelists talk about, though, is the grind. Social media activity is hard work. The grind is real and can be exhausting. There are days when you'll be sick of it. If you are starting from the ground up with no followers or a small audience, it can take from six months to two years to get traction. That's working relentlessly, day in and day out.

To be consistent, you must be disciplined and push through the desire to take a day off. Getting value from and adding value to the social channel requires consistent, focused, and regimented discipline.

However, you must be careful not to allow social media activity to take over your life. It is crucial that you balance playing the long-game on social media with putting opportunities into your pipeline today.

The most important action you can take is to block time for social media on your calendar and limit the time you spend there, strictly within those time blocks. For example, I block 6:30 a.m. to 7:30 a.m. and 5:30 p.m. to 6:30 p.m. each day specifically for social media activity. Once those blocks are over, I move on to other things.

Limiting my time on social media forces me to be efficient and effective—getting as much done as possible, in the least amount of time, with the greatest possible outcome. Posting activity outside of my designated time blocks is accomplished automatically through my marketing automation platform.

Short, daily time blocks (one hour per day is plenty for most salespeople) and the deployment of tools that automate some of the activity are the keys to making the grind bearable. You may feel that you are not accomplishing much in one hour a day, but the cumulative impact of daily activity, over time, is enormous.

There are several tools that automate social media activity. I've included a list at https://www.salesgravy.com/vskit

Connecting

Network = net worth is a perpetual mantra for highly successful people. Network connections are the heart of the social media channel. Connections get you in the door and in front of the right people faster. When your connections introduce or refer you to people inside of their network or company, you have instant credibility.

When you engage in a conversation on a social platform with a prospect, send them a connection request. Following interactions with stakeholders by phone, on video calls, or in-person, send a connection request. This is when you have the highest probability of acceptance.

Three Ways to Make Connections

Followers: When you consistently publish high-value original or curated content that connects with your audience, people will follow you. When they choose to follow you, more of your content will rise to the top of their feed.

Followers are akin to fans. The more they see you and your content, your familiarity grows, and the more they like you.

Most social platforms allow you to view and manage your followers. This opens up the door to building targeted prospecting lists.

Reciprocal: With Twitter and Instagram in particular, when you follow people, they have a tendency to reciprocate and follow you back. The probability that they will reciprocate is determined by their level of familiarity with you, your profile, and the quality of the content that is posted on your feed. When you follow other people, you'll see their posts and gain awareness of trigger events and buying signals.

Direct: On both LinkedIn and Facebook you may initiate a direct request for a connection. On Facebook, the process is straightforward: You just click "Send a Friend Request." Though Facebook has primarily been an entertainment tool for keeping up with family and friends, I'm connected with many customers there and business conversations are often initiated through Facebook messenger.

On LinkedIn, you have the option of sending a standard, generic connection request (you may be asked to say how you know the person) or you may customize your connection request. I highly recommend sending a personalized note with each LinkedIn connection request giving the reason for your request and referencing past interactions. A personalized note improves the probability that your request will be accepted.

Sadly, far too many people make the mistake of sending connection request messages that are either spammy pitches or direct requests for a meeting. This does not work. It is a total turn-off. Your connection request will be denied, you may be blocked by that person, and it can get you in trouble with LinkedIn.

If you don't know a prospect and there is no familiarity, it is certainly OK to send a connection request without a message. Though not optimal, it is far better than a pitch. A better way, though, is to like, comment, and share (LCS) their posts for a few weeks prior to sending your connection request.

LCS both builds familiarity and taps into the law of reciprocity. When you LCS someone's post, it is a gift of attention and makes them feel important. This increases the probability that they will accept your request because they feel an obligation.

Avoid the Connection Request Bait and Switch

It is very bad form to pitch someone as soon as they accept your connection request. It's self-serving and rude.

Social selling is about nuance. There is no nuance in rewarding your prospect for accepting your connection request with a sledge-hammer to the forehead. "Thank you for connecting, now buy from me!" is a total turn-off that results in your connection being rescinded, your message potentially reported as spam, and you being blocked.

Once your connection request is accepted, be patient. Spend a little time gaining trust and building familiarity with an LCS routine on their posts. Fill up the obligation bank account with these gifts. Then send a well-constructed text, video, or voice message. Better yet, pick up the phone and call them. Your conversion rate will increase exponentially when you follow this process.

Social Proximity

On LinkedIn, once a person connects with you, you gain the ability to see their connections. This helps you develop a more detailed buyer and influencer map and determine your proximity to the people in accounts that you want to meet. With this information, you can develop a social proximity path to getting introductions to these stakeholders.

This is why it is in your best interest to send a connection request every time you interact with a prospect, new stakeholder, and people you'd like to have in your professional network. The more connections you have, the closer your social proximity is to key decision makers.

Content Curation

Intuitively, we know that salespeople who can educate, offer insight, and solve problems are far more valuable than those whose primary sales strategy is to pitch products and services. However, to add value, you must be valuable.

In the social channel, the primary way you provide value is through content that educates, builds credibility, anchors familiarity, and positions you as an expert who can solve relevant problems. The right content shared at the right time with the right prospects can create important connections and convert passive online relationships into real-time conversations.

The challenge is that the social channel is a voracious and insatiable beast that devours content. It must be fed daily for you and your message to remain relevant and present. You'll never be able to create enough original content to keep up.

The solution to this problem is curation. A simple analogy for curation is the act of clipping articles from magazines and newspapers and sending them to someone. Except that on social media, you are doing this digitally and amplifying the impact by going from a one-to-one analog footprint to one-to-many digital distribution.

Instead of publishing your own original content, you leverage the content that is being created and published by others. Essentially, you become a maven who aggregates the most relevant content for your audience and shares it through your various social media newsfeeds.

The beautiful thing about content curation is that even though you didn't produce the content, some of the credit for the content rubs off on you.

Three Pillars of Content Creation

Awareness: You need to be aware of what is happening in your industry—trends, competitors, and movers and shakers. Have your eyes and ears open, pay attention to what is going on around you, and consume industry-specific information.

Sources: You'll need good sources for content.

- Pull from your company blog, podcast, and YouTube channel. Many forward-leaning companies have libraries full of content that you may post.
- Leverage industry blogs and trade publications.
- Tap into the thought leaders who are shaping the dialog in your industry.
- Grab relevant articles from news sources like the *Wall Street Journal*.

Intent: Rather than just randomly and disparately sharing, be intentional about your curation strategy. Take time to read and understand what you are sharing, so that you may include comments and insightful takeaways with the content you share. Your added insights shift content curation closer to content creation.

There are tools that will help you with sourcing and distributing content. I've included a list at https://www.salesgravy.com/vskit

Content Creation

Creating and publishing original content is the most powerful way to build your personal brand and helps burnish your reputation as an expert in your field. Original content is more likely to pull in comments and be shared.

Social media algorithms place greater emphasis on original content—especially content that is posted natively. Native means that your post isn't a link to an article, podcast, or video on another website.

Best Content to Post

Original content can include slide presentations, e-books, white papers, infographics, and podcasts. However, the best forms of original content that are the easiest for sales professionals to create and post include:

Long-Form Posts: These are two to three paragraph single topic, text posts of 175 words or less, with no outbound links.

Articles: LinkedIn allows you to post full-length original articles. These articles may include images, videos, and links to other resources (good for lead gen). An easy way to extend original articles is to pull excerpts from them and leverage for long-form posts.

Videos: As you learned in Chapter 18, online video consumption is voracious and growing. It's easy to shoot and upload original videos right from your video sales call set, or just press record on your phone and start talking. Some ideas include:

- Short videos of you expounding on a subject
- Behind the scenes at your office or place of work
- Micro-demos
- Product delivery or installation at a customer account
- Customer testimonials
- Webinars
- Interviews

You may post videos on all the major social channels, including YouTube. The length of the video you are allowed to post depends on the channel. You may expand your content by breaking long videos such as webinars and interviews into many small videos. You can also convert your videos into MP3 files to build podcasts.

Pictures: Images are the fastest, easiest way to add original content.

- Fun pictures of you and your colleagues on the job
- Company events

- Charitable work
- You receiving an award
- Customers receiving a big order
- You with your customers
- You with new products
- Behind the scenes videos
- Relevant pictures of you with your family or hobbies

The Authority Principle

Following the guidance of experts makes it easier to navigate uncertainty in a complex world. Uncertainty increases cognitive load and slows us down. To move faster, we look to experts for advice.

This is a heuristic called the *authority principle*. It is easier to make decisions based on expert recommendations than to dig through all of the information and work out the answer on our own.

When you publish original content that is relevant and valuable and you confidently project yourself as a subject matter expert in your field, it draws prospects to you like a magnet and entices them to engage. As they engage, you gain insight into the problems they are facing, opportunities to help them, and influence over their buying decisions.

34 | Personal Branding

You must constantly ask yourself three questions as you engage on social media platforms:

1. Does my presence here support my reputation and credibility?
2. Does it help people become familiar with my name, face, and personal brand in a positive way?
3. Does my activity balance building and strengthening my personal brand with supporting and creating awareness for my company's brand?

If the answer to any of these questions is "no" or "I'm not sure," then stop and adjust your strategy.

At the center of building familiarity on social media is honing your personal brand. Your goal is positioning yourself as a capable, knowledgeable professional who brings value to the table and solves problems. Secondarily, you have a fiduciary responsibility to the company that is paying your salary and writing your commission checks to create awareness of its brand.

Virtual First Impressions

Like most people, you make quick judgments or build quick impressions about others when you are introduced for the first time. It is just how we operate as human beings.

To deal with an overwhelming amount of incoming data and avoid cognitive overload, your brain has evolved to quickly look at patterns and compile that information into snapshots of other people (remember cognitive load and heuristics from Chapter 13). These snapshots form your first impressions—regardless of how valid they may be.

When you meet someone face-to-face, those first impressions matter greatly. You meet in the lobby and shake hands. They size you up—what you are wearing, how you carry yourself, body language, and facial expressions. The whole package. At the subconscious level their brain decides, based on the pattern it perceives, if you are likeable and trustworthy.

That first impression may be negative. However, as the conversation progresses, you have the opportunity to change their impression of you. In person, you at least get a second chance to make a good first impression.

It is exponentially more difficult to change first impressions that are made about you online. When potential customers view the "online you" and don't like what they see, it can create an insurmountable hurdle.

Before virtual meetings, stakeholders will look you up online in an effort to get the gist of who you are and what you are all about. They'll look at your headshot, bio, and review your posts. What they find will cause them to make instant judgments about you. Those judgments will impact your ability to influence and persuade them to make commitments to give up time, resources, and money.

Don't Post Stupid Sh★T on Social Media

Not long ago, a prominent author asked me to endorse his new book with a blurb for the back cover and his website. He sent over a copy of the book and it was excellent. Based on the quality of the work, I felt comfortable putting my name on it. Before I sent my blurb, though, I looked him up on Facebook.

What I found changed my mind. His feed was full of emotionally charged, profanity laden, political rants. It was an instant turnoff because many of his posts were in direct opposition to my core values and the values we live by at Sales Gravy.

I considered the negative implications of aligning my personal brand with his. What if one of my clients saw my name on the back of his book and looked him up too? How might my employees feel? How might it reflect on my personal brand?

After thinking it through, I reluctantly declined to give him my endorsement. When I explained why, he became furious. He argued that his Facebook feed was personal and had nothing to do with business. It was his "First Amendment right" to post anything he wanted there.

I politely explained that people viewing his social media presence do not make the distinction between personal and business. To others, *who you are online is who you are.* If you wish to sell books, or software, or capital equipment, or sales training, it is just dead stupid to post anything that has the potential to turn off or piss off potential buyers.

Certainly, in the United States, you have the First Amendment right to post pretty much whatever you want. In turn, your customers have the right to vote with their wallets and do business with someone else. Your employer also has the right to fire you if your posts damage or reflect poorly on its brand.

For this reason, you must carefully and intentionally manage everything you allow other people to see on social media. You must refrain from posting anything that has the potential to be controversial. You won't need to look much further than the news to be reminded of the fragility of our social media presence. Hardly a day passes in which some poor soul hasn't lost their job or seriously damaged their reputation for posting something stupid on social media.

As sales professionals, we must consider the unintended consequences of our posts—to our credibility, reputation, and income. In other words, *if you like money, don't post dumb sh*t on social media.*

We live in a hypersensitive world. People are easily offended by the smallest things. The wrong words, wrong like, wrong comment can make it impossible for your prospect to do business with you and in extreme cases, can go viral and ruin your career. You want people to know your name and face, but in the sales profession, "all publicity is not good publicity."

Familiarity is a double-edged sword. When impressions of you are positive, familiarity can cut through a lot of friction and help you gain appointments, build relationships faster, and advance deals through your pipeline. When prospects have a negative impression of you, they will erect walls to keep you out.

Keep it neutral and inoffensive, all the time, on all social media platforms. Think before you post. If you are emotional about a topic, STOP. Walk away for a few hours and cool off. This will save you an immense amount of pain. This admonition extends to provocative business posts that can garner lots of attention but may turn-off potential buyers—especially deep-pocket large companies—who shy away from controversy of any kind.

Social Media Profiles—A Powerful Snapshot of You

Of course, the vast majority of sales professionals have the good sense not to berate their boss, post inflammatory political or religious commentary, or toot their horn about how drunk they got the night before on social media. Instead, you are much more likely to damage your personal brand through a failure to optimize your social media profiles.

On each social media platform, you have a profile. It is your home base and personal branded page on that platform and in web search. Your social media profiles are a direct reflection of your personal brand and the tip of the social selling spear.

Before engaging in any other social media activity, invest time in developing and perfecting your social profiles. Today, not tomorrow, take action to ensure that your profiles cast you in the best light:

- Your headshots are current and professional.
- Profile hero images support your personal and company brand.
- Profile bios and headlines are complete, truthful, and tell your story well.
- Profile keywords make it easy for people to find you in a search.
- Remove posts that could be construed as offensive, extreme, or could damage your credibility.
- Project a consistent personal brand across all major social networks.

Headshot

According to PhotoFeeler.com, a website that helps people choose the right photo for online profiles, "Profile photos are so essential to modern communication that a good one's become a basic necessity. And that couldn't be truer than for those of us whose professional lives are tied to social media profiles."

Ensure that you have a professional headshot on all your profiles—including Facebook, Instagram, Twitter, Snapchat, YouTube, Direct Messaging apps, etc… Professional means you leave your cat, dog, kids, vacation, college buddies, cool sunglasses, and bottle of beer out of the picture.

Your headshot should be taken in good light, at a flattering angle, on a neutral background. Lose the cheesy poses—like with your arms crossed, hand on your chin, staring wistfully into the distance, or cocking your eyeglasses. These poses are a turn-off and can cause you to come off like a self-centered schmuck.

Instead, look into the camera, put a pleasant look on your face, and SMILE. In a study based on over 60,000 ratings, Photo Feeler found that a genuine smile has a significant impact on other people's perceptions of your competence, likeability, and influence based only on your profile picture.[1] As we discussed in Chapter 15, few things create positive impressions faster than an genuine smile.

A best practice for personal brand consistency is to place the same headshot on all of your social media profiles. Your image is like your logo. You want it to be familiar and stick.

Cover or Hero Image

Most social media sites allow you to upload a cover/hero image to your profile. This is the large background image in the header of your personal profile page. The reason there are signs outside of businesses is exactly why you need to customize your social media profile cover images. It is a free way to let an image tell your story.

The image dimensions and specs for each social platform are different and have a tendency to change. A quick Google search will help you find the current image size specification for each social media platform.

It is easy to build cover images with free tools like Canva.com. If you prefer help from a graphic designer, you'll find plenty of affordable options at Fiverr.com

Headline and Bio

Depending on the social media platform, you'll have the option of posting a profile headline and bio. With platforms like LinkedIn you get a headline and a long-form bio, whereas on Instagram and Twitter you only get a short and sweet headline.

Your headline and bio serve three purposes:

- Keywords so people can find you in search
- Telling your story
- A hook that entices visitors want to learn more about you

There are dueling philosophies on how headlines and bios should be written. Some experts advise that your headline should be descriptive—why people choose you or how you help customers. Others advise that headlines should be professional and straightforward—your role and occupation.

Likewise, some experts advise that your bio should be conversational and written in first person. Still others advise that a professional biography be written in third person.

The advice that experts and trainers offer on headlines and bios is mostly conjecture and is based on their own personal preference. They'll usually spout statistics that support their position while leaving out competing data that does not.

Personally, I prefer that professional headlines and bios be straightforward with no fluff. But that doesn't mean that my way is the right way or the only way. It's simply my preference.

My advice for headlines and bios is to do what makes you feel most comfortable, test out different formats to see what connects best, and don't be afraid to change things up. It's your story; the key is expressing it in a format that compels people to want to learn more about you.

Writing headlines and bios that connect with profile visitors and draws them in requires thoughtfulness and effort. They should be well written, compelling, truthful, and descriptive of who you are, your values, what you do best, and why customers and clients count on and trust you to solve their problems.

Media and Links

Ensure that you are cross-linking each social profile page to your other profile pages, along with any place you are blogging or contributing content. With LinkedIn, you may add rich media to your profile, including documents, photos, links, videos, and presentations. Add media that will be interesting to your prospects, educate them, give them a reason to connect with you, and support your personal brand.

Contact Information

Privacy? Forget about privacy. You are in sales. The very best thing that can happen is that a prospect calls and interrupts you. If you make it hard for them, they won't. If you don't provide contact information, they can't. So, make it easy. Put your contact information, including phone number, email, and website on your social media profiles.

Custom URLs

Most social media sites will allow you to choose a custom URL for your page. It is not automatic. This is an option you must choose in account settings. For example, my LinkedIn profile URL is https://www.linkedin.com/in/jebblount/

A custom URL is an extension of your personal brand, helps you build familiarity, makes it easier for you to share your profile, and makes it easier for people to find you in Google searches.

Update Your Profiles Regularly

Be sure to complete your entire profile. Don't leave gaps, holes, or partially completed profiles. Make a commitment to manage your online presence by reviewing, updating, and continuously improving all of your online profiles at least once a quarter. Things change. Make sure your profiles are changing with you and that they stay fresh. As you review your profiles, step into the shoes of visitors and answer this question: Would you buy you?

PART VII

Virtual Selling Is Still Selling

35

The Truth about Jedi Mind Tricks

Your overriding focus as a sales professional, from the time you wake in the morning to the time you lay your head down at night, is improving the win probability of the deals in your pipe. Each step, question, the demo, the presentation, every word you utter and everything you do as you advance through the sales process should be calculated to bend win probability in your favor.

In each sales situation, there will be multiple paths to a closed deal and multiple communication channels you may *blend* into the sales process. Like a chess master, you must choose the path that gives you the highest probability of getting a win.

Of course, there are a few basics that will give you the highest probability of closing the sale:

- Actively targeting qualified prospects that are in the buying window.
- Being fanatical about prospecting.

- Building and sustaining a robust pipeline full of qualified opportunities.
- Executing the sales process.
- Maintaining momentum by advancing deals to the next step on every call.
- Building relationships with stakeholders and delivering a positive buying experience.
- Presenting a compelling business case for doing business with you.
- Consistently and confidently asking for information, introductions, next steps, and ink.

Keys to Mastering Virtual Selling

Still, during our Virtual Selling Skills courses I get peppered with questions about magic words that will bring stalled deals back to life and make prospects say yes on prospecting calls.

Each day of my professional life, I'm approached by salespeople who are looking for Jedi mind tricks. They are desperately seeking Obi-Wan Kenobi style tactics that allow them to close deals on virtual sales calls with a sweep of the hand: "These aren't the droids you're looking for."

That's the kind of power we all want. But, alas, it only happens in the movies. The real secret to effective virtual selling is not a sexy, cool Jedi mind trick. It's something much more boring. *It's faithfully executing the sales process.*

Perhaps the greatest virtual selling challenge is staying on track with the sales process, because virtual sales calls:

- are technology driven and fast-paced, which makes it very easy to allow speed to fool you into taking shortcuts with the sales process;
- are bereft of many of the signals and cues inherent in face-to-face interactions, making it easy to miss buying signals or when stakeholders are just not that into you;
- can make you feel insecure, causing you to hesitate rather than confidently asking for the next step.

On virtual calls, you want to feel in control. You want to feel confident. You want to feel comfortable. But there is no trick, easy button, magic fairy dust, or Jedi mind trick that is going to do this for you.

The keys to virtual sales excellence are practice, repetition, and remembering that virtual selling is still selling. Virtual selling outcomes are predictable, based on how you leverage, execute, and move deals through the sales process. This is the most important truth in this book.

To be successful with virtual selling, you must put the entire sales process puzzle together (Figure 35.1). Follow a well-designed sales process with qualified prospects that are in the buying window, and you will close more deals at higher prices. It's the truth, and it's a guarantee.

Figure 35.1 The Sales Process Puzzle

1. Prospecting
2. Qualifying
3. Initial meetings
4. Aligning the sales and buying processes
5. Mapping stakeholders
6. Gaining consistent micro-commitments
7. Discovery, discovery, discovery
8. Solution mapping and stakeholder consensus
9. Presenting a lock-tight business case
10. Getting past objections
11. Negotiating
12. Asking for the sale

I'm not going to do a deep dive into the sales process because I've already written those books. Read them because they are the perfect companions to *Virtual Selling*.

- *Sales EQ*
- *Objections*
- *Inked*
- *People Buy You*

Instead, I'm going to highlight two important skill sets that are crucial for excellence on virtual sales calls and will immediately improve the probability that you close pipeline opportunities: *Asking questions and asking for the next step.*

Less Talking, More Asking

The primary reason salespeople struggle with closing is they talk and pitch rather than ask questions. This results in shallow discovery and a weak business case because they did not uncover needs, problems, pain, opportunities, or the stakeholders' desired business outcomes.

In sales, questions are the beginning and the end. Alpha and omega. If sales were a language, it would be a language of questions—strategic, artful, and fluid questions asked in the context of the conversation. It's simple: the more questions you ask, the more sales you will make.

Yet, effective discovery is more than just asking questions. It's asking the right questions, and the right questions are open-ended questions.

Open-ended questions such as, "How is that impacting you?" or "What happens when your workers' compensation costs increase?" encourage stakeholders to talk and elaborate.

Conversely, closed-ended questions like, "How many of those do you use?" or "Are you happy with that?" elicit short, limited responses.

It is more difficult to get stakeholders to open up on virtual calls. After you ask a stakeholder a discovery question, the awkward silence or clipped answers can rattle you. Impatience and insecurity take over. To compensate, you ask closed-ended questions and start talking.

This is a big problem on virtual sales calls because once you go down that road, it's difficult to get discovery calls back on track. When stakeholders don't feel like you are listening or the time spent with you is being wasted, they are more likely to disappear. On virtual sales calls, closed-ended questions give you the illusion of control. Yet, they create poor emotional experiences for stakeholders who are subjected to these interrogations.

Daniel J. Boorstin once said, "The greatest obstacle to discovery is not ignorance. It is the illusion of knowledge."[1] The root cause of making such false assumptions in sales is asking closed-ended questions.

On virtual calls, you must have the patience and emotional discipline to encourage stakeholders to open up. The objective is to leverage open-ended questions to encourage them to express the issues that are most important to them and provide the information you need to build a compelling business case for why they should do business with you.

In sales, 99 percent of your questions (and questioning statements like "Tell me more" or "Walk me through that process") should be open-ended. I'm especially fond of the *statement and pause* approach for getting prospects to talk. I'll say something like, "Wow, it sounds like that's been really challenging." Then I pause and allow silence to do the rest of the work.

Ask for the Next Step

From the CEO to frontline sales reps, everyone is looking for ways to unstick deals, shorten sales cycles, and increase pipeline velocity. This is where virtual selling gives you an advantage.

Virtual selling is fast. Because virtual sales calls are easier to schedule and conduct, you can rapidly advance deals through the pipeline.

Except for one small challenge. Salespeople, more often than not, fail to ask for and get a commitment to a next step on virtual calls. The failure to consistently set next steps lengthens the sales cycle, bogs down the process, and causes deals to stall.

When I conduct pipeline reviews with my clients' sales teams, my default question with every opportunity is, "What's the next step?" Following this question, I watch salespeople squirm in their seats and search for answers, because rather than firm next steps, they have excuses:

- "I'm waiting to hear back."
- "I'm calling back next week to set the next appointment."
- "I've put a proposal together and I'm hoping to get on the decision maker's schedule."
- "Can't understand why everything suddenly went dark."
- "Trying to get back in touch."
- "My contact is taking the proposal to her boss. I'm hoping to hear back this week."

- "The prospect seemed interested in doing business with us. I keep leaving messages to check in, but he doesn't return my calls."

Stalled deals plague the sales profession, clogging pipelines, ruining forecasts, and causing untold frustration. I've heard all the sad excuses, but it's always the same root cause: *The salesperson failed to ask for and get a commitment to a next step.*

Setting a Firm Next Step

Let's be clear, though. Emailing a presentation is NOT a next step. Neither are statements like, "I'll call you next week," or, "Just call me when you are ready," or, "I'll email my pricing."

Last year I caught one of my salespeople as she was just about to make a big mistake. We were in the early stages of a potentially monster training deal.

The prospect was a Fortune 50 company seeking a training partner to help them with prospecting and top-of-funnel strategies. Their sales enablement team engaged us because they'd heard about the success of our Fanatical Prospecting Boot Camps.

Following the second discovery meeting, they'd asked for a presentation on our training methodology and an overview of our curriculum before they would agree to level us up to the executive who was the ultimate decision maker. It was a classic move by influencers to retain power.

My sales rep spent three days building and customizing the presentation. I stopped by to check on how it was going. She responded, "I'll be ready to email it over in the morning."

"Whoa. Big mistake! What happens after you send her the presentation?" I asked.

Silence, thinking, searching for a response. But there was none. She knew the truth. After she emailed the presentation and the stakeholder had what she wanted, the likelihood that the deal would stall was high.

"How many hours have you sunk into crafting this presentation?" I asked.

"At least ten?" she muttered.

"So, you've invested all of this time and effort. And now you plan to email the presentation without getting anything in return?" I was shaking my head in disapproval. "What should you be asking for?"

At first, she wasn't tracking, but finally she realized what she needed to do.

"I need to ask them to schedule a video call to review the proposal and use it as a stepping-stone to level up to the decision maker."

"Exactly!" I responded. "I also want you to go back and think about how you managed to leave the last call without setting the next step and consider the additional work you need to do now to fix that mistake."

She tracked down the stakeholders and they agreed to meet. The video call and presentation opened up a robust conversation. The stakeholder group was impressed enough that they agreed to set up a meeting with the decision maker—a micro-commitment that advanced the deal.

A firm next step requires a commitment to action from both you and your stakeholder—*and* a date on which you will meet again to review those actions. Finally, that date must be written in stone on your calendar and your stakeholder's calendar. This also means that you must send a calendar invite for the next step immediately after you end your call and consider sending a video message to make it stick.

Prospects are so crazy busy that as soon your call ends, they will have already forgotten about you and moved on to the next pressing issue on their priority list. If you don't have a firm next step on their calendar, you'll spend the next month chasing them down.

On virtual sales calls, your job is to keep the ball rolling. You should never expect stakeholders to do this for you. Therefore, it pays to follow this simple cardinal rule: *Never leave a virtual sales call (or any sales call), without gaining a commitment for a firm next step from your stakeholder. Ever!*

The Most Important Discipline

Asking is the most important discipline in sales. You must ask for what you want, directly, assumptively, assertively, and repeatedly. In sales, asking is everything. *When you fail to ask, you fail.*

If you are having a hard time getting the next appointment, getting to decision makers, getting information from stakeholders, leveling up higher in the organization, or closing the deal, it's not because you lack prospecting skills, presentation skills, closing skills, the right words to say, or Jedi mind tricks.

Nine times out of 10, you are insecurely and passively beating around the bush because you are afraid to hear the word *no*. In this state, confident and assertive asking gets replaced with wishing, hoping, and wanting. You wait for your prospects to do your job for you and set the next step themselves. But they don't.

Only direct, confident, assertive asking gets you to the next step and closes the sale. Everything in sales begins with and depends on the discipline to *ask*.

36 | Selling Invisible Trucks

It was 2008, deep in the middle of the global financial crisis. With the economy crashing, the large transportation and logistics company needed to rapidly reduce the size of its commercial truck fleet. This meant decommissioning trucks and putting them up for sale.

At that time, the organization offloaded its used trucks to wholesalers. The challenge was that wholesale prices for used commercial trucks were plummeting while, the number of trucks that it (and other large fleets) needed to offload was increasing.

It was here, facing the cruel head winds of supply and demand economics, that Jack and Bob found themselves between a rock and a hard place. Jack and Bob were responsible for moving used trucks out of company's massive fleet, as fast as possible and profitably.

With wholesalers offering pennies on the dollar and the pressure mounting to get the used trucks off of the books, they were running out of time and options. If they let the trucks sit until the market improved, the cash that was sorely needed would be wrapped up in the equipment. If they sold the equipment on the wholesale market, the losses would be massive.

They quickly realized that the only way out of this pickle was to shift their focus away from the wholesale market. Instead, they would sell the trucks directly to retail customers where they'd have more control of prices and profits.

Going direct to retail, though, created a whole new set of problems. Direct selling was a completely different sales motion than wholesaling. On the wholesale market, they would bundle dozens of trucks together and then sell them all in a single transaction. With direct sales, though, it was one truck at a time.

Ever since used commercial trucks have been sold, face-to-face, belly-to-belly is how selling has been done. Dealers purchased used trucks from wholesalers and parked the trucks on their lots. There, salespeople engaged customers, who "kicked the tires" and went for test drives before buying.

Jack and Bob had no infrastructure for direct selling used equipment. They didn't have commercial lots where they could park used trucks, nor did they employ used truck salespeople.

A Light-Bulb Moment

With the clock ticking and the financial crisis worsening, they scratched their heads searching for an answer to this conundrum. Then, almost by accident, they stumbled on the answer that was soon to change everything.

While heading into a meeting to discuss a direct sales strategy, they overheard a call. A small business owner was looking to purchase a used truck. The person on their team who took the call turned the potential customer away because, at the time, they did not sell used trucks on the retail market.

Jack and Bob surmised that if there was one call, there must be more; and they were right. A little bit of digging uncovered dozens of calls from business owners who wanted to purchase used trucks. All of them had been turned away.

The light bulbs clicked on. Though they did not have the physical infrastructure to sell used trucks, they did have phones. In a moment of clarity, they dumped the entire model for selling used trucks on its head and went virtual.

Virtual Selling Changes Everything

They immediately began routing all incoming calls from people looking to purchase used trucks to a project manager on their team. That person sold 10 trucks within a few weeks.

Encouraged by this early success, they pulled some strings to get a sales rep from another part of the company transferred to their team. The new sales rep was even more successful.

They quickly added a second and third salesperson. The small team worked the phones, email, and text messages to move trucks.

When they sold 100 trucks in a single month, Jack and Bob knew that things would never be the same. They leveraged virtual selling to climb out of the financial hole created by the 2008–2009 recession and then went on to disrupt the entire used truck market.

Selling Invisible Trucks

In the early days, they gained a tremendous competitive advantage because the costs of selling a truck via the virtual channel were much lower than for their competitors that sold trucks from physical lots. In head-to-head matchups with competitors, when price was a factor, they were almost always in a position to win.

At first, the new used truck sales team sold decommissioned trucks that were parked at the company's various shops across the country. But, as the financial crisis waned, the large inventory of trucks that had weighed so heavily on Jack and Bob became depleted.

Without inventory to sell, their competitive advantage began to shrink. When customers needed a particular type of equipment, it was the truck specs, not the price, that mattered most. Once again, Jack and Bob had to innovate.

Because the organization is always upgrading the fleet with newer models, a large number of trucks in the fleet are set to be decommissioned at any given time. The traditional process, though, was to take a truck out of the fleet first, and then sell it. This meant that the truck would cease to produce revenue while continuing to depreciate as it sat waiting to be sold.

But what if trucks could be sold while they were still on the road with customers, generating revenue? This might be the answer to the inventory problem, because it opened up a large swath of the working fleet that could be offered to customers.

Leveraging this methodology would give the used truck sales representatives access to one of the largest inventories of used trucks in the world. It would also significantly reduce the cost of sales, widening their competitive advantage.

By this time, the used truck sales team had become so skilled at virtual selling that they could easily shift into selling trucks that were still on the road being driven by customers—sight unseen. In effect, they began selling invisible trucks. It was virtual selling at its best.

Virtual Selling Is Still Selling

Today, this company dominates the retail used truck market. Because more than 90 percent of the trucks they sell are through virtual channels, they are far more agile than their competitors. Last year they sold over 25,000 used trucks this way.

I count these sales professionals among the best in the world. As a lifelong student of sales, I am in awe at their ability to convince a buyer in Dallas to purchase a truck while it is still on the road with a customer making deliveries in Chicago. For me, this is the apex of professional selling.

Jack and Bob's secret to success is not really a secret. It is the tried-and-true formula of all great sales organizations:

- Hire talented sales professionals and sales leaders.
- Consistently follow and execute a well-designed sales process.
- Provide regular and ongoing sales training and coaching to keep skill levels high.
- Leverage framework-based sales techniques that flex to individual customer situations.
- Focus on human-to-human connections.
- Deliver a legendary customer experience.
- Constantly innovate.
- Move fast.
- Foster a performance-driven culture.

This is why, when the global coronavirus pandemic hit, Jack and Bob's sales organization never missed a beat. They were already ahead of the curve.

Lessons

As you blend virtual selling into your business development, sales, and account management processes, remember these important lessons:

1. Most important among them is, just because something has always been done one way doesn't meant that it is the only way.

2. When you relentlessly adhere to basics and fundamentals of sales excellence, you will bend win probability in your favor.

3. When you blend virtual selling into your sales process, you will become more agile and productive.

4. When you focus on building and investing in human-to-human relationships, you will gain a decided competitive edge.

5. When you keep your mind open to new possibilities, you will be unstoppable.

Notes

Chapter One

1. Stewart Wolpin, "The Videophone Turns 50: The Historic Failure That Everybody Wanted," *Mashable,* April 20, 2014, https://mashable.com/2014/04/20/videophone-turns-50/.

Chapter Two

1. Alan Kozarsky, ed., "How Important Are Our Eyes?" *WebMD,* May 10, 2019, www.webmd.com/eye-health/qa/how-important-are-our-eyes.
2. E. Hatfield, J. Cacioppo, and R. L. Rapson, *Emotional Contagion* (New York: Cambridge University Press, 1994). ISBN 0-521-44948-0
3. Shirley Wang, "Contagious Behavior," *Observer* (February 2006), https://www.psychologicalscience.org/observer/contagious-behavior.

Chapter Eight

1. Antonio Damasio, *Descartes' Error: Emotion, Reason, and the Human Brain* (New York: Putnam, 1994; rev. ed., Penguin, 2005).

Chapter Eleven

1. Insights Team, "Five Reasons Why Your Company Needs to Embrace Video Conferencing Now," *Forbes* (October 30, 2017), www.forbes.com/sites/insights-zoom/2017/10/30/5-reasons-why-your-company-needs-to-embrace-video-conferencing-now/#3f6c054e47c4.
2. Infographic, "Wondering How to Look Good on Video? You're Not Alone," Highfive, 2020, highfive.com/resources/infographics/how-to-look-good-on-video.

Chapter Thirteen

1. Katrin Schoenenberg, Alexander Raake, and Judith Koeppe, "Why Are You So Slow? Misattribution of Transmission Delay to Attributes of the Conversation Partner at the Far-End," *International Journal of Human-Computer Studies* 72, no. 5 (May 2014): 477–487, www.sciencedirect.com/science/article/abs/pii/S1071581914000287.
2. Manyu Jiang, "The Reason Zoom Calls Drain Your Energy," BBC (April 22, 2020), www.bbc.com/worklife/article/20200421-why-zoom-video-chats-are-so-exhausting.
3. Lauren Geall, "Have You Got Zoom Fatigue? Why You're Finding Video Calls So Exhausting," *Stylist* (April 2020), www.stylist.co.uk/life/zoom-fatigue-video-call-virtual-drinks-exhaustion-tiring/376846.
4. Richard Culatta, "Cognitive Load Theory (John Sweller)," *InstructionalDesign.org*, 2015, www.instructionaldesign.org/theories/cognitive-load.html.
5. Vocabulary.com, "heuristic," Vocabulary.com Dictionary, https://www.vocabulary.com/dictionary/heuristic.
6. Lori A. Harris and A.P. Cliffs, *Psychology* (Hoboken, NJ: John Wiley & Sons Inc., 2007), p. 65.
7. Daniel Kahneman, *Thinking, Fast and Slow* (New York: Farrar, Straus and Giroux, 2011).

Chapter Fifteen

1. https://www.psych.ucla.edu/faculty/page/mehrab

2. https://www.paulekman.com/

3. Practical Psychology, "MicroExpressions — Reading Facial Expressions Are Better Than Reading Body Language," YouTube, December 2, 2017, https://www.youtube.com/watch?v= tu1uzG_EBGM&feature=youtu.be

4. P. Ekman and W. V. Friesen, "Constants Across Cultures in the Face and Emotion," *Journal of Personality and Social Psychology*, 17, no. 2 (1971), 124–129.

5. Amy Cuddy, "Your Body Language May Shape Who You Are," YouTube, Ted, October 1, 2012, https://youtu.be/ Ks-_Mh1QhMc.

6. James Clear, "How to Be Confident and Reduce Stress in 2 Minutes Per Day," http://jamesclear.com/body-language-how-to-be-confident.

7. Belle Beth Cooper, "The Science Behind Posture and How It Affects Your Brain," *LifeHacker,* November 13, 2013, lifehacker. com/the-science-behind-posture-and-how-it-affects-your-brai-1463291618.

8. Susan Weinschenk, "Your Hand Gestures Are Speaking for You," *Psychology Today*, September 26, 2012, www.psychologytoday. com/us/blog/brain-wise/201209/your-hand-gestures-are-speaking-you

9. Linda Talley, Samuel Temple, "How Leaders Influence Followers Through the Use of Nonverbal Communication," *Leadership and Organization Development Journal,* March 2, 2015, www.emerald .com/insight/content/doi/10.1108/LODJ-07-2013-0107/full/ html.

10. Jeb Blount, *Sales EQ* (Hoboken, NJ: John Wiley & Sons 2017), pp. 107–108.

11. David Ludden, "Your Eyes Really Are the Window to Your Soul," Psychology Today, December 31, 2015, www.psychologytoday. com/us/blog/talking-apes/201512/your-eyes-really-are-the-window-your-soul

12. Jennifer Marlow, Eveline van Everdingen, and Daniel Avrahami, "Taking Notes or Playing Games? Understanding Multitasking in Video Communication," *CSCW*, February 27-March 2, 2016, https://dl.acm.org/doi/pdf/10.1145/2818048.2819975

13. Jon Porter, "iOS 13 Will Fix the FaceTime Eye Contact Problem," *Vox,* July 3, 2019, https://www.theverge.com/2019/7/3/20680681/ios-13-beta-3-facetime-attention-correction-eye-contact

14. "Making Distance Disappear," *360 Magazine,* 2020, https://www.steelcase.com/research/360-magazine/making-distance-disappear/

15. Heather Schwedel, "Staring at the Gargoyle on My Screen," *Slate,* December 2, 2019, https://slate.com/human-interest/2019/12/video-conferencing-is-the-worst.html

16. Anne Quito, "We're All Distracted by How Terrible We Look on Video Calls. Here's How to Fix It," *Quartz,* August 22, 2016, https://qz.com/637860/video-call-tips-for-skype-and-facetime-steelcase-researchers-are-solving-your-appearance-barrier-on-video-calls/

17. Fraser W. Smith and Stephanie Rossit, "Identifying and Detecting Facial Expressions of Emotion in Peripheral Vision," PLOS One, May 30, 2018, https://journals.plos.org/plosone/article?id=10.1371/journal.pone.0197160.

18. Manyu Jiang, "Video Chat Is Helping Us Stay Employed and Connected. But What Makes It So Tiring – And How Can We Reduce 'Zoom Fatigue'?" BBC, April 22, 2020, www.bbc.com/worklife/article/20200421-why-zoom-video-chats-are-so-exhausting?ocid=ww.social.link.email

19. Egan Jiminez, "In a Split Second, Clothes Make the Man More Competent in the Eyes of Others," EurekaAlert! Princeton University, Woodrow Wilson School of Public and International Affairs, December 9, 2019, www.eurekalert.org/pub_releases/2019-12/puww-ias120919.php

20. Ti Kiisel, "You Are Judged by Your Appearance," *Forbes,* March 20, 2013, www.forbes.com/sites/tykiisel/2013/03/20/you-are-judged-by-your-appearance/#523930726d50.

21. Nasim Mansurov, "What Is Moiré and How It Can Ruin Your Photos," *Photography Life*, December 24, 2019, photographylife.com/what-is-moire.

22. Gauri Sardi-Joshi, "What You Wear Changes That Way You Think," Brain Fodder, https://brainfodder.org/psychology-clothes-enclothed-cognition/

23. Hannah Yasharoff, "Viral Reporter Returns to 'GMA' after 'Hilariously Mortifying' Video Appearance with No Pants," *USA Today*, April 28, 2020, www.usatoday.com/story/entertainment/tv/2020/04/28/quarantine-woes-gma-abc-reporter-mistakenly-appears-tv-without-pants/3039932001/

24. "Super Bowl XXXVIII Halftime Show Controversy," Wikipedia, April 27, 2020, en.wikipedia.org/wiki/Super_Bowl_XXXVIII_halftime_show_controversy.

Chapter Sixteen

1. Cheryl L. Grady, Anthony R. McIntosh, M. Natasha Rajah, and Fergus I. M. Craik, "Neural Correlates of the Episodic Encoding of Pictures and Words," *PNAS* 95, no. 5 (March 3, 1998): 2703–2709, https://www.pnas.org/content/95/5/2703

2. Rachel Gillett, "Why We're More Likely to Remember Content with Images and Video (Infographic)," *Fast Company* (September 18, 2014), https://www.fastcompany.com/3035856/why-were-more-likely-to-remember-content-with-images-and-video-infogr

3. "Polishing Your Presentation," 3M Meeting Network, http://web.archive.org/web/20001102203936/http%3A//3m.com/meetingnetwork/files/meetingguide_pres.pdf

4. Tversky, A., and D. Kahneman, "Judgment under Uncertainty: Heuristics and Biases" *Science* (New Series) 185 (1974), 1124–1131.

5. Carmine Gallo, "Neuroscience Proves You Should Follow TED's 18-Minutes Rule to Win Your Pitch," *Inc.* (February 21, 2017), https://www.inc.com/carmine-gallo/why-your-next-pitch-should-follow-teds-18-minute-rule.html

6. Holdcroft Nissan Hanley, "Holdcroft Nissan Virtual Showroom," (April 14, 2020), https://youtu.be/jbDk9wRGQ2M

Chapter Seventeen

1. Walter B. Cannon, The Wisdom of the Body, New York, W.W. Norton & Company, Inc., 1932.
2. Katrin Schoenenberg, Alexander Raake, and Judith Koeppe, "Why Are You So Slow? – Misattribution of Transmission Delay to Attributes of the Conversation Partner at the Far End," *International Journal of Human-Computer Studies* 72, no.1 5 (May 2014): pp. 477–487. www.sciencedirect.com/science/article/abs/pii/S1071581914000287.

Chapter Eighteen

1. https://www.marketingcharts.com/digital/video-109907
2. Cisco, "Cisco Annual Internet Report," March 9, 2020, https://www.cisco.com/c/en/us/solutions/collateral/executive-perspectives/annual-internet-report/white-paper-c11-741490.html
3. SalesLoft, "Using Personalized Videos in Modern Sales Engagement, https://salesloft.com/resources/blog/using-personalized-videos-in-modern-sales-engagement/
4. Juliana Nicholson, "With Video: A HubSpot Experiment," HubSpot, July 12, 2019, https://blog.hubspot.com/marketing/video-prospecting
5. Sandy Natarajan, "Re-imagining the Sales Strategy—What Makes It the Need of the Hour?" Hippo Video, May 4, 2020, https://www.hippovideo.io/blog/re-imagining-the-sales-strategy-what-makes-it-the-need-of-the-hour/.
6. Laura Frances Bright, *Consumer Control and Customization in Online Environments: An Investigation into the Psychology of Consumer Choice and Its Impact on Media Enjoyment, Attitude, and Behavioral*

Intention (Austin: The University of Texas, 2008), https://reposi-tories.lib.utexas.edu/handle/2152/18054

7. Robert B. Cialdini, *Influence: The Psychology of Persuasion* (New York: William Morrow and Company, 1993).

Chapter Nineteen

1. Evan Cohen, "The Humble Phone Call Has Made a Comeback," *The New York Times*, April 9, 2020, www-nytimes-com.cdn .ampproject.org/c/s/www.nytimes.com/2020/04/09/technology/ phone-calls-voice-virus.amp.html

2. "Return of the Phone Call: Why Talking Beats Texting When You're in Isolation," *The Guardian*, March 17, 2020, www .theguardian.com/lifeandstyle/2020/mar/17/return-of-the-phone-call-why-talking-beats-texting-when-youre-in-isolation

3. Chris Orlob, "If You're Selling without Video, You're Doing It Wrong (This Data Explains Why)," Gong.Io, November 27, 2018, www.gong.io/blog/if-youre-selling-without-video-youre-doing-it-wrong-this-data-explains-why/

Chapter Twenty Two

1. E.J. Langer, A. Blank, and B. Chanowitz "The mindlessness of ostensibly thoughtful action: The role of 'placebic' information in interpersonal interaction," *Journal of Personality and Social Psychology* 36(6) (1978), 635–642.

Chapter Twenty Three

1. Tara Bennett-Goleman, *Emotional Alchemy* (New York: Harmony Books, 2002).

Chapter Twenty Six

1. Velocify, "Text Messages for Better Sales Conversions Report," http://pages.velocify.com/rs/leads360/images/Text-Messaging-for-Better-Sales-Conversion.pdf.

Chapter Twenty Seven

1. Nigel Davies, "It's Probably Time to Stop Announcing the Death of Email," *Forbes* (June 24, 2019), www.forbes.com/sites/nigeldavies/2019/06/24/its-probably-time-to-stop-announcing-the-death-of-email/#13f6e4737a41.
2. "Email Statistics Report, 2018-2022," The Radicati Group, Inc. (March 2018), www.radicati.com/wp/wp-content/uploads/2018/01/Email_Statistics_Report,_2018-2022_Executive_Summary.pdf.
3. Dena Cox, Jeffrey G. Cox, and Anthony D. Cox, "To Err Is Human? How Typographical and Orthographical Errors Affect Perceptions of Online Reviewers," *Computers in Human Behavior* 75 (October 2017), 245–253, www.sciencedirect.com/science/article/pii/S0747563217303205?via%3Dihub
4. "Smiley Emojis in E-Mails Could Create Frowns, says BGU Study," Ben-Gurion University of the Negev (August 14, 2017), https://in.bgu.ac.il/en/pages/news/smiley_emojis.aspx

Chapter Twenty Eight

1. Sara Radicati, "Email Statistics Report, 2014–2018," The Radicati Group, Inc., April 2014, http://www.radicati.com/wp/wp-content/uploads/2014/01/Email-Statistics-Report-2014-2018-Executive-Summary.pdf
2. Michael C. Mankins, Chris Brahm, and Gregory Caimi, "Your Scarcest Resource," *Harvard Business Review,* May 2014, https://hbr.org/2014/05/your-scarcest-resource.

3. Kimbe MacMaster, "3 Reasons Video Is a Phenomenal Sales Tool [Infographic], *Vidyard,* January 18, 2017, https://www.vidyard .com/blog/video-sales-tool-infographic/

Chapter Thirty

1. "Messaging App Usage Worldwide: eMarketer's Updated Forecast, Leaderboard, and Behavioral Analysis," eMarketer, July 20, 2017, https://www.emarketer.com/Report/Messaging-App-Usage-Worldwide-eMarketers-Updated-Forecast-Leaderboard-Behavioral-Analysis/2001939
2. "The Messaging Apps Report: Messaging Apps Are Now Bigger Than Social Networks," Business Insider Intelligence, September 20, 2016, https://www.businessinsider.com/the-messaging-app-report-2015-11.

Chapter Thirty One

1 The History of Live Chat Software," Whoson, https://www .whoson.com/our-two-cents/the-history-of-live-chat-software/
2. CCW Digital, Live Chat Benchmark Report 2018, Comm100, 2018, https://www.ec3.co.za/uploads/2/6/3/7/26378480/ comm100-live-chat-benchmark-report-2018.pdf
3. Dom Price, "Yes, Chat Bots Are Incredibly Efficient. But Your Customers Hate Them." Inc., March 27, 2018, www.inc.com/ dom-price/yes-chat-bots-are-incredibly-efficient-but-your-customers-hate-them.html
4. Stephen McDonald, "25 Reasons Live Chat Can Grow Your Business," SuperOffice, May 18, 2020, www.superoffice.com/ blog/live-chat-statistics/
5. Megan Burns, et al., "Understanding the Impact of Emotion on Customer Experience," *Forrester,* July 13, 2015, https://www .forrester.com/report/Understanding+The+Impact+Of+Emoti on+On+Customer+Experience/-/E-RES122503

Chapter Thirty Four

1. "New Research Study Breaks Down 'The Perfect Profile Photo,'"
   https://www.photofeeler.com/blog/perfect-photo.php.

Chapter Thirty Five

1. Carol Krucoff, "The 6 O'Clock Scholar," *The Washington Post,*
   January 29, 1984, https://www.washingtonpost.com/archive/
   lifestyle/1984/01/29/the-6-oclock-scholar/eed58de4-2dcb-
   47d2-8947-b0817a18d8fe/

Acknowledgments

In one of my favorite quotes, Nolan Bushnell, the mind behind the Atari video game system, said that "Everyone who's ever taken a shower has had an idea. It's the person who gets out of the shower, dries off, and does something about it who make a difference."

In late-March 2020, as the global coronavirus (Covid-19) pandemic raged across the globe like a wildfire, I stepped out of the shower and dried off.

As I called the one person that I knew would understand my crazy idea, I could hear Bushnell's words buzzing in my head.

Shannon Vargo, vice president and publisher at John Wiley & Sons, picked up the call on the first ring. She listened as I pitched *Virtual Selling* and the insane idea to write and publish a full-length book in just 60 days. When I finished, all she said was, "Let's do it."

The truth is, *it is the person who gets out of the shower with an idea, dries off, and has a team of people around them that are willing to do something about that idea who makes a difference.*

Shannon, you are rare and special person. I am deeply grateful to you for trusting me and for your willingness to move barriers so that *we* can make a difference.

Likewise, a massive thank you to Sally Baker and Deborah Schindlar who were with me every step of the way while writing, editing, and preparing *Virtual Selling* for publication.

Thank you to David Monostori, Trey LaMarr, and Jeb Blount Jr. for your enormous help with working through the technical elements of video sales calls and video messaging.

Keith Lubner and Jason Eatmon, thank you for taking the helm of Sales Gravy while I focused all of my attention on writing this book. The peace of mind you afforded me was invaluable.

Finally, to my beautiful wife, Carrie. Without you, by my side, supporting me, there would be no *Virtual Selling* book. I love you!

Training, Workshops, and Speaking

Sales Gravy offers a comprehensive suite of training programs and workshops for sales professionals, leaders, account executives, SDRs, account managers, customer service professionals, and channel managers.

Our virtual instructor-led training programs, classroom-based instructor-led training programs, self-directed e-learning courses, and workshops include:

Virtual Selling Skills

Sales Negotiation Skills

Business Outcome Selling Strategies

Sales Objections Bootcamp

Sales EQ

Fanatical Prospecting Bootcamp

Complex Account Prospecting Skills

Prospecting Sequencing Excellence

Webchat Bootcamp

Fanatical Military Recruiting

Situational Coaching

Coaching Ultra-High Performance

Message Matters Sales Presentation and Communication Skills

Business Guidance Selling (cloud, SaaS, IoT)

Enterprise Account Sales Skills

Customer Experience Selling (B2C)

Adaptive Account Management

Customer EQ

Adaptive Partnering (channel management)

Adaptive Mentoring

All training programs are delivered by our certified professional trainers or may be licensed and delivered by your learning and development team. We offer self-directed learning via the Sales Gravy University Platform (https://www.SalesGravy.University) or we can deliver e-learning content to your LMS.

The training media, educational design, and delivery connect with adult learning preferences and are responsive to multigenerational learning styles. We employ an active learning methodology that blends interactive instruction with experiential learning elements and roleplaying scenarios to create reference experiences that anchor key concepts and make training stick.

In addition to training, we specialize in developing custom sales onboarding learning paths for new hires and sales playbooks.

For more information, please call 1–844–447–3737, or visit https://www.SalesGravy.com.

About the Author

Jeb Blount is the author of 13 books and among the world's most respected thought leaders on sales, leadership, and customer experience.

As a business leader, Jeb has more than 25 years of experience with Fortune 500 companies, small and midsize businesses (SMBs), and startups. His flagship website, SalesGravy.com, is the most visited sales-specific website on the planet.

Through his global training organization, Sales Gravy, Jeb and his team train and advise a who's who of the world's most prestigious organizations.

Jeb's books include:

Virtual Selling (John Wiley & Sons, 2020)

The Virtual Training Bible (John Wiley & Sons, 2020)

Inked (John Wiley & Sons, 2020)

Fanatical Military Recruiting (John Wiley & Sons, 2019)

Objections (John Wiley & Sons, 2018)

Sales EQ (John Wiley & Sons, 2017)

Fanatical Prospecting (John Wiley & Sons, 2015)

People Love You: The Real Secret to Delivering a Legendary Customer Experience (John Wiley & Sons, 2013)

People Follow You: The Real Secret to What Matters Most in Leadership (John Wiley & Sons, 2011)

People Buy You: The Real Secret to What Matters Most in Business (John Wiley & Sons, 2010)

Connect with Jeb on LinkedIn, Twitter, Facebook, YouTube, and Instagram.

To schedule Jeb to speak at your next event, call 1–888–360–2249, email brooke@salesgravy.com or carrie@salesgravy.com, or visit www.jebblount.com. You may email Jeb directly at jeb@salesgravy.com.

Index